Beethoven

The Symphonies
An Anthology of Selected Writings

BEETHOVEN
As depicted by the life mask taken by Franz Klein in 1812
(derived from a copy in the author's possession)

BEETHOVEN
THE SYMPHONIES

AN
ANTHOLOGY
OF
SELECTED WRITINGS

Terence M. Russell

Jelly Bean Books

The right of Terence Russell to be identified as the
Author of the Work has been asserted by him in accordance
with the Copyright, Designs and Patents Act 1988.

Copyright © Terence M. Russell 2025

Published by
Jelly Bean Books
136 Newport Road
Cardiff
CF24 1DJ

ISBN: 978-1-917022-71-2

www.candyjarbooks.co.uk

All rights reserved.
No part of this publication may be reproduced, stored in a
retrieval system, or transmitted at any time or by any means,
electronic, mechanical, photocopying, recording or otherwise
without the prior permission of the copyright holder. This book is
sold subject to the condition that it shall not by way of trade or
otherwise be circulated without the publisher's prior consent in any
form of binding or cover other than that in which it is published.

CONTENTS

AUTHOR'S NOTE	I
INTRODUCTION	IX
EDITORIAL PRINCIPLES	XII
BEETHOVEN'S FINANCIAL TRANSACTIONS	XV

BEETHOVEN: AN ANTHOLOGY
OF SELECTED WRITINGS:

Gerald Abraham	1
Theodor W. Adorno	3
Allgemeine musikalische Zeitung (AmZ)	5
Boito Arrigo	11
Vladimir Ashkenazy	12
Daniel Barenboim	14
Philip Barford	16
Béla Bartók	19
Arnold Bax	19
Paul Bekker	20

Luciano Berio	23
Hector Berlioz	23
Leonard Bernstein	30
Arthur Bliss	32
Ernst Bloch	34
Eric Blom	37
Mark Evan Bonds	40
Leon Botstein	42
Pierre Boulez	45
Johannes Brahms	46
Alfred Brendel	47
Gerhard von Breuning	49
Alfred Peter Brown	52
Cive Brown	54
Michael Broyles	56
Anton Bruckner	58
Neville Cardus	60
Elliott Carter	64
Pablo Casals	67
Alfredo Casella	68
Carlos Chávez	69
Edward T. Cone	70
Barry Cooper	72
Martin Cooper	74
Aaron Copland	77
John Crabbe	79
William Crotch	82
Louise Elvira Cuyler	83
Carl Czerny	84
Carl Dahlhaus	86
Peter Maxwell Davies	89
Collin Davis	90
Basil Deane	92
Claude Debussy	93

Frederick Delius	97
David B. Dennis	98
Domenico Dragonetti	106
Antonín Dvorák	108
Alfred Einstein	108
Frederick Freedman	109
Wilhelm Furtwängler	111
Hans Gal	118
Charles Gounod	121
Percy Grainger	122
Franz Grillparzer	124
George Grove	125
François-Antione Habeneck	129
William Henry Hadow	130
Charles Hallé	133
Hamilton Harty	136
Christopher Headington	141
E. T. A. Hoffman	142
Gustav Holst	144
Arthur Honegger	145
Anthony Hopkins	147
Peter le Huray and James Day	148
Vincent d'Indy	149
David Wyn Jones	151
Karl August Kahlert	153
William Kinderman	154
Otto Klemperer	155
Raymond Knapp	158
Nikolai Rimsky-Korsakov	158
Siegfried Kross	160
Constant Lambert	162
Paul Henry Lang	165
Ernest Markham Lee	168
Raymond Leppard	169

Franz Liszt	171
Edward Macdowell	174
Charles Mackerras	176
John B. McEwan	177
William Mcnaught	179
Gustav Mahler	180
Nicholas Marston	186
Denis Matthews	187
Wilfrid Mellers	189
Felix Mendelssohn	191
Yehudi Menuhin	197
Olivier Messiaen	204
Paul Mies	206
Darius Milhaud	208
Ignaz Moscheles	209
Charles Münch	211
Modeste Musorgsky	213
Brian Newbould	213
Ernest Newman	215
Richard Osborne	219
Hubert Parry	221
Philharmonic Society	222
Sergei Rachmaninoff	227
Simon Rattle	228
Maurice Ravel	230
Johann Friedrich Reichardt	232
Hans Richter	236
Ferdinand Ries	237
Nikolay Rimsky-Korsakov	240
Romain Rolland	240
Stephen Rumph	243
Camille Saint-Saëns	245
Malcolm Sargent	247
Anton Felix Schindler	248
Johann Aloys Schlosser	250

Percy Alfred Scholes	253
Harold C. Schonberg	254
Robert Schumann	255
Roger Sessions	258
Ignaz von Seyfried	261
George Bernard Shaw	263
Jean Sibelius	267
Robert Simpson	269
Nicolas Slonimsky	272
Alexander Brent Smith	274
Maynard Solomon	275
Oscar George Sonneck	278
Louis Spohr	280
Charles Villiers Stanford	282
Preston Stedman	284
Karl Heinrich Stockhausen	288
Richard Strauss	290
Igor Stravinsky	294
John William Sullivan	297
Karol Szymanowski	298
Peter Tchaikovsky	300
Alexander Wheelock Thayer	305
Virgil Thomson	307
Michael Tippett	314
Arturo Toscanini	320
Donald Francis Tovey	325
Cosima Wagner	329
Richard Wagner	332
Ernest Walker	346
Felix Weingartner	347
Hugo Wolf	350
BIBLIOGRAPHY	355
INDEX	390
ABOUT THE AUTHOR	393

AUTHOR'S NOTE

I have cherished the idea of making a study of the life and work of Beethoven for many years. This statement requires a few words of personal reflection. I first encountered Beethoven in my early piano lessons — Minuet in G major, WoO 10, No. 2. At the same time I became acquainted with his piano pupil Carl Czerny — *Book One, Piano Studies*. My heart sank when I discovered the rear cover advertised a further *99* books in the same series — scales, arpeggios studies for the left hand, studies for the right hand — all the way to his Op. 824! By coincidence, my *Czerny Book One* was edited by Alec Rowley — who had the same surname as my music teacher. In my childish innocence, I often wondered why *he himself* never appeared to give me a lesson!

In my teenage years I found myself drawn ever closer

to Beethoven's music in the manner that ferromagnetic materials are ineluctably held captive in the sway of a magnetic field. The impulse to which I yielded is well described in words the conductor Bruno Walter gave in one of his rare public addresses: 'It is my belief that young people at that age are more easily impressed by what is heroic and grandiose; that they more easily understand works of art in which passionate feelings are violently uttered in raised accents, and that the lighter sounds of cheerfulness are less impressive to them.' I do indeed recall the stirring effect made on me on first hearing the Overture *Egmont*, the unfolding drama of the Fifth Symphony and the declamatory opening chords of the *Emperor* Piano Concerto.

I resolved to read everything I could about Beethoven, starting with Marion Scott's pioneering English-language study of the composer in *The Master Musicians series*. My father took out a subscription for me for *The Gramophone* magazine, enabling me to read reviews of the new 'LP' recordings – none of which though I could afford! The LP was then – 1950s – beginning to supplant the 78 rpm shellac records, stacks of which could be purchased for as little as six pence each in 'old' money. I listed to the radio to hear Anthony Hopkins 'Talking about music' and to other musicological luminaries including Howard Fergusson, Hans Keller, Paul Hamburger, Denis Matthews, and Peter Stadlen.

At this same time I had the privilege of hearing Beethoven's music performed by the *Hallé Orchestra* under the baton of Sir John Barbirolli, and experienced the *Carl Rosa Opera Company* perform the composer's only opera *Fidelio*; I borrowed the piano-reduction score from the City Library to become better acquainted with this moving work – only to find the score's fists full of notes were well beyond my capabilities. Nonetheless, since then *Fidelio's* every note has been woven into my DNA. I also recall the period when the *London Promenade Concerts* were designated 'Friday night is Beethoven night'.

Through these influences I resolved to visit Vienna to see where Beethoven had lived and worked. But how? The support for such travel was beyond the means of my family. Fortunately in my final year at school (1959) an opportunity presented itself. I saw a poster that stated **WUS – World University Service** – required volunteers to work in the Austrian town of Linz to help relocate refugees who were living there in improvised wooden shacks – displaced and dispossessed victims of the Second World War. To those participating all expenses would be paid together with free accommodation – in one of the crumbling wooden shacks! From Linz, I planned to make my way to Vienna.

I applied to **WUS** and, despite being a mere school-leaver, I was accepted. The **WUS** authorities doubtless reasoned the building-trade skills I had acquired during my secondary education in the building department of a technical school would be useful. This proved to be the case. At the refugee camp I dug trenches and was allowed to assist as a bricklayer. All about me were wide-eyed children eager to help but mostly getting in the way. I recall one afternoon when a reporter from *The Observer* newspaper paid a visit to our construction site to gather material for an article he was writing on European post-war recovery – he generously admired my trenches and brickwork!

Of lasting significance was another visit, this time from a Belgian priest. He took a group of us to the nearby *Mauthausen* Concentration Camp, recently opened as a silent and solemn memorial to those who had perished there. It was a deeply moving experience. Years later I learned of the views of the ardent Beethovenian Sir Michael Tippet. After the horrors of the *Holocaust*, he posed the question for mankind: 'What price Beethoven now?' He posited: 'Could we any longer find solace in Beethoven's setting of Schiller's *Ode to Joy* and its utopian vision — "Be embraced you Millions"?'

My refugee contribution duly came to end and Vienna beckoned. On arrival there I found scenes reminiscent of *The Third Man* and *Harry Lime*. I recall, for example, encountering cobblestones piled high in the streets waiting to be replaced after having been disturbed by the heavy armoured vehicles that had so recently passed over them. But Vienna was welcoming. I visited the houses where Beethoven had lived and worked and paused outside others associated with him that were identified by a commemorative plaque and the Austrian flag. A particularly memorable occasion was attending a recital in the great salon within the palace of Beethoven's noble patron Prince Lobkowitz — the very one where the *Eroica* Symphony had been premiered. Ultimately, my steps led me to the composer's first resting place in the *Währinger Ortsfriedhof*. I paid silent homage to the great man and, as I did so, discovered nearby the resting place of Franz Schubert to whom Beethoven was an endless source of admiration and inspiration.

I felt a youthful impulse to discover yet more about Beethoven and his music. But absorption in musicology would have to take second place. My chosen career beckoned in the guise of architecture — 'the mother of the arts' and 'the handmaid of society'. There was room though for Beethoven's music and from that time on it has been my constant companion through attendance at recitals, in concerts and music-making in the home. And at home a reproduction of Franz Kline's 1812 study of the composer has greeted me each day for more than half a century.

On my retirement from a career in architectural practice, research and university teaching, the opportunity finally presented itself for me to devote time to researching Beethoven musicology. Having attained my eightieth year also emboldened me to make progress with my good intentions!

With these autobiographical remarks outlined I will say a few remarks about my working method— see also the comments made in *Editorial Principles*.

As a member of staff of The University of Edinburgh, I had the good fortune to have access to the *Reid Music Library*, formed from a nucleus of books bequeathed by General John Reid and augmented over the years by such custodians as Sir Donald Francis Tovey, sometime *Reid Professor of Music* and renowned Beethoven scholar. Over a period of three years, I made a survey of the many works in the Reid collection. I consulted each item in turn making records on paper slips — many hundreds — that I deemed to be relevant for my researches. I confined my searches to book-publications, as reflected in my accompanying bibliography. All of this was quite some years ago, the cut-off date for my researches being 2007. Beyond this date I have not surveyed any further works. I am mindful though that Beethoven musicology and related publication continue to be a major field of endeavour in the manner of the proverbial 'ever rolling stream'.

In the intervening years since completing my archival researches, personal tribulations associated with family illness and bereavement slowed my progress in giving expression to my projected intentions. Latterly, however, with renewed energy, and more time at my disposal, I have been able to make progress. My studies take the form of a set of monographs. The first set of these, trace the creation origins and reception history of each of Beethoven's piano sonatas and string quartets. The resulting texts also incorporate contextual accounts of Beethoven and his contemporaries. Also included in my musicological surveys are two related Beethoven anthologies. The set of monographs in question, identified by short title, are:

Beethoven: An anthology of selected writings.
Beethoven: The piano sonatas: An anthology of selected writings.

The Piano Sonatas:
Op. 2–Op. 28
Op. 31–Op. 81a
Op. 90–Op. 111

The String Quartets:
Op. 18, Nos. 1–6
Op. 59, Nos. 1–3 (Razumovsky); Op. 74 (The Harp); Op. 95 (Quartetto serioso)
Op. 127, Op. 132 and Op. 130 (Galitzin)
Op. 131, Op. 135; Grosse Fuge, Op. 133 and Op. 134 (Fugue transcription)

I provide further information about these studies in the introduction to each individual monograph. Suffice it for me to state here the basic premise upon which my work is founded. I believe it is rewarding, concerning the life of a great artist, to find connections between who he *was* and what he *did*; in Martin Cooper's words 'between his personality, as expressed on the one hand in human relationships, and on the other in artistic creation'. (*Beethoven, The Last Decade*) That is not to say I consider it essential to the enjoyment of Beethoven's music to know this or that fact about it. His music can be enjoyed, as millions do, with – in Robert Simpson's apt phrase –'an innocent ear', for what it is and how it reaches out to us in purely musical terms without any prejudging of its merits based upon extra-musicological facts. Maynard Solomon expresses similar thoughts: 'It is doubtless true that we need have no knowledge whatever of a composer's biography, or knowledge of any other motivating factor of any kind, to appreciate the artwork on some fundamental level.' (*Beethoven Essays*, 1988, p. 116)

I must make a further point. I am mindful that a scholar who ventures into a field of study that is not rightly his may be regarded with some suspicion. In this regard I can but ask the reader to place his or her trust in me in the following way. I have attempted to bring to my work the care which publishers and their desk editors have required of me in my book writings relating to architecture — listed elsewhere.

As inferred, it is now more than sixty years since I paid homage to Beethoven in Vienna's *Währinger Ortsfriedhof* and my warmth of feeling towards the composer and his music have grown with the passing of the years. My studies are not intended to be propaedeutic — that would be pretentious. However, if in sharing with others what I have to say contributes to their knowledge and understanding of the composer, and thereby increases their own feelings towards him and his works, my own pleasure in bringing my work to completion will be all the more enhanced.

When Beethoven arrived in Vienna, he was unknown. He was armed though with a note of encouragement from his youthful friend and benefactor Count Ferdinand Waldstein. It contained the often-quoted words: 'Receive Mozart's spirit from Haydn's hands.' Some forty years later Beethoven passed away in the House of the black-robed Spaniards at 200 *Alservorstädter*, the *Glacis* where he had lived since the autumn of 1825. Soldiers had to be called to secure the doors to the inner courtyard of the house from the pressure of onlookers. His body was blessed in the

Alservorsttädt Parish Church, schools were closed and perhaps as many as 10,000 people formed a funeral procession — an honour ordinarily reserved for monarchs. The *Marcia Funebre* from the composer's Op. 26 Piano Sonata was performed at the funeral ceremony. Franz Grillparzer read the funeral oration. Franz Schubert, who, as remarked in life so admired Beethoven, was one of the pallbearers. The composer's mortal remains were lowered into a simple vault. Beethoven now belonged to history.

Dr Terence M. Russell
Edinburgh 2020

To the foregoing I am pleased to add the following works:

The Piano Concertos
The Symphonies: An Anthology of Selected Writings
Symphony No. 1 In C Major, Op. 21
Symphony No. 2 in D Major, Op. 36
Symphony No. 3 in E-flat Major, Op. 55
Symphony No. 4 in B-flat Major, Op. 60

TMR
2024

INTRODUCTION

As the title to this work implies, it consists of a compilation of texts that bring together views bearing on Beethoven's symphonic compositions. As such, it provides a collective estimation of the composer's achievements as expressed through the writings and remarks of fellow musicians, musicologists and performing artists. In selecting the texts for inclusion, my primary intention has been to make available to the reader the opinions of recognised authorities concerning such considerations as: the composer's aesthetic and creative impulse; his philosophical and intellectual outlook; the expressive nature of his writing — his instrumentation; the challenges with which he confronts the performer — relating to questions of interpretation and performance; and, above all, the continuing legacy of his musical inheritance. Where applicable, prefatory remarks are incorporated together with the selected texts so as to provide the reader with the original context from which the various writings have been derived.

The *Anthology* incorporates a number of writings that, although not directly concerned with Beethoven's symphonies, contribute to our wider understanding and appreciation of the composer and his music. The bibliography at the close of the work will also be of value to the reader wishing to discover more about the original sources and other publications not cited in the text.

Writing of Beethoven's uniqueness, in the context of symphonic writing, Paul Mies states:

> 'It is remarkable that even the names of the symphony-composers of Beethoven's time are hardly remembered today and that their works have almost disappeared. To a greater extent that at any other time one composer — Beethoven — overshadowed all his contemporaries ... To a certain extent this was true even in Beethoven's own day. When a critic, writing of the performance of the Fourth Symphony at the *Niederreinisches Musilkfest* in 1828, declared that "nothing more magnificent of this kind has probably ever been written, nor ever will be written", that was not an isolated judgement but one constantly reaffirmed by Beethoven's contemporaries. If not all his works were fully valued at once, if contemporaries were for a while placed by his side, he was in his own day already regarded as the greatest living composer.'

Of Beethoven's position in musical history Mies affirms:

> 'The uniqueness of Beethoven's historical posi-

tion, standing as he does between two ages and two philosophies, is nowhere more apparent than in his attitude towards the symphony. The symphony in the nineteenth century was essentially an aristocratic entertainment; to the Romantics it was a vehicle for self-confession on a grandiose scale. For Beethoven it was neither. It was a public work, not a private one. It did not reflect his immediate personal situation, nor did it use it to symbolize an immediate human relationship ... Beethoven's public was mankind, and he was mankind's spokesman. In his symphonies and overtures he proclaimed his concepts about life, concepts which, he believed, are of universal application: love of nature, desire for peace, freedom and brotherhood, the reality of conflict, of defeat, of triumph. To achieve his aim, it was necessary for him to forge a new symphonic language, one direct in its impact, yet capable of a hitherto unexplored range of expression. The story of the symphonies is the story of his creation and extension of this language.'

Paul Mies, *The Orchestral Music of Beethoven's Contemporaries* in: Philip Radcliffe, *The Age of Beethoven, The New Oxford History of Music*, Vol. VIII, Gerald Abraham, editor, 1988.

TMR

EDITORIAL PRINCIPLES

By its very nature a study of this kind draws extensively on the work of others. Every effort has been made to acknowledge this in the text by indicating words directly quoted or adapted with single quotation marks. Wherever possible, for the sake of consistency, I have retained the orthography of quoted texts making only occasional silent changes of spelling and capitalization. Deleted words are identified by means of three ellipsis points ... and interpolations are encompassed within square brackets [ ]. Quoted words, phrases and longer cited passages of text remain the intellectual property of their copyright holders.

The texts to each piano concerto are presented 'freestanding' so they can be read independently of each other – rather in the manner of a recital programme-note. However, the circumstances bearing on Beethoven's life, and the origins of his compositions, unite his works in various ways. With this in mind, the reader, so inclined, may read this book in the conventional way — from cover to cover. Thereby, insights may be gained into the nature of the interrelationships between the various piano concertos and the circumstances bearing on their creation origins. A number of individuals recur in our narratives. To introduce these afresh, in the text to each concerto, would become repetitive. I have therefore adopted the principle of describing a particular individual at their *first* appearance with subsequent citations being made in summary form. I occasionally make cross-references between texts, but these have been kept to a minimum. The Index is presented in the form of a timeline and serves as a guide to who and what appears in the texts in their chronological sequence.

I address the reader in the second person notwithstanding that the work is my own — produced without the benefit of a desk editor. It follows that I must bear the responsibility for any errors of misunderstanding or misinterpretation for which I ask the reader's forbearance. A collaboration I must acknowledge is the help I received from the librarians of the *Reid Music Library* at the University of Edinburgh. Over the three-year period it took me to compile my reference sources, they served me with unfailing courtesy, often supplying me with twenty or more books at a time. In converting my manuscript into book-format, I wish to thank my editorial coordinator, William Rees, for his support and painstaking care. I would also like to thank Shaun Russell (no relation) for his work designing the covers for each of the volumes.

My admiration for Beethoven provided the initial impulse to commence this undertaking and has sustained me over the several years it has taken to bring my enterprise to completion. That said I am no Beethoven idolater. I am mindful of the danger that awaits one who ventures to chronicle the work of a great artist. I believe it was Sigmund Freud who suggested that biographers may become so disposed to their subject, and their emotional involvement with their hero, that their work becomes an exercise in idealisation. In response to such a putative charge let me say. First, I am no biographer. I do however make reference to Beethoven's personal life and his relationships with his contemporaries, consistent with my sub-title. Second, I acknowledge Beethoven has his detractors. Accordingly, I have not shrunk from allowing dissentient voices, critical of Beethoven and his work, to be heard. These, however, are few and are silenced amidst the adulation that awaits the reader in support of the endeavours of one of humanity's great creators and one who courageously showed the way in overcoming personal adversity.

TMR

BEETHOVEN'S FINANCIAL TRANSACTIONS

Beethoven's negotiations with his music publishers make many references to his compositions. Today they are recognised for what they are — enduring works of art — but referred to in his business correspondence they appear almost as though they were mere everyday commodities — for which he required an appropriate remuneration. Beethoven resented the time he had to devote to the business-side of his affairs. He believed an agency should exist, for fellow artists such as himself, from which a reasonable sum could be paid for the work (composition) submitted, leaving more time for creative enterprises. In the event Beethoven, like Mozart before him, had to deal with publishers largely on his own. Beethoven, though, did benefit in his business dealings from the help he received from his younger brother Kasper Karl (Caspar Carl). From 1800, Carl worked as a clerk in Vienna's Department of

Finance, in which capacity he found time to correspond with publishers to offer his brother's works for sale and — importantly — to secure the best prices he could. In April 1802, Beethoven wrote to the Leipzig publishers Breitkopf & Härtel: '[You] can rely entirely on my brother who, in general, attends to my affairs.' Whilst Carl promoted Beethoven's interests with determination, he appears to have lacked tact and made enemies. For example, Beethoven's piano pupil Ferdinand Ries — who for a while also helped the composer with his business negotiations — is on record as describing Carl as being 'the biggest skinflint in the world'.

The currencies most referred to in Beethoven's correspondence are as follows:

> Silver gulden and florin: these were interchangeable and had a value of about two English shillings.
> Ducat: 4 1/2 gulden / florins: valued at about nine shillings.
> Louis d'or: This gold coin was adopted during the Napoleonic wars and the French occupation of Vienna and Austria more widely. It had a value of about two ducats or approximately twenty shillings, or one-pound sterling.

Beethoven was never poor — in the romantic sense of 'an artist starving in a garret'. On arriving in Vienna, in 1792, he was fortunate to receive financial support from his patron Prince Karl Lichnowsky who conferred on him an annuity of 600 florins — that he maintained for several years. Between the months of February and July of 1796, Beethoven undertook a concert tour taking in Prague, Dresden, Leipzig and Berlin. He was well-received and wrote to his other younger brother Nikolaus Johann: 'My art is winning me friends and what more do I want? ... I shall make a good deal of money.' Later on, in 1809, Napoleon Bonaparte's youngest brother Jérôme Bonaparte offered Beethoven an appointment at his Court with the promise of an income of 4,000 florins. Alarmed at the prospect of losing Beethoven — now the most celebrated composer in Europe — three of Vienna's most notable citizens, namely, the Archduke Rudolph (Beethoven's only composition pupil), Prince Kinsky and Prince Lobkowitz settled on the composer the same sum of 4,000 florins. Inflation, however, brought about by the Napoleonic wars, soon eroded its value; personal misfortune to Lobkowitz and Kinsky also took its toll.

Beethoven undoubtedly had to work hard to secure a reasonable standard of living. Notwithstanding, despite his occasional straitened circumstances, he contributed generously to the needs of others. For example, he allowed his works to be performed at charitable concerts without seeking any benefit to himself; in 1815 his philanthropy earned for him the honour of Bürgerrecht — 'freedom of the City'.

Beethoven earned a great deal of money when his music was performed, to considerable acclaim, at several concerts held in association with the Congress of Vienna (1814–15). He did not, though, benefit from it personally; he invested it on behalf of his nephew Karl. It is one of the misfortunes of Beethoven's life that in money-matters he was in some ways culpably improvident. This is poignantly evident in a letter he wrote on 18 March 1827 to the Philharmonic Society of London — just one week before his death; the Society had made him a gift of £100. He sent the Society 'His most heartfelt thanks for their particular sympathy and support'.

TMR

*'Beethoven was born, it would seem, to write symphonies...
Beethoven's nine symphonies have stood for more
than a century and a half as ideals for others to emulate.
There is neither an uncertain composition nor a genre
of work among the nine. Each is a confident, individual
statement from an artist for whom music was the
supremely expressive language. Beethoven restored music
to the proud pinnacle it had occupied in earlier times
when, along with arithmetic, geometry, and astronomy,
it was included in the quadrivium of liberal arts.
He proclaimed himself a Tondichter (tone poet).
In so doing, he set himself apart from his craftsmen-
forebears of the eighteenth century, and he placed his art
on a par with literature, philosophy, and religion,
as a means to uplift, instruct, and heal mankind.'*

Louise Elvira Cuyler, The Symphony, *New York,
Harcourt Brace Jovanovich, 1973.*

SELECTED WRITINGS

GERALD ABRAHAM
The English-Jewish musicologist Gerald Abraham wrote extensively about music both in his capacity as Professor of Music at the University of Liverpool (1947–62) and as President of the Royal Musical Association (1970-74). He was General Editor to the multi-volume *New Oxford History of Music* (1982–85–88). Introducing Volume Eight in this series he writes:

> 'The title of no other volume of the *New Oxford History of Music* includes the name of a composer. But no other period of musical history is so completely dominated by one composer; in popular thought the years 1790–1830 are the *Age of Beethoven* ... In the first years of maturity he

had opened a great symphony with an heroic theme and rivaled Cherubini with a rescue opera which owes musical ideas as well as its subject to a French source and borrows its most dramatic stroke from Méhul's *Hélèna*. A few years later he opened his greatest piano concerto with a quasi-military *allegro* ... But the spirit of the age is more comprehensively captured and preserved in Beethoven's first eight symphonies (1799—1812), his chamber music from the *Razumovsky* Quartets of 1806 to the *Archduke* works of 1811—12, and the piano sonatas from the *Pathétique* (1799) to Op. 90 (1814).'

Of Beethoven the putative romantic Abraham cautions:

'In Beethoven there are plenty of premonitions of romanticisms but not its full ripening. The romantic instrumental composers were more and more concerned with the expression of defined emotions, even pictorial or literary images: Beethoven during his last ten or twelve years was, except in the Mass and Ninth Symphony, almost exclusively concerned with the ineffable. He had become a more and more isolated figure, immensely respected but detached in spirit from the musical scene rather than at its centre ... [The] *Age of Beethoven* was above all an age of transition. Yet Beethoven, who had played the leading role in the process for so long, now stood apart, times had changed and he had changed, but not with them. He does not belong to German Romanticism.'

Gerald Abraham, *The Age of Beethoven, 1790–1830*, Vol. eight: *The New Oxford History of Music*, Oxford, New York, Oxford University Press, 1988, pp. v–vi.

In his role as Ernst Bloch Professor (1968–69), Abraham declared (Lecture VI):

> 'All the great masters have derived from tradition. Some have affected it much more than others: for instance, Beethoven very much more than Mozart. This has nothing to do with "Greatness", which is not a measurable quality anyhow. Beethoven possessed qualities that specially appealed to the Romantic age.'

Gerald Abraham, *The Tradition of Western Music*, London, Oxford University Press, 1974, p. 112.

THEODOR W. ADORNO

The German philosopher, sociologist and composer Theodor W. Adorno spent many years compiling notes for a projected study of Beethoven. His work remained in this form at the time of his death but was edited and collated by the writer and philosopher Rolf Tiedemann, being published in English translation (Edmund Jephcott) as *Beethoven: The Philosophy of Music, Fragments and Texts*, Cambridge: Polity Press, 1998). Adorno worked on his projected Beethoven text through the years 1938–56. Despite this long period of gestation, his work did not progress beyond a great accumulation of diverse texts – 'fragments' – arbitrarily arranged in his files. In his reworking of this material, Tiedemann recast Adorno's texts into 370 numbered sub-texts to which he appended scholarly commentaries. Thereby, he sought 'to organize the material as Adorno himself might have done, had he written the projected book' (*Preface*). Discussing Beethoven's symphonies, Adorno writes — in typically challenging fashion:

> 'In principle, Beethoven's symphonies are simpler than his chamber music despite their substantially more lavish apparatus, and this very simplicity showed what effects the many listeners had in the interior of the formal edifice. It was not a matter of adjusting to the market, of course; at most, perhaps it had to do with Beethoven's intent to "strike fire into a man's soul". Objectively, his symphonies were orations to mankind, designed by a demonstration of the law of their life to bring men to an unconscious consciousness of the unity otherwise hidden in the individual's diffuse existence.' p. 117.

Adorno considered Beethoven's chamber music and symphonies to be complimentary:

> 'The first, largely dispensing with pathos in gesture and ideology, helped to express the self-emancipating status of the bourgeois spirit without as yet directly addressing society. The symphony took the consequence, declaring the idea of totality to be aesthetically void as soon as it ceased to communicate with the real totality.' pp. 117–18.

Of Beethoven's symphonic construction, Adorno states:

> 'In a Beethoven symphony the detail work, the

latent wealth of interior forms and figures, is eclipsed by the rhythmic-metrical impact; throughout, the symphonies want to be heard simply in their temporal course and organisation, with the vertical, the simultaneity, the sound level left wholly unbroken. The exception remained the wealth of motifs in the first movement of the *Eroica* — which in certain respects, of course, is the higher peak of Beethoven's symphonies as a whole.' p. 118.

ALLGEMEINE MUSIKALISCHE ZEITUNG (AMZ)

The *Allgemeine musikalische Zeitung* (*General music newspaper*) was a German-language periodical that commenced publication in 1798 under the direction of its owner and founder Gottfried Christoph Härtel. Its publisher was Breitkopf & Härtel of Leipzig with whom Beethoven had many negotiations. The periodical reviewed musical events taking place in the German-speaking nations and in other countries. As such, it was amongst the first to bring to the attention of the musically-minded public an awareness of Beethoven's compositions and of their originality — that the periodical's contributors frequently found to be disturbing. In 1800, the *AmZ* published a review in celebration of Joseph Haydn, to whom it accorded 'the first place' with regard to his symphonies and quartets 'wherein no one has yet surpassed him'. Beethoven, a still relatively unknown composer, is not, however, overlooked; the reviewer comments how he may even usurp the venerable master 'if he calms his wild imaginings'. In 1803, a contributor to the *AmZ* endeavoured to define the orchestral symphony as follows:

'Symphonies are the triumph of this art. Unlimited and free, the artist can conjure up an entire world of feeling in them. Dancing merriment, exultant joy, the sweet yearning of love and profound pain, gentle peace and mischievous caprice, playful jest and frightful gravity pour forth and touch the sympathetic strings of the heart, feeling, and fantasy; the complete multitude of instruments is at his command.'

The *AmZ* contributor acknowledged Mozart and Haydn had produced works of art in the genre of instrumental music 'that deserve great admiration'. (Mozart had died in 1792 but Haydn was still alive.) He described Mozart's symphonies as 'colossal masses of rock, wild and abundant, surrounding a gentle, laughing valley'. Haydn's symphonies he compared with a Chinese garden 'created by cheerful humour and mischievous caprice'. Although by now Beethoven had composed his First Symphony (1799–1800) and his Second (1802), the *AmZ's* contributor regarded him as still being 'a novice in art' but recognised how he was already 'approaching the great masters'.

Christian Michaelis, a professor of philosophy, was a regular contributor to the *AmZ* and its sister Journal the *Berliner musikalische Zeitung* (*BmZ*). Writing in the *BmZ* issue 1 of 1805, he placed Beethoven alongside Haydn and Mozart as a creator of 'great symphonies' in whose work he found 'a spirit similar to the grand plan and character of a heroic epic'. Beethoven's First Symphony – the longest to date in the repertoire – had been published in 1801 and the Second in 1804. Michaelis then set out to further define the symphony:

'A simple introduction prepares the listener for the rich presentation that follows in a slow meaningful section in which exuberant melody is not dominant ... The other sections are added in which a great theme is developed. Its content becomes clearer in all its depth and opulence ... The individual features of its musical portrait intermesh marvellously, to make one another necessary, and form a large, effective, magnificently organised whole.'

On 22 February 1806, the *AmZ*'s music correspondent reported on a concert that had taken place in Leipzig. Featured on the programme were symphonies and overtures by Haydn and Mozart followed by 'a more recent work by Beethoven'. According to the correspondent's account, the music's 'profoundly serious fantasy and imaginative artistic depth' filled the audience with such enchantment that it was felt long after the concert. The Beethoven work in question was most probably one of the first two symphonies.

By 1814, Beethoven's symphonies were well established in the repertoire and were the subject of critical scrutiny. Audiences would also have had some familiarity with his more recent creations: for example, the Seventh Symphony was first performed in December 1813 and the Eighth in February 1814. Thereby, audiences would be aware of the composer's spirited interpretation of the *scherzo*. Ordinarily conceived as a vigorous, light or even playful movement, in Beethoven's hands it had become much more. So much so that in the July issue of the *AmZ*, the contributor felt obliged to sympathise with those somewhat bewildered by Beethoven's most recent innovations. He writes: 'Many lovers of music — and it is certainly not to be held against them — are not just a little astonished at many of the scherzos in Beethoven. They don't just seem to be *playful* at all. Well, they are right in their way!' In Beethoven's defence he posited: 'But is there not a *jest*, which according to its own innermost nature, as well as in its sound, is related to *pain*?' For those not able to grasp this relationship, the reviewer conceded they had no more hope of understanding a Beethoven scherzo than comprehending Egyptian hieroglyphics!

Later in the year, a fellow contributor to the *AmZ* accepted that Beethoven's symphonies — and his personality as expressed through them — posed a challenge to their assimilation. Resorting to vivid word-imagery, he likened the composer's music to violent, terrestrial phenomena:

> 'Beethoven's great instrumental compositions, seen from one point of view, are to a certain degree like volcanoes that pour out their rivers of fire in all directions. Like the former they are destructive, but, and that is the difference, they destroy only impermanent, common, and conventional things. Like volcanoes, they fructify, only faster. More richly even, and more magnificently.'

Turning to a consideration of Beethoven's psyche, he elaborates:

> 'His soul is like the sea: when it is peaceful, the sky with all its constellations is mirrored in its tides. If, however, the almighty breath of nature passes across it, it too billows upon the shore, foaming and surging. So too with *him*. If his soul is peaceful and quiet, then an endless abundance of friendly, illuminating beams break forth from him in all directions and a world of wonders is opened up to us with its magical glow.'

The following year, October 1815, the *AmZ* contributor — perhaps the same one? — likened Beethoven to a navigator:

> 'Beethoven is unquestionably the boldest sailor on the tides of harmony. Every one of his journeys on the sea is a voyage of discovery. If it occasionally seems as if he is off-course, the fixed star of the North Pole always shines for him, and at last he always lands in a new world. But to settle down there calmly is certainly not his way.'

The Leipzig philosopher and music theorist Amadeus Wendt is considered to be one of Beethoven's foremost contemporary music critics. Writing in the November 1822 issue of the *Allgemeine musikalische Zeitung* he contributed an article titled. *On the Condition of Music in Germany.* Directing his subject to orchestral music he expounded: 'The symphony is a tone-painting that is produced through the collaboration of orchestral instruments. The masters who have devoted themselves to this genre, and they are the greatest composers of our nation, have elevated German orchestras greatly by the demands that they made on instruments in their symphonies.' Wendt acknowledged instruments had been improved 'by many and new inventions' — for example the French horn had been supplied with valves — and, he added, 'the expanding art of virtuosity supported these demands'.

These developments, Wendt suggested, had enabled composers to engage 'the masses of sound of the orchestra' as 'a master engages the sound of a pianoforte on which he improvises in a free flight of fantasy'. In this he acknowledged Beethoven's role: '[This] happened through *Beethoven* [Wendt's italics] and others who in this regard have brought forth unexcelled original works.' Wendt considered it was in response to such works that orchestras had 'achieved a high degree of perfection' enabling them 'to overcome difficulties now that otherwise would have been considered insurmountable'. Wendt recognised, though, that Beethoven's orchestral music still posed a challenge: 'However, the gigantic works of *Beethoven* seem to frighten off his descendants in this area.'

A year after Beethoven's death in March 1827, the August 1828 issue of the *AmZ* published an article in which the contributor reflected on Beethoven and his music. He acknowledged he 'understood his peculiarities somewhat more', but conceded he was aware Beethoven's originality would for some always remain 'somewhat incomprehensible'. He then contributed an obituary-style encomium:

> 'Musical fate has selected a genius richly endowed by nature who, neither bound, borne, nor oppressed by middle-class familial relationships, made music his kingdom, his world. With self-confidence he transferred this peculiarity in his way of thinking and acting to art in a peculiar and singular manner ... His slightest musical developments were listened to intensely, his artistic moods were received sympathetically, and he saw the sounds of his poetry immediately performed publicly in the liveliest form by a circle of excellent artists. With the passing of the years, he was excluded from friendly, soothing human contact because of his loss of hearing. He sought to compensate for everything that fate did to aid and injure him ... in a musical dream-world that could no longer adjust to its phantoms to reality.'

Wayne M. Senner, Robin Wallace and William Meredith, editors, *The Critical Reception of Beethoven's Compositions by his German Contemporaries*, Lincoln: University of Nebraska Press, in association with the American Beethoven Society and the Ira F. Brilliant Center for Beethoven Studies, San José State University, 1999, Vol. 1, p. 29 p. 34, p. 37, p. 42, p. 43, p. 55, and p. 127.

BOITO ARRIGO

The Italian Boito Arrigo is remembered today for his collaboration with Giuseppe Verdi, notably for supplying the libretti to his operas *Otello* and *Falstaff*. In his day, however, Arrigo enjoyed a reputation for being a poet and writer on music. Arrigo's musical articles adopt vivid word-imagery to convey his thoughts about the character of a composer. Thus:

> 'Haydn proceeds from Bach as the flowering laburnum from the terrible rock' and Schuman is 'the sail of a ship before the wind'. In Arrigo's scheme of things: 'Beethoven [is] a solar intelligence, a nature almost divine, amphibian of sky and earth'. Arrigo pronounced Beethoven to be 'the greatest of all' in stature: 'Bach comes up to his chest, Mendelssohn to his heart, Schumann to his elbow, Haydn to his knee, Wagner to the clavicle of his foot.'

Frank Walker, *The Man Verdi*, London, Dent, 1962, p. 454.

In an essay on what constitutes beautiful, Arrigo wrote:

'The Beautiful can come to life in many kinds of forms, the most bizarre, the most varied, the most different; regarding the sublime, one can only point to its great form, the divine form, universal and eternal: the form of the sphere. The horizon is sublime; the sea is sublime; the sun is sublime. Shakespeare is spherical, Dante is spherical, Beethoven is spherical.'

Mary Jane Phillips-Matz, *Verdi: A Biography*, Oxford, Oxford University Press, 1993, p. 474.

VLADIMIR ASHKENAZY

In an interview with the American pianist and author David Dubal, and the Russian-born pianist and conductor Vladimir Ashkenazy, Beethoven became the subject of conversation, prompting the following exchange:

> DUBAL: 'Which brings to mind Beethoven and his hard-fought creative developments. Do you know the little book called *Beethoven: His Spiritual Development*, by J. W. N. Sullivan?'

> ASHKENAZY: 'It is my favourite book on Beethoven and perhaps on music itself. It's such a marvelous little volume.'

> DUBAL: 'Sullivan felt that music on the level of Beethoven's communicates great depths of consciousness that contain invaluable lessons for humanity.'

> ASHKENAZY: 'How much he understood of

Beethoven, one of the great geniuses? That we have a Beethoven in our midst is a great solace and a never-ending experience.'

David Dubal, *The World of the Concert Pianist*, London: Victor Gollancz, 1985, p. 42.

On another occasion Ashkenazy compared Beethoven with Mozart:

'I have always been puzzled by the fact that Beethoven composed with great difficulty while Mozart did so effortlessly and very, very fast. And most of his music is so incredible, so transcendental, that there are no words to describe it. Beethoven's case seems more understandable because the greatness of the music was the result of so much effort. He certainly had the feeling, the musical idea and the image corresponding to his feeling. But it took a lot of time, anguish and torment before his ideas crystallized into something that could be written on paper, in notes. He did hundreds of sketches. But we know what finally came out. And when it is imperfect or clumsy from the formal point of view, as it very occasionally is, it is still perfect from the point of view of communicating ultimate reality — or, in other words, true to life.

'When I say that I can understand Beethoven's case more easily, I am not saying that he is closer to me, but merely that he reflects life in all its states. Mozart, on the other hand, is so elevated, so perfect that he almost seems removed from life — because life is not perfect. But Mozart is.

Maybe he represents some essence of life, a transcendental essence, the ultimate meaning of life. But I can't explain it. I don't know and can't reconcile the apparently easy process of composition with the unfathomable depth and complete, integral, organic vision contained in his music. Some critics and musical people say that the music was already made up, stamped in his mind all the time. I don't believe this, but cannot provide any answers of my own, either. Perhaps the only conductor who came close to explaining this mystery was the late Josef Krips who stopped an orchestra during a rehearsal of a Mozart symphony, tapped his baton and said, "Gentlemen, please! Remember: Beethoven *goes* to heaven: Mozart *comes* from heaven!" '

Helena Matheopoulos, *Maestro: Encounters with Conductors of Today*, London, Hutchinson, 1982, pp. 478–9. See also the entry for J. N. W. Sullivan.

DANIEL BARENBOIM

In his autobiography *A Life in Music*, the Argentine-Israeli born pianist and conductor Daniel Barenboim outlined his views on the nature of Western European music, as we typically know it in recital and concert. Here, he reflects on the changing nature of musical appreciation and its relevance in today's education of the young:

'Nowadays, millions of people appreciate music. Before the invention of the gramophone record, music lovers had to content themselves with playing the Beethoven symphonies in four-hand arrangements for piano in their homes. This did mean, though, that they were actively in contact with the music. They were not simply passive listeners and, therefore, their actual knowledge of the music was greater. The size of the audience is much larger now, but the knowledge they possessed was greater before and, in addition, people were able to read music — an ability which has almost totally disappeared today. If only education authorities would appreciate how easy and necessary it is to teach children to read music, and how much their lives would be enriched by it, either as players or simply as listeners in adult life.'

Drawing on his experience as a concert pianist, Barenboim asserts:

'I also believe that you cannot conduct or bring out the full significance of what you as a musician can see in a Beethoven symphony unless you know the piano sonatas, the string quartets, and a few other pieces as well. Certain cycles represent the essence of a composer's creation. In the case of Beethoven, I think it is in the piano sonatas and the string quartets, with Mozart the piano sonatas and operas.'

Turning his attention to Beethoven's symphonic repertoire, Barenboim contends:

'The difference between the *Eroica* and the *Pastoral* Symphony can be far greater than the difference between two composers whose works are similar. Beethoven was able to, or felt a need to adopt or create a new musical idiom for almost every piece he wrote. You need to know these pieces so as to apply your knowledge to the interpretation of the one you are actually performing.'

Daniel Barenboim, *A Life in Music*. London, Weidenfeld & Nicolson, 1991, pp. 85–86 and p. 198.

PHILIP BARFORD

In his portrait of *Beethoven as Man and Artist* the musicologist Philip Barford expresses candid and uncompromising views:

'Totally opposed to the romantic image of "Beethoven the Creator and Conqueror" is the psychological, psychiatric, even clinical view. Beethoven was a genius with the characteristic marks of genius — neurotic without a doubt, unstable, oscillating between moody introspection and depression on the one hand and back-slapping exaltation and enthusiasm on the other, with his own view of himself enlarged by solid convictions of his own worth and tainted by excursions into self-pity. He was aggressive, over-sensitive, restless, undisciplined in his life, gross and crude with an "unbuttoned" sense of humour, devious, intolerant and sometimes hypocritical. He suffered a great deal of ill-health.'

Notwithstanding these many personal shortcomings, Barford offers the following affirmation of Beethoven's continuing relevance to humankind — almost as an antidote to his previous raw candor:

> 'Beethoven's enduring monument is his music. There, in the notes, are his intellectual functions revealed. Beethoven *is* the music. The symphonies, quartets, sonatas — these are the very structure of his consciousness, the framework of his being enshrined in symbols, which reveal the truth to us in the only language that matters ... And yet the traditional romantic images must be given their due. A bust, an engraving or a painting that is a true work of art brings something through which is true to its subject, something discerned intuitively by the artist who has made it, however fleetingly, living contact with the inner life behind the appearances. From this point of view, images projected in idealized busts and portraits by artists who never even saw Beethoven could be allowed their measure of truth.'

Barford considers Beethoven in the context of Freedom:

> 'Beethoven believed in Freedom and in God, and like many others in his day and ours saw no reason to waste time saying what he meant by these terms. Like many he had felt the impact of the French Revolution. Unlike most his notion of freedom rose quite above political considerations and the local circumstances of his life, although he was interested in politics and freely criticized politicians and the police during a period of Viennese history when it was unwise to do so. His cavalier treatment of sonata conven-

tions reveals a mind which, of its own creative momentum, had broken through previously accepted limitations.'

Barford identifies Beethoven's personal credo by which he sought to live:

'Freedom from theological restraints is clearly indicated in Beethoven's credo, which he adopted from an inscription on a temple in Jean-François Champollion's *Pictures of Egypt.* "I am that which is. I am everything that is, that was, and that will be. No mortal man has raised my veil. He is of himself alone, and it to this aloneness that all things owe their being." Beethoven copied out these words, framed them, and kept them on his desk.'

Of Beethoven's continuing legacy Barford states:

'Beethoven is still very much before us, not only as a musical genius but as a challenge to the further growth of humanity, the symbol of man's eternal rejection of negative attitudes to life, and all narrow cleaving to petty ambitions of the finite self. The forces of his personality, which overflowed into unrefined excesses and offensive behaviour, were reflections of forces transmuted at a higher level of his being — the level of his better self, his individuality — into music.'

Phillip Barford, *Beethoven as Man and Artist*, In: Denis Arnold and Nigel Fortune, editors, *The Beethoven Companion*, London, Faber and Faber, 1973, p. 22, p. 31 and p. 37.

BÉLA BARTÓK

The Hungarian composer, pianist and ethnomusicologist Béla Bartók expressed his thoughts about music throughout his lifetime in a number of essays. In his *On Beethoven's Genius* (1911) he stated: 'It is not given to every composer to be able, like Beethoven, to break down every difficulty himself and to create perfection in every single work.' In his essay *The Influence of Peasant Music on Modern Music* (1931), Bartók reflected on the manner in which Beethoven had given expression to such an influence in his music:

> 'It is a well-known fact the Viennese classical composers were influenced to a considerable extent by folk music. In Beethoven's *Pastoral* Symphony, for instance, the main motive of the first movement is a Yugoslav dance melody. Beethoven obviously heard this from bagpipes, perhaps even in Western Hungary; the *ostinato*-like repetition of one of the measures, at the beginning of the movement, point to such an association.'

Benjamin Suchoff, *Béla Bartók, Essays*, University of Nebraska Press, Faber and Faber (reprint), 1992, p. 340 and p. 453.

ARNOLD BAX

In an essay *First Music*, the English composer, poet, and author Sir Arnold Bax revealed the origins of his youthful inclination to orchestral music:

> 'My earliest distant acquaintance with the orchestra came when I was taken for the first time to

one of the Crystal Palace Saturday Concerts [where Beethoven symphonies were regularly performed]. My father had been a subscriber since 1860, and unfailing attendance at 'the Palace' every Saturday afternoon was for him a religious observance, almost comparable with the obligation laid upon the devout Catholic to hear Mass every Sunday.'

Cited in: Lewis Foreman, editor, *Farewell, My Youth, and other Writings by Arnold Bax*, Aldershot, Scolar Press, 1992, p. 7.

In an essay on Bax, the English musicologist Burnett James touched upon the composer's observations concerning Beethoven. Drawing on his personal knowledge of Bax, he affirmed he was acutely aware of Beethoven's symphonic achievement, remarking: 'I once heard him assert that the first movements of the *Eroica* and Ninth Symphonies represented the ultimate in symphonic thought and construction.' Regarding Bax's own symphonic music, he stated:

'In the first movement of the Third, the woodwind set up an insistent rhythm at the end of the introduction which acts as a bridge to the movement proper. It is strikingly similar to the corresponding section of the Beethoven Seventh.'

Quoted in: Lewis Foreman, *Bax: A Composer and his Times*, London: Scolar Press, 1983, p. 242.

PAUL BEKKER

The German musicologist Paul Bekker is remembered for

his pioneering study of Beethoven, from which we quote the following in which he gauges the measure of the composer's symphonic achievement:

> 'The symphonies rise like a great nine-pointed peak from the mountain range of Beethoven's works; they do not perhaps pierce the clouds at the altitude of his other works but they are visible from the greatest distances. The first Beethoven symphony was first performed on April 2nd, 1800, the last, the Ninth Symphony, on May 7th, 1824, so that about a quarter of a century, from his thirtieth to his five-and-fiftieth year comprise his whole symphonic work. In his youth and in his last years he produced nothing in this branch of music. The complete story of his development as a composer cannot, therefore, be read in the symphonies, but they form a comprehensive cycle of his work during his prime, when he surveyed the world about him most keenly and rendered an account of what he saw in his art. No other work of his has so many, and such vital, points of contact with a wide range of human culture, or has made so deep an impression upon the artistic consciousness of the masses. The symphonies are the most popular of Beethoven's works, indeed they are the most popular of all serious instrumental music.'

Bekker attributed the success of Beethoven's symphonies, in the first place, 'to the concentration of his creative power', which, in contrast to previous such works in the genre he considered to be 'stupendous'. In his desire to select and concentrate his material into the shortest possible musical formulae, Bekker recognised Beethoven imposed a severe task upon himself — as evident in his many painstaking sketches — but, he argues, this 'arose from a new conception of the basis of symphonic work'. He elaborates:

> 'His ideas were too big for the narrow bounds of the music *salons* of the nobility, and he did away with the intimate and chamber-music character which had hitherto clung to the symphony. He calculated on a far wider sphere of influence, and exchanged the range of thought and feeling of a particular class for the whole range of human interest of his period ... They are a confession of his outlook upon common human problems, not, like the sonatas, a subjective revelation of his own particular nature. He strips away everything personal and seeks the eternal and typical in the problems before him.'

Bekker maintains Beethoven *speaks* to us through his symphonies:

> 'The symphonies might well be described as speeches to the nation, to humanity. Because the sense of human solidarity then existed as a strong and unbrocken force, it inspired the greatest composer of the time to write symphonies which, in the width of their appeal, far surpassed any previous work of the kind.'

Paul Bekker, *Beethoven*, London, J. M. Dent & Sons, 1925, pp. 146–47.

LUCIANO BERIO

The musicologist-authors Rossana Dalmonte and Bálint András Varga invited the Italian composer Luciano Berio to express his views about Beethoven and his music. He responded:

> 'There are pieces by Beethoven, those that I think I know particularly well and to which I feel very close, that I perceive and "feel" globally, without a beginning and an end, like an organic, non-chronological whole, or a huge process of mutation ... The fact is that with Beethoven, the great gesture, the great process, the great musical event (whether it be the Third or Fourth Symphony, Fourth Piano Concerto, Opp. 106, 111, 135, etc.) seems to emerge every time, dripping with precedents, from a totality that contained that great process, and from which Beethoven, like Michelangelo, has hacked it out "*a forza di levare*". We thus have a totality that "speaks" the piece, and to which the piece continually alludes through innumerable, and disconcerting ways.'

David Osmond-Smith, editor and translator, *Luciano Berio: Two Interviews with Rossana Dalmonte and Bálint András Varga*, New York, London, Boyars, 1985, p. 67.

HECTOR BERLIOZ

Hector Berlioz's enthusiasm for the music of Beethoven is well documented. He himself gave expression to it in his *A Travers Chants, Etudes Musicales, Adorations, Boutades et Crtiques,* an English edition of which was translated and edited by Edwin Evans and was published in 1911 under the title *A Critical Study of Beethoven's Nine Symphonies, with a Few Words on his Trios and Sonatas, a Criticism of Fidelio and an Introductory Essay on Music*, London, W. Reeves, 1911.

More than thirty years after Beethoven's death his works were little known in France. Those that were performed, in particular the orchestral works, were usually premiered in severely edited and truncated form and were typically received with hostility. The symphonies were condemned for being 'bizarre, incoherent, diffuse, bristling with harsh modulations and wild harmonies, bereft of melody, over the top, too noisy, and horribly difficult to play'. Berlioz recalls the effect made upon him personally on 'discovering' Beethoven's music:

> 'It sometimes happens that in the life of an artist one thunderclap follows another as swiftly as it does those great storms in the physical world ... I had scarcely recovered from the visions of Shakespeare and Weber when I beheld Beethoven's giant form looming above the horizon. The shock was almost as great as that I had received from Shakespeare, and a new world of music was revealed to me by the musician, just as a new universe of poetry had been opened to me by the poet.'

Ernest Newman, annotated and translated, *Memoirs of Hector Berlioz from 1803 to 1865, Comprising his Travels in Germany, Italy, Russia, and England*, New York, Knopf, 1932, pp. 75–76.

Berlioz reflected on the reception of Beethoven's symphonies in France in his essay *The Art of Music* (1837):

'Some thirty-six or thirty-seven years ago, Beethoven's works, which at the time were completely unknown in France, were tried out at the Opéra's *Concerts Spirituels*. Today, it would be hard to believe the storm of criticism from the majority of musicians that greeted this wonderful music ... To satisfy the demands of men of good taste, who at the time held sway at the *Académie Royale de Musique*, M. Habeneck, who later organised and directed with such care the performance of the symphonies at the Conservatoire, found himself obliged to make monstrous cuts in them, of a kind that would not be tolerated in a ballet by Gallenberg or an opera by Gaveaux. Without such *corrections*, Beethoven would not have been granted the honour on the programmes of the *Concerts Spirituels* between a solo for bassoon and a flute concerto.'

Berlioz next describes the response of the French violinist and conductor Rodolphe Kreutzer — remembered as the dedicatee of Beethoven's Violin Sonata No. 9, Op. 47, known as the *Kreutzer* Sonata — to the unwarranted editing of Beethoven's symphonies:

'At the first hearing of those passages that had been marked with a red pencil, Kreutzer took to flight blocking his ears, and he had to summon all his courage to steel himself to listen at the rehearsals to *what was left* of the Symphony in D major, No. 2. Let us not forget that M. Kreutzer's opinion on Beethoven was shared by ninety-nine per cent of musicians in Paris at that time, and that without the persistent efforts of the tiny fraction who took the opposite view, the greatest composer of modern times would probably still be largely unknown today. The mere fact that fragments of Beethoven were performed at the Opéra was therefore of considerable significance ... since without this the *Société des Concerts du Conservatoire* would probably not have been founded.'

Elizabeth Csicserry-Ronay, translator and editor, *Hector Berlioz: The Art of Music and other Essays: (A Travers Chants)*, Bloomington, Indiana University Press, 1994, p. 9. See also: Michel Austin, translator, *Berlioz, Predecessors and Contemporaries, The Hector Berlioz website.* Originally published in: Hector Berlioz, *The Art of Music and other Essays (A Travers Chants)*.

Berlioz likened music to language that, uniquely he maintained, could 'designate silence and specify its length'. He asserted, with typical Gallic passion: 'If all human languages should perish [music] would still remain the greatest and most poetic of the arts — and the most free.' With a typical flourish he concluded: 'What is a Beethoven symphony but sovereign music in all its majesty?'

Hector Berlioz, *The Musical Madhouse (Les Grotesques de la Musique)*, Rochester, New York, University of Rochester Press, 2003, p. 138.

In 1828, Berlioz heard Beethoven's Third and Fifth Symphonies for the first time when they were performed at the Paris Conservatoire — an experience he found overwhelming. In the same year he submitted an entry in a bid to secure the coveted *Prix de Rome*. His composition, a cantata *Herminie,* was one of four attempts; it was not until

1830, though, that he was eventually successful. In his *Memoires*, Berlioz writes of the passion for Shakespeare that Beethoven's music had stirred within him:

> 'I was haunted by my Shakespearean passion, which had been painfully intensified by the effect produced on me by Beethoven; and [I] was at that time a dreamy, savage creature, silent to the verge of dumbness, disorderly in my attire, as great a burden to my friends as to myself, and my only occupation the occasional production of a small and shapeless article on music.'

On 10 December 1831, Berlioz wrote enthusiastically to his fellow countryman Victor Hugo; Berlioz was by then becoming more fully aware of Beethoven's music:

> 'Oh! You are a genius, a man of power, a colossus who is both tender, pitiless, elegant, monstrous, raucous, melodious, volcanic, affectionate and *scornful*. This last constituent of genius is certainly the rarest, neither Shakespeare nor Molière had it. Beethoven alone among the *great* gauged correctly the size of the human insects that surrounded him and on his level I see none but you.'

Hugh Macdonald, editor: *Berlioz: Selected Letters*, London: Faber and Faber, 1995. p. 95.

An entry from Berlioz's *Memoires* from 1837 bears testimony to the slow progress Beethoven's music was taking in France to infiltrate into even the more musically enlightened circles. This realization derives from remarks made by the then Director of the Fine Arts. Berlioz discretely withholds his name but describes him as being the 'arbiter of the destinies of art and artists' who, apparently, did not condescend to recognise the worth in any music except that of Rossini. One day, in conversation with Berlioz, the individual in question endeavoured to recall the names of past and present musicians whom he considered to be of standing. He appeared to falter, stopped and remarked: 'But surely there must be another – what is his name? A German, whose symphonies they play at the Conservatoire. You must know *him*, M. Berlioz. Beethoven? Ah, Beethoven. Well, *he* was not devoid of talent.' Berlioz later recalled, that he was scarcely able to contain his disdain: 'I myself heard the Director of the Fine Arts express himself thus, and admit that Beethoven *was not devoid of talent*.'

In 1854, Berlioz was asked to supply biographical details for his *Memoires* and to explain the grounds why he himself had encountered such opposition in Paris as a composer. It is worth recalling what a modernist Berlioz was. His *Symphonie Fantastique* was composed only seven years after the death of Beethoven and occupies an entirely new and different musical landscape. Depicting 'An episode in the life of an artist', Leonard Bernstein described the *Symphonie Fantastique* as 'the first musical expedition into psychedelia' because of its hallucinatory and dream-like nature.

Berlioz's response to the request he had received for details for his *Memoires*, provides further evidence, albeit indirectly, of the challenges Beethoven's music was proving to be almost thirty years after his death. He first states:

> 'The principal reason for the long war raged against me, lies in the antagonism existing

between my musical feeling and that of the great mass of the Parisian public. Many of them looked upon me as a madman.'

Berlioz concludes:

'All music deviating from the beaten track of the manufacturers of *opéras-comiques* necessarily seemed to these people the music of madmen, just as Beethoven's Ninth Symphony and colossal pianoforte sonatas are to them the compositions of a lunatic.'

Ten years later, in 1864, Berlioz was reunited with his son who had been away in Mexico. He relates:

'Towards evening, as we walked along the banks of the Seine and talked of Shakespeare and Beethoven, I remember we got into a state of immense excitement, in which my son only shared as far as Shakespeare was concerned, he being still unacquainted with Beethoven. We ... agreed finally, however, that it was good to be alive, to worship the beautiful, and that, if we could not destroy its opposite, we must rest satisfied with despising and forgetting it as far as possible.'

Ernest Newman, annotated and translated: *Memoirs of Hector Berlioz from 1803 to 1865, Comprising his Travels in Germany, Italy, Russia, and England*, New York, Knopf, 1932, p. 81, p. 95, pp. 180–1, pp. 483–4 and p. 510.

LEONARD BERNSTEIN

The American composer, conductor, pianist, educator and humanitarian Leonard Bernstein was described by the music critic Donal Henaham as 'one of the most prodigiously talented and successful musicians in American history'. Bernstein's admiration for Beethoven approached reverence. This is evident in the many recordings he made of the composer's music alongside his equally numerous performances of the five piano concertos. Moreover, he expressed his thoughts about Beethoven's music in lectures, not least when he held the tenure of the Charles Eliot Norton Professorship of Poetry at Harvard University (1973–74). His lectures on Beethoven's symphonies, originally destined for television, are today available on *You Tube*. The following is a characteristic Bernstein-Beethovenian utterance:

> 'When you get the feeling that whatever note succeeds the last is the only possible note that can rightly happen at that instant, in that context, then the chances are you're listening to Beethoven ... Our boy has the real goods, the stuff from Heaven, the power to make you feel at the finish: "Something is right in the world". There is something that checks throughout, that follows its own law consistently: something we can trust that will never let us down — But that is almost a definition of God — I meant it to be.'

Leonard Bernstein, *The Joy of Music*, New York, Simon and Schuster, 1959.

In one of his YouTube recordings, Bernstein states:

'I have studied [Beethoven's music] and re-studied it, rehearsed and performed it over and over again and I may report that I have never tired of it for a single moment. The music remains endlessly satisfying, interesting and moving and has remained so for almost two centuries and to all kinds of people. In other words, this music is not only infinitely durable but perhaps the closest music has ever come to universality and that dubious cliché about music being the universal language almost comes true with Beethoven. No composer has ever lived who speaks so directly to so many people, to young and old, educated and ignorant, amateur and professional, sophisticated and naive, and to all these people of all classes, nationalities and racial backgrounds, this music speaks a universality of thought of human brotherhood, freedom and love.'

Bernstein about Beethoven's Music, You Tube.

The Greek-born author and biographer Helena Matheopoulos interviewed Leonard Bernstein and asked him when he was writing his own compositions, did he take into consideration the possibilities that other conductors of his work might experience? He answered making reference to Beethoven:

'[Being] a composer makes me conduct more like a composer, more like *the* composer of each work, I hope. And being a conductor makes me compose more like a conductor, with more attention paid to problems of performance, unlike Beethoven. In this respect, I am the exact opposite of Beethoven, who wrote in any old way and left you to bloody well do it, somehow.'

Helena Matheopoulos, *Maestro: Encounters with Conductors of Today*, London, Hutchinson, 1982, p. 16.

ARTHUR BLISS

The English composer Arthur Bliss writes of his early musical experiences whilst at preparatory school:

> 'I shall always be grateful to the self-effacing and dedicated music master there who introduced me to the Beethoven Sonatas ... My introduction to Beethoven through practising his *Andante con Variazioni*, Op. 26, and then through hearing in London his *Coriolan* Overture and Fifth Symphony fired me with a longing to find out all there was to know about his personality and life.'

Later Bliss wrote about the capacity of Beethoven's music to heal:

> '*All* Beethoven's music is a continual protest against the cruelty, misery and evil in this world, but he *does*, after a lifetime's struggle, supply and answer in the music of his last period, envisaging a world of compassion and serenity. I believe that through whatever changes and transformations music is passing it must unswervingly keep its idealistic aim; otherwise, it may cease to retain its mysterious power of healing and of giving joy, and just dwindle into an excitant aural sensation, and nothing more.'

*

In the spring of 1934, Bliss was invited to deliver a series of lectures at the Royal Institution. H. G. Wells was in the audience of one of these and later invited Bliss to compose the music to Alexander Korda's film-adaptation of his *Things to Come*. In discussing unity and form in music, Bliss made passing, but significant, reference to Beethoven:

> '[Unity] in diversity [is] the employment not of one idea that spreads, but of two or more antagonistic ideas that are gradually compelled to harmonize and form one complete whole. This implies drama and struggle, and is the formal idea lying behind the first movement of a Beethoven sonata, for instance. The first develops from a single thematic idea, the second is based on the interaction of several contrasted ones.'

Arthur Bliss, *As I Remember*, London, Thames Publishing, 1989, pp. 18–19, p.102 and p. 247.

In a BBC radio broadcast delivered on the Overseas Service on 3 October 1941 — published under the title *Music in Wartime* — Bliss conveyed his impressions of musical appreciation in England — his audience being American. In this he remarked:

> 'In serious music there is one composer whom the people need and demand above all others, and he is Beethoven. In the recent Promenade Concerts in the Albert Hall the top galleries were filled on a Beethoven night — this generally happens only on boxing nights, or when there are great spectacular shows. Before the Queen's Hall

was destroyed by bombing, Basil Cameron gave a series of five Beethoven concerts there. It was impossible to get a seat. Beethoven has supplanted Bach in general favour.'

At a Royal College of Music prize-giving held on 18 July 1974, an address was read on behalf of Bliss to the students by the Director of the College David Willcocks — Bliss was unwell at the time. His address touched upon what Bliss referred to as 'the mysterious, magical world of sound' and of the pleasure to be derived from making music with others and of the privilege of being a composer endeavouring 'to extend the boundaries of our art'. Calling Beethoven to mind, he quoted the composer's then acknowledged authority:

> 'I think it was Donald Tovey who said of Beethoven that when we are listening to him there come rare moments when we seem for an instant to be standing at the same high inspirational summit. The sad difference between Beethoven and us is simply that while he can remain there, we cannot.'

Gregory Roscow, editor, *Bliss on Music: Selected Writings of Arthur Bliss, 1920–1975*, Oxford, Oxford University Press, 1991, p. 73, p. 179 and pp. 278–279. See also: Toscanini.

ERNST BLOCH

The philosopher Ernst Bloch is known for his Marxist views and outlook for a humanistic world free from oppression and exploitation. Alongside his major intellectual interests, he also had close friendships with musicians, including Bertold Brecht and Kurt Weill, and writers on music including Theodor Adorno. Concerning the latter, he once remarked:

> 'I have from Beethoven that whenever something seems to me false, absurd or unreal (in his music), I should defer entirely to him and seek fault in myself.'

Theodor W. Adorno, *Beethoven: The Philosophy of Music; Fragments and Texts*, Cambridge: Polity Press, 1998.

In his colourful, spirited and deeply thoughtful essay, relating to the structures and moods to be found in aspects of Beethoven's music, Bloch's text is interpolated with such expressions and imagery as '*Luciferan* music', 'flashes of lightning', 'notes [that] spiral upwards', 'architectonic', 'growing intensity', and the 'the struggle or soul of the emergent relationship'. With the foregoing in mind, he offers the following generalization about the music of Beethoven:

> 'Hence in Beethoven's music the detail is nothing and vitality in the broad context is everything — energy, directness, conflict-torn departure and resolution which is not re-possession but entirely gain. Thus, in his developments, so thoroughly torn apart, Beethoven never acknowledges the theme's opportunity for delicate, calm, solitary self-enrichment. He recognises only the emotive quality of its exploration as the boldness, the *élan* of an adventure stated in the intrinsic harmonic-rhythmic substance. With Beethoven we enter

the room and breathe the relationship. We have the most vivid feeling that here, everything is compressing itself by turns, and thus through the changing atmospheric pressure, so to speak, we ascertain the height and depth of the terrain — more than that, we acquire a true sailor's instinct and even genetic instinct for the atmosphere and its laws.'

Bloch also considers the rhythm and energy to be found in Beethoven's music:

'Above all, rhythm in Beethoven's music has taken possession of harmony, contributed a dynamism with strong drive and capped it with this dynamism's *rhythmic cultivation of the tonic.* The respiration of the rhythm no longer allows the parts to give themselves out simply as chords, vertically, or even to relax homophonically, any more than it permits all the parts to state uniform conviction, by which we mean the frictionless fugal self-differentiating of a single idea. Instead the rhythmicising energy constructs in depth. It annexes a polyphonic action by encompassing the vertical segments and, notwithstanding its tendency towards filigree polyphony, by showing a preference for climaxes which settle in a single layer, passages where the notes fit together to form sonic columns supporting the achieved splendour and are thereby capable of subordinating highly daring, self-intensifying, self-deciding dynamic-rhythmic harmony to a new form, *sequential counterpoint.*'

Later Block adds:

> 'Another element arises continuously and with growing intensity: the struggle or soul of the emergent relationship. Hence, in Beethoven's music, the detail is nothing and vitality in the broad context is everything — energy, directness, conflict-torn departure and resolution which is not re-possession but entirely gain.'

Ernst Bloch, *Essays on the Philosophy of Music*, Cambridge: Cambridge University Press, 1985, p. 32, p. 70 and pp. 109—110.

ERIC BLOM

The Swiss-born, British musicologist Eric Blom is perhaps most widely known for being the music correspondent for the *Manchester Guardian* and the editor of *Music & Letters* and of the fifth edition of Grove's *Dictionary of Music and Musicians*. In addition, he wrote extensively on a wide range of music subjects. In his essay *A Beethoven Movement and its Successors*, he traces the influence of the *Allegretto* of Beethoven's Seventh Symphony on the symphonic writing of Schubert, Berlioz, and Mendelssohn. First, he opens with some generalisations:

> 'Volumes have been written, and will continue to be written, on the amount and importance of the influence Beethoven exercised upon his successors in the field of the symphony. Any study of this influence will, above all, have to answer two main questions: How was Beethoven's symphonic technique taken over

by later symphonists? And in what light did they regard his symphonic ideas, the spiritual world that he embodied in his great works? Though the first is a technical and the second a philosophical question, the two are closely linked, for Beethoven's symphonic work is perhaps the most striking example of the idea behind creating and shaping its appropriate means of expression.'

When Beethoven's Seventh Symphony was first performed in Vienna on 8 December 1813, the *Allegretto* was received with such acclaim that the audience demanded an encore, and the Viennese music critic present at the concert hailed the movement as 'the crown of the more modern instrumental music'. Blom believes other composers took Beethoven's *Allegretto* as a model for one or other of their own symphonic movements. The first of these, he suggests, was Schubert in the *Andante* of his C major Symphony. Of this he states:

'It is very likely that he was much impressed by this *Allegretto*, the whole character of which is curiously Schubertian ... I suggest that the Schubert *Andante* is essentially a symphonic march built upon the lines of Beethoven's *Allegretto*, yet with the difference that the heroic expression of the latter is here superseded by a feeling of wistful melancholy. Schubert's *Andante* stands for the same idea as Beethoven's *Allegretto*, that is, the symphonic march as the musical symbol of tragic fate, but conceived by a different mind and temperament.'

In Blom's opinion, the next composer after Schubert to follow Beethoven's precedent, of introducing music of a Beethovenian character into symphonic writing, was Berlioz. He cites the *Marche au Supplice* of his *Symphonie Fantastique* and the *allegro* section of Berlioz's first movement — *Scènes de Mélancholie, de Bonheur et de Joie*. Blom offers further evidence of the influence of Beethoven on Berlioz:

> 'Let us now turn to the *Marche de Pélerins* in the *Harold Symphony*. Like the *Allegretto*, it is a second movement and an *allegretto* march ... Like Beethoven, Berlioz opens and concludes the movement with a "curtain" of sustained chords; the first theme is in strict periodical form and square-cut, only that Beethoven's "full-stop" rests are here filled in with the so-called murmuring of the pilgrims. The chant-like tune itself moves along in heavy, monotonous [crochet] rhythm that is kept up throughout the movement, just as in the Beethoven *Allegretto*.'

With regard to the influence of Beethoven on Mendelssohn, Blom makes reference to the latter's *Italian Symphony*. He considers this, like Berlioz's *Harold in Italy*, seems to have been modelled in three of its four movements on Beethoven's Seventh Symphony:

> 'The key is A major, the *allegro vivace* first movement in 6–8 time reminds one very much of the corresponding movement in the Beethoven Symphony, and its finale, the "Saltarello", is a wild, exuberant dance movement exactly like Beethoven's *allegro con brio*. And there is some

local colouring in both the finales — Hungarian and Russian in Beethoven's and Italian in Mendelssohn's.'

Eric Blom, *Classics Major and Minor: With some other Musical Ruminations*, London, J. M. Dent, 1958, pp. 9–20.

MARK EVAN BONDS

Mark Evan Bonds is Professor of Music at the University of North Carolina and has served as editor-in-chief of the *Beethoven Forum*. He is known particularly for his writing on the aesthetics and philosophy of music as, for example, in *Music as Thought: Listening to the Symphony in the Age of Beethoven* (Princeton, 2006). In his earlier work, *After Beethoven* (Harvard, 1990), he considered the challenge Beethoven's symphonic achievement posed to other composer's following after him. He postulates:

> 'Would-be symphonists were compelled to confront Beethoven. Many turned to other instrumental genres, most notably the concert overture and its outgrowth the symphonic poem. Other composers, like Wagner, declared the symphony to have exhausted itself and proclaimed the "music drama" to be the "artwork" of the future.'

Bonds characterises the inhibitions felt by later composers as the "anxiety of influence" and suggests those who fell under its intimidating spell included, in varying degrees: Franz Schubert — Ninth Symphony, that draws on Beethoven's *Ode to Joy theme* in its last movement; Franz Liszt — *Faust* Symphony; Anton Bruckner — Symphony No. 5; César Franck — Symphony in D minor; and Antonín

Dvořák — *New World* Symphony. He further cites Hector Berlioz, Felix Mendelssohn, and Gustav Mahler as also recognising Beethoven's influence. To these, perhaps most notably, may be added Johannes Brahms who, allegedly, was given to remark 'You do not know what it feels like to be followed by *Him*' — Beethoven. By as late as 1901, Claude Debussy — an occasional harsh critic of Beethoven who personally avoided symphonic writing — asserted: 'It seems to me that the proof of the futility of the symphony has been established since Beethoven.'

Bonds draws attention to the fact that even in Beethoven's own time, music critics were questioning what might be his legacy? He cites the observations of the composer and music theorist Gottfried Weber. Writing in 1826, Weber contemplated the aesthetic challenge he considered Beethoven's Ninth Symphony would pose for subsequent generations:

> 'What other nation has anything to compare to the symphonies of our Haydn and Mozart? Or to the still more boldly intensified symphonies of the great hero of instrumental music in our own time of our Beethoven, whose latest ... grand symphony with chorus indeed seems to point towards an ominous culmination and turning point in this realm of music.'

Bonds cites words written by the playwright and music critic Franz Rochlitz in his 1827 obituary notice to Beethoven:

> '[For] some time now, not one of his competitors has dared even to dispute his supremacy in the realm of instrumental music. Strong composers avoid him on this ground; weaker ones

subjugate themselves, in that they labour mightily to imitate him'.

Rochlitz's perception unjustly overlooks the symphonic achievements of Beethoven's youthful contemporary Franz Schubert. As Bonds remarks:

'The one outstanding exception from the 1820s, Schubert's *Great* C Major Symphony, remained unknown for practical purposes until its rediscovery by Schumann in 1839 and its premier later that same year by the Leipzig Gewandhaus Orchestra under the direction of Mendelssohn'.

Bonds concludes:

'[In] the end, Beethoven remained both a model and a nemesis for the large majority of symphonists from 1830 onward, including Mendelssohn and Schumann themselves. For it was Beethoven, more than any other composer, who was perceived to have redefined the nature of the genre.'

Mark Evan Bonds, *After Beethoven: Imperatives of Originality in the Symphony*, Cambridge, Massachusetts, London, Harvard University Press, 1996, pp. 1–13.

LEON BOTSTEIN

In his essay *Sound and Structure in Beethoven's Orchestral Music*, the Swiss-American conductor, educator and music scholar Leon Botstein suggests the impact of Beethoven's symphonies has been twofold. The latter part of what he has to say is consistent with the remarks of Mark Evan Bonds, as outlined above:

> 'On the one hand, after his death, the symphony as a genre achieved a unique prestige as an experience of solidarity (i.e. the objective and universal) and personal engagement (i.e. the subjective and the individual) at the same time it remained tied to highly-prized aristocratic traditions of taste and connoisseurship ... Beethoven's example was paralyzing through its evident novelty and boldness, making imitation by successors impossible and deviation from the Beethovenian model daunting at best.'

Quoting Paul Bekker (see above), Botstein considers the manner in which Beethoven's orchestral music was revolutionary through its sheer volume and presence of sound:

> 'Beethoven opened up the sonic power implicit in the orchestral forces of Mozart and Haydn, and the symphony now became more than a sonata for orchestra. Bekker suggested that Beethoven composed with a new "idealized picture of the space and listening public" in mind; his goal was to reach a "mass" of public with the symphony, and to create a "community" through the act of shared listening.'

Thereby, Beethoven's music was far-reaching and extended beyond the confines of the aristocracy who had initially welcomed Beethoven into their salons. His contribution, Botstein avows, 'was the transformation of the tradition of the sublime and dignified [as exemplified in the late symphonies of Mozart and Haydn] towards monumentality, dramatic intensity, and universality, conceived in a political and social as well as aesthetic sense'.

Botstein considers Beethoven's orchestration:

> 'A remarkable aspect of Beethoven's use of the orchestra is the sheer variety and extreme range of colour, texture, and sound that he achieved without adding substantially to the forces used by Haydn and Mozart. Only Symphonies 3, 5, 6, and 9 use more instruments than can be found in Haydn and Mozart: doubled winds (flute, oboe, clarinet, bassoon), doubled brass (two horns, two trumpets), tympani, and strings. The *Eroica* Symphony, which marks the first time Beethoven used more than the traditional compliment of two horns in an orchestra, employs only one additional French horn. In the Fifth Symphony, three trombones, piccolo, and a contrabassoon appear, but only in the last movement ... In Symphony No. 6 the parallel to [Haydn's] *The Seasons* is apparent, since the trombones appear for the first time in the remarkable "Storm" of the fourth movement.
>
> 'The Ninth Symphony tells a different story. Four horns are part of the basic sound. Trombones appear in the scherzo and again, with contrabassoon, piccolo, and percussion (triangle, bass drum, and cymbal), in the last movement.'

Leon Botstein, *Sound and Structure in Beethoven's Orchestral Music*, in: Glenn Stanley, editor, *The Cambridge*

Companion to Beethoven, Cambridge, New York, Cambridge University Press, 2000, pp. 165–85.

PIERRE BOULEZ

In an interview with Pierre Boulez, the American musicologist and lecturer on music James R. Briscoe invited Boulez to remark on the response of an audience to music. Boulez answered:

> 'I find there are always works that communicate with a large group and those that communicate with fewer. For instance, I might take Beethoven, the epitome of a musician known everywhere. If you play the Ninth Symphony, everyone would flock to the performance. If the Mass [D minor Op. 123], then many fewer. And if you play the last quartets, then you reduce to a few. I find that I am not at all shocked by that. One day Beethoven must express himself in a quite expansive way but on another much more for himself. Shakespeare wrote dramas that are played constantly, but he also wrote the sonnets, known by very few people. I do not find it unrealistic to expect a different appreciation from audiences.'

James R. Briscoe, editor, brief description: *Debussy in Performance*, New Haven, Yale University Press, 1999, pp. 89–90.

On another occasion Boulez compared the audience that might attend a popular sporting event to that which might be attracted to a Beethoven concert:

'Even the greatest conductor with the most standard repertoire does not have the popularity of, for instance, a boxing match. You have, for a football match, let's say two hundred thousand people and, even for a Beethoven symphony, you have only five thousand.'

Michael Oliver, editor, *Settling the Score: A Journey through the Music of the Twentieth Century*, London, Faber and Faber, 1999, p. 299.

JOHANNES BRAHMS

It is well reported that Brahms, as a young composer, found it difficult to escape from Beethoven's shadow, remarking 'You do not know what it's like to be followed by Him' — or words to that effect depending on the translation. In conversation with the Austrian music critic and teacher Richard Heuberger, Brahms shared some thoughts about his predecessor:

'I understand very well that the new personality of Beethoven, the new outlook, which people found in his works, made him greater, more important in their view [than in Mozart's later works]. But 50 years later this judgment has been altered. The attraction of novelty must be differentiated from inner value. I admit that the [Third Piano] Concerto of Beethoven is more modern, but not so important! I am able to understand, too, that Beethoven's First Symphony did impress people colossally. In fact, it was the new outlook! But the last three symphonies by

Mozart are much more important! Some people are beginning to feel that now.'

Originally published in Richard Heuberger, *Erinnerungen an Johannes Brahms: Tagebuchnotizen aus den Jahren 1875-1897*, editor K. Hofman, Tutzing, 1970. The quotation is derived from: John L. Holmes, *Composers on Composers*, New York, Greenwood Press, 1990, p. 14.

Brahms shared many views about music with Clara Schuman. The following is an extract, from a letter he wrote to her on 14 August 1855:

> 'Incidentally I ought to tell you that Shakespeare made a close study of Plutarch. In *Coriolanus, Julius Caesar* etc., whole speeches are taken bodily out of Plutarch, and in *Coriolanus* particularly the action is based entirely upon him (the sequence of scenes). Beethoven also loved to read Plutarch, and when listening to his music one often imagines that one can see the outline of one of Plutarch's heroes.'

Berthold Litzmann, editor, *Letters of Clara Schumann and Johannes Brahms, 1853–96*, New York, Vienna House. 2 Vols., 1971, Vol. 1, p. 44.

ALFRED BRENDEL

Alfred Brendel is universally acknowledged for being among the most respected interpreters of Beethoven and has the distinction of being the first to record his complete solo works for piano. In conversation with Brendel, the Swiss writer Martin Meyer invited him to consider the proposition:

'[Don't] you think that the history of interpretation is gradually reaching a state of exhaustion?' Brendel responded:

> 'I see no signs of that. With the Beethoven symphonies there was perhaps a certain sense of exhaustion after the old generation had stepped down, a generation of conductors who had lived permanently with these works and maintained them at the centre of the repertoire — with orchestra's, for whom these were the canonical orchestral works that taught their members how to listen to each other. That is no longer the case. Mahler's symphonies have now, at least for the time being, taken on this role, and are instilled into the orchestras, certainly with some good reason, by today's conductors. Meanwhile, we have a number of recordings which serve up Beethoven's symphonies in a new way, following Beethoven's own metronome markings. One can certainly no longer imitate Furtwängler or Klemperer today. And neither should one. There are, however, not only historically oriented performers, but also conductors like Sir Simon Rattle, who draw inspiration from both sources. Simon has turned his attention to early performance practices, and has at the same time taken a most admiring view of Furtwängler.'

Alfred Brendel, *The Veil of Order: Alfred Brendel in Conversation with Martin Meyer*, London, Faber and Faber, 2002, p. 213.

GERHARD VON BREUNING

Gerhard von Breuning was the son of Beethoven's lifelong friend, Stephan von Breuning. Beethoven held a particular affection for Gerhard, whom he knew as a child, referring to him as *Hosenknopf* – 'trouser button' – because he considered he attached himself to him like a button on his trousers. In the last two years of his life, Beethoven had rooms in the so-called *Schwarzspanierhause. Unlike many of Beethoven's other residences it has not survived, being demolished in 1903–4.* Von Breuning is remembered in musicology today for his reflections on Beethoven in the title of which he adopted the name of *Schwarzspanierhause.* These were originally published in Vienna in 1874 under the title *Aus dem Schwarzspanierhause: Erinnerungen an L. van Beethoven aus meiner Jugendzeit,* known today in English translation as *Memories of Beethoven: From the House of the black-robed Spaniards.* This work has the authority of being one of only three book-length writings written by authors who knew Beethoven personally, the other two being the *Biographische Notizen über Ludwig van Beethoven – Remembering Beethoven: the Biographical Notes of Franz Wegeler and Ferdinand Ries* – and Anton Schindler's *Biographie von Ludwig van Beethoven – Beethoven as I Knew him.* In his editorial commentary to the modern-day edition of von Breuning's study (1992) Maynard Solomon describes it as 'a minor classic of the Beethoven literature, [and] an important source for our knowledge of the composer's later years'. From this text we have derived the following extracts:

> '[Beethoven] was powerful-looking, of medium height [in fact, Beethoven was of short stature being no more than 168 cms. – 5 feet 2 inches tall], vigorous in his gait and lively in movements,

his clothing [was] far from elegant or conventional and there was something about him overall that did not fit into any classification.' [When von Breuning knew the composer, he had become negligent in his dress but as a young man he took greater care of his appearance].

Von Breuning inherited a piano that Beethoven had owned early in his career as a virtuoso pianist. This disposed him to exclaim:

'When one looks at the [Josef] Brodman grand piano ... considered one of the best makes at that time, with its tiny tone and its mere five and a half octaves, one finds it hard to conceive how it could have been adequate for Beethoven's tempestuous improvisations, while realizing that it was as a consequence of Beethoven's sonatas that the piano was altered and strengthened into its present state, indeed it had to be almost made afresh.'

Later in life, Beethoven owned a full six-octave Brodman grand that today forms part of the Berlin Collection of Musical Instruments. (See: Tilman Skowroneck, *Beethoven the Pianist*, Cambridge University Press, 2010, p. 128.) It is from von Breuning that we learn how completely deaf Beethoven was in his final years. He recalls a visit to see the composer at the period when he was at work on the so-called Galitzin String Quartets. He tells us how he entered unnoticed by Beethoven who was preoccupied at his desk. He continues:

'I was quiet for a while and then went over to the

Graf piano [Conrad Graf loaned one of his 6 1/2 octave grand pianos to the composer around 1825–6] ... and began to strum lightly on the keys ... I kept looking in his direction to see whether he might be bothered. When I saw that he was completely unaware of it, I played louder ... I had no more doubts. He heard nothing and kept on writing.'

In the months just before his death, Beethoven derived pleasure in leafing through a forty-volume edition of Handel's collected works that he had received as a gift, in December 1826, from the London harp manufacturer Johann Stumpff. The young von Breuning assisted the now ailing composer to enjoy these works:

'I began to bring one volume after another over to his bed. He leafed through them one volume after another ... sometimes stopping at particular passages ... [He] started to sing the praises of the great Handel and to call him the most classic and most accomplished of all composers.'

Gerhard von Breuning was in Beethoven's presence until half an hour before he passed away. At the ensuing internment, the poet and dramatist Franz Grillparzer wrote the funeral oration. Later in life, von Breuning's father presented him with a copy of Grillparzer's text. (See also: Franz Grillparzer)

Gerhard von Breuning, edited and part-translated by Maynard Solomon: *Memories of Beethoven: From the House of the black-robed Spaniards*, Cambridge, Cambridge University Press, 1992, p. 19, p. 38, p. 72, and p. 96.

ALFRED PETER BROWN

In his survey *The Symphonic Repertoire*, the American musicologist Alfred Peter Brown summarized Beethoven's contribution to the genre of the symphony:

> 'Beethoven's accomplishments in the realm of the symphony reformulated the genre. Whereas symphonies by Haydn and Mozart were made up of individual movements, mostly united by key and character, for Beethoven, the cycle additionally gained its coherence through patterns of tonality, rhythms, motifs, and anything else that his logical imagination could draw upon. The practice of distributing the movements of a symphony through an evening of arias, concertos, etc., was no longer tenable. Beethoven's symphonic movements demanded juxtaposition not separation.'

Brown considers the significance of Beethoven's tonality:

> 'Perhaps more than any other element, tonality contributed to the organic conception. Key definition became a structural issue, not an accepted premise. In the first movement of nearly every Beethoven symphony, the same question can be asked: where, how, and how strongly is the tonality first asserted? As a result tonal tensions and resolutions were what the piece was all about ... Tonal breadth and action were often coordinated with melodic materials that lent themselves to expression and contraction. The implications of an idea could be played to their fullest or reduced to the smallest perceptible unit. In

Beethoven's music these processes were no longer abstractions understood only by the analyst, but were easily perceived and understood by the uninitiated.'

Brown next remarks on the special qualities of Beethoven's orchestral sound:

'[Beethoven] exploited orchestral sound both colouristically and dynamically. A wider range of dynamics went hand in hand with the expression of the orchestra beyond the classical model, resulting in music more powerful and varied. The piccolo, contrabassoon, and extra pairs of horns, and trombones were now admitted to symphonic composition. At the same time, the technical requirements were greater: to recall only a few instances: the flute in the finale of the Third Symphony, the bassoon in the finale of the Fourth Symphony, the oboe in the scherzo of the Sixth, the string bass in the third movement of the Fifth and the finale of the Ninth Symphonies, the horns in the first and last movements of the Seventh Symphony.'

Brown concludes with reference to the challenge Beethoven's symphonic writing posed to the composers following after him:

'Beethoven provided a new standard for the composers of the nineteenth century, whether it be Schubert in contemporary Vienna, Schumann in Germany, or Berlioz in France. Radical or conservative, they ultimately drew upon

Beethoven's symphonies as worthy models for imitation. But at the same time, Beethoven's "Nine" provided the genre with a new prestige and with it a new anxiety. Though Beethoven became an unavoidable influence, some composers avoided big instrumental genres and, when they did compose symphonies, wrote fewer works, sometimes without striving for his sublime language.'

Alfred Peter Brown, *The Symphonic Repertoire*. Vol. 2, *The First Golden Age of the Viennese Symphony: Haydn, Mozart, Beethoven, and Schubert*, Bloomington, Indiana, Indiana University Press, 2002, pp. 555–56. Brown provides an extensive 'Bibliographic Overview' in which he lists many works devoted to the analysis of Beethoven's symphonies. Of this body of writings, he comments: '[Every] Beethoven symphony has elicited and stimulated important observations from critics of different backgrounds and agendas.'

CLIVE BROWN

Clive Brown is recognised as an authority in the academic world of musicology and historical performance. He is the author of what many consider to be the definitive work *Classical and Romantic Performing Practice from 1750–1900*. He contributed the introduction to Christopher Hogwood's recordings of the Beethoven Symphonies, on period instruments, from which we cite the following:

> 'Since the time of their performances, Beethoven's Symphonies have been a constant and important part of the orchestral repertoire.

In the ... years since the premiere of the First Symphony, each generation has claimed Beethoven for its own and has performed his work according to its own taste. Instruments have evolved and styles have changed so gradually that the transformation has hardly been perceptible, but there is no doubt that modern performances of Beethoven's Symphonies differ from those heard by his contemporaries, both the sound and the style are quite unlike those the composer would have imagined when he conceived them.

'The performance of Beethoven's symphonic masterpieces on the instruments for which they were written, with the sort of orchestral forces which first performed them, and with due consideration to the style of playing familiar to the composer, is more than merely a pious gesture or a dry academic exercise. Just as cleaning successive layers of restoration and dirt from an old painting uncovers the colours and details of the original, revealing the artist's intentions as regards balance and intensity, so it is with the authentic performance of old music. Sounds are far less tangible than paint, but modern research has given us the means to recreate with a substantial degree of certainty the sort of sound which Beethoven would have had in mind, and there is every reason to believe that he had as sensitive and discriminating an ear for timbre as a great artist for the pigmentation on his palette.'

Clive Brown, Introduction to, *Beethoven, Symphonies*, The Academy of Ancient Music conducted by Christopher Hogwood, DDD Music.

MICHAEL BROYLES

The American musicologist Michael Broyles outlines Beethoven's contribution to the transformation of the classical world in music:

> 'The ten years in Beethoven's life, from approximately 1800 to 1809, comprise one of the crucial decades in the history of Western music. During that time Beethoven not only wrote an astonishing number of major compositions which still form the core of the concert repertory — the first six symphonies, the Third, Fourth and Fifth Piano Concertos, the Triple Concerto, the *Razumovsky* Quartets, as well as fourteen piano sonatas that include the *Moonlight*, the *Tempest*, the *Waldstein*, and the *Appassionata*, in addition to *Fidelio* and other large vocal pieces — but created a body of works of such individuality that their shadows haunted composers throughout the nineteenth century. In 1800, Beethoven's compositions still resided in the Classical world of Haydn, Mozart and Clementi. By 1809 Beethoven had fundamentally reordered that world.'

Discussing the evolution of Beethoven's later 'heroic style' in his symphonic writing, Broyles elucidates:

> '[The] Classical symphony became a relatively insignificant factor as an independent compositional approach for Beethoven after the *Eroica*. Yet Beethoven continued to write symphonies, and the six symphonies composed after 1804 rank amongst his most well-known and respected compositions. To later generations of musicians

they have formed the innermost core of the symphonic ideal, defining more than any other body of works the very concept of the symphony.'

Broyles perceives the musical values enshrined in Beethoven's Op. 50s and Op. 60s being gradually eroded and displacing older ones. At the same time, he considers the composer's interest in the genre of the concert overture that helped to shape his symphonic writing:

'In the overtures, Beethoven discovered that orchestral composition did not necessarily imply a symphonic basis and that the orchestra was particularly well suited to a poetic-rhetorical style. It was more difficult for Beethoven to adapt that style to the symphonies, however. The symphony as a genre was too well-defined by 1800, and, as witnessed by the dual stylistic path Beethoven pursued in the years 1800–03, the identification between style and genre became almost complete for Beethoven once he began writing symphonies.'

Turning to Beethoven's later symphonic achievement, Broyles contends:

'In the later symphonies of Beethoven, we find a gradual evolution away from the Classical symphonic ideal. While the outward structure of the symphony was maintained, the style-change of the heroic decade affected and gradually reshaped the content. In tone and rhetoric some of Beethoven's later symphonies are decidedly unsymphonic. Early Beethoven had attempted to maintain the stylistic tendencies of the sonata genres against the almost constant intrusion of symphonic elements. The opposite occurs in the later Beethoven symphonies — he attempted to continue in the symphony style, but the style-changes of the years 1804–07 were always there, reshaping and reorienting the works, sometimes in the most fundamental way.'

Michael Broyles, *Beethoven: The Emergence and Evolution of Beethoven's Heroic Style*, New York, Excelsior Music Publishing Co., 1987, p. 1, pp.173–74, and p. 222.

ANTON BRUCKNER

The Austrian composer and organist Anton Bruckner is known for his monumental symphonies — once pejoratively described by Brahms as 'symphonic boa constrictors' — and religious music including several masses and motets. Notwithstanding his musical originality he was deferential to other composers, notably Wagner, to whom he showed humility often bordering on subservience. He was in awe of Beethoven as is illustrated by the following anecdote. After a triumphant performance of his *Te Deum* in Berlin, in 1891, he learned that a music critic had favoured him by likening him to 'a second Beethoven'. This was a novel experience for Bruckner who normally had to endure criticism of his music, in particular from the Viennese critic Eduard Hanslick. On this occasion, however, being compared with Beethoven was too much for the modestly inclined Bruckner who is reported to have exclaimed: 'Good Lord, how could anyone say such a thing?' Being profoundly religious he promptly crossed himself to expunge the possibility of sin.

Originally published in: Max Graf, *Legend of a Musical City*, New York, 1945 and quoted in: *The Book of Musical Anecdotes*, editor, Norman Lebrecht, London: Andre Deutsch, 1985, p. 187.

The Dresden composer and conductor Jean Louis Nicodé visited Bruckner in March 1891. Bruckner was then age 67 and was enjoying his hard-earned celebrity. Nicodé was greeted by Bruckner at the door to his apartment whilst still wearing his nightshirt and holding a candle before him. As they entered the composer's music room Nicodé noticed Bruckner's eyes began to gleam with tear drops shining in them. His recollection continues: 'Finally he led us next door into his bedroom, which was just as big as his study. He pointed to the portraits of Beethoven and Wagner above his bed and said: "They are my dear Masters".' As further testimony to his modesty, Nicodé describes Bruckner making a deferential gesture to the portraits.

Carl Hruby studied with Bruckner and published reminiscences of the composer in his *Meine Erinnerungen an Anton Bruckner* – 'My recollections of Anton Bruckner'. He describes the morning when he arrived for a lesson and found Bruckner seated at the piano lost in thought, not initially acknowledging his pupil's entry. Collecting himself he then remonstrated against the injustice he felt towards the critics who found fault in his music, disposing him to exclaim: 'Beethoven! Beethoven! Recalling this years later, Hruby writes:

> 'For Bruckner [Beethoven] was the incarnation of everything lofty and sublime in music. He connected that hallowed name with all the twists of fortune in his own life, and at crucial moments

he often asked how Beethoven would have behaved in the same situation.'

In 1863 Beethoven's remains were exhumed, together with those of Franz Schubert. Bruckner was invited to take part in the official ceremony that took place in Vienna's old Währinger cemetery. After some discussion, it was decided to open Beethoven's coffin as part of the proceedings. This provided Bruckner with the opportunity to press forward and stare at Beethoven's mortal remains. According to Hruby, Bruckner was 'deeply moved' and 'shaken to the core'. On the way home it was only after some reflection that Bruckner realized, in his eagerness to stand close by the remains of the composer he so revered, his eyeglasses had fallen into the coffin. The thought they would be reinterred with Beethoven's remains according to Hruby gave Bruckner 'great delight'.

The composer Franz Marschner recounts:

> 'Bruckner certainly knew the symphonies of Beethoven. Hearing the Ninth in 1866 was a seminal musical experience. But, according to Karl Waldeck [Bruckner's close friend], it was the *Eroica* (No. 3) that Bruckner rated highest. Bruckner's own copy of the score shows how intensively he analysed the harmonic and periodic structure of this symphony.'

Stephen Johnson, *Bruckner Remembered*, London, Faber and Faber, 1998, pp.157–58 and pp. 168–169.

NEVILLE CARDUS
The English writer and critic Sir Neville Cardus was widely

read for his contributions to *The Manchester Guardian* on both music and cricket. He counted several distinguished musicians amongst his personal friends. In 1962 he contributed an article to an issue of *The Manchester Guardian* in which he outlined his feelings towards Beethoven and his music:

> 'Today, more than one hundred and thirty- five years after his death, Beethoven's music remains close to the consciousness and feeling of ordinary humanity. Time hasn't diminished its significance or its power. On the contrary, it comes home to us more urgently that ever before. The clash of man's ideas, ambitions, and vanities, the struggle between the individual will and the irresistible massed stupidity of instinct, the littleness of the ego in the fact of the tidal waves of the changing years — Beethoven has told us of the mysterious immensities and fluctuations which, since the revolution in his own period, created in the nineteenth-century, setting into motion forces that have caused the greatest upheaval in civilization of all.'

Turning to the present day — we recall Cardus was writing in the 1960s — he continues:

> 'At the present time Beethoven is neither to be claimed by the "new" or the "old". He is neither of the "right" nor of the "left". He himself was a rebel, but one who didn't run away from the past. "I have never believed in the *Vox populi*" he once said, yet in the finale of the Ninth Symphony he strove to embrace the "millions". He was, in fact,

aristocratic in intellect and a democrat in sympathies. He was perhaps not the most truly and wholly musical of all composers, the most *suffused* by music. This distinction is Mozart's. But Beethoven was the greatest man ever to live and find a way of life in music.'

Cardus believed, as in the case of many another genius, Beethoven had become a legend and, thereby, his life and work had become distorted through the prism of history. As he put it:

'He is often thought of as a grim perpetually heroic, fate-driven Prometheus, setting himself against the order and propriety of the ordained gods of music.' Cardus acknowledged Beethoven had 'shattered the immaculate palace of the eighteenth-century symphony', remarking how a mere eighteen years separated the G minor Symphony of Mozart and Beethoven's *Eroica* Symphony and argued that in no other art had such an advance been taken in a single step. Cardus was of the view that in the genre of the symphony, Beethoven had dramatized its classical patterns and procedures and, for the first time, had made it 'an organic, single-minded, single-purpose whole'.

Neville Cardus, *Talking of Music*, London, Collins, 1957, pp. 47–50.

In 1927 the Manchester music fraternity commemorated Beethoven's Death Centenary with a celebratory concert, about which Cardus reflected:

'Beethoven's imaginative world was vast and multitudinous. In this respect the Centenary Concert must have done some excellent service, for centenary criticism of Beethoven has tended to make the average man think that the composer lived utterly in a shadowy realm of introspection, and that he even standardized the expression of his tragic isolation. No symphonic writer could thrive if he were less than a full man; the symphony itself is a universe for the musical imagination to fill or enter at all. The extent of Beethoven's emotional experience was so immense that to this day writers, poets, and philosophers seek in vain, after the manner of Schopenhauer, to find in his works a sort of first-principle giving a hint of the meaning of the world "as in itself it really is". It is Beethoven's range, indeed, that has led many of his admirers to call him Shakespeare.'

Cardus qualifies Beethoven's comparison with Shakespeare:

'But that description rather runs counter to Beethoven's essentially personal way of experiencing emotion and giving expression to it. A Shakespeare mingles his genius with the passing show of things; like Childe Harold, he says, "I live not in myself, but I become Portion of that around me". Beethoven's art is not protean in this sense; he did not project his imagination into the external world, but rather drew life into his own consciousness and made it part of himself. We can all find points of contact in Beethoven; we can all pass through, by means of his music, most of the moods and emotions known to man. But we must worship Beethoven always in his own image; he is not Hamlet today, Anthony tomorrow, Prospero the day after. His music is the full man himself; as we hear it we hear his voice and nobody else's; we can even see the godlike shape of him through all the sounds that fall on our ears. His marvellous power of making a synthesis of what he lived through elevates personal and particular emotion to the realms of the universal. In this sense he is the most democratic of composers; every man jack of us comes into his world and finds there some echo of the music we have at one time or other tried to make for the purposes of self-expression.'

Neville Cardus, *Talking of Music*, London, Collins, 1957, pp. 45–46.

ELLIOTT CARTER

The American composer Elliott Carter must be a candidate for holding the record for being the oldest amongst active composers, living to the remarkable age of 104. More significantly, he won the coveted Pulitzer Prize twice, composed forty works between the ages of 90–100 and twenty more after he had turned 100, in 2008. In conversation with the American writer on music Allen Edwards, Carter was asked how precisely did he expect the listener to consciously follow music? Carter responded:

'The question of how much you can expect most listeners to hear is a problem in itself — I wonder how many people hear themes coming back in the tonic in a Beethoven symphony. And furthermore, Beethoven himself, with functional harmony at his disposal, always presented many effects coordinated with the return of themes to the tonic at the beginning of a recapitulation — some emphatic non-harmonic effect such as, for instance, a pause or a long pedal, so that when the theme returns in the tonic it's very obvious that *something* has happened, whether a listener recognizes it's the tonic or not.'

Allen Edwards, *Flawed Words and Stubborn Sounds: A Conversation with Elliott Carter*, New York, Norton & Company, 1971, pp. 208–09.

In his essay *To be a Composer in America* (1953), Carter makes passing reference to Beethoven:

'Everybody knows, for example, that listening to Beethoven is not best done by cataloguing themes. What counts in listening to music is following the grand line, its forward motion, its reversals and dramatic and expressive moments.'

In a later essay *Music Criticism* (1972), Carter considered the question of the influence of music criticism on a composer. Beethoven himself was not immune to criticism. There was the occasion, for example, when he felt obliged to write to the Leipzig publishers Breitkopf & Härtel to complain about what he considered to be the unjust treatment of his music, as expressed in their journal *Allgemeine musikalische Zeitung* (see above). He asserted, unfounded criticism could be discouraging to a young composer.

Carter's response to criticism was for the composer to find inner resolve as he developed his art:

> 'Within the confines of his own development the composer has only two critics in our situation: his own works and his alter ego — his self-critical activity. His works, as they mount up, each tend to suggest new paths of development, or, having fulfilled their particular vein, bring it to a halt. It is quite a common pattern for composers to write successive works exploring opposing areas of experience or technique — the comparison of Beethoven's Eighth and Ninth Symphonies shows this, as do the like-numbered ones of Mahler, as indeed do the three symphonies Mozart wrote in 1788.'

Jonathan W. Bernard, editor, *Elliott Carter: Collected Essays and Lectures, 1937–1995*, Rochester, New York, Woodbridge, University of Rochester Press, 1998, p. 341.

In a BBC broadcast in the summer of 1972, Elliott Carter discussed the problem in musical appreciation of attaching words and meaning to sounds. He made a wry reference to Beethoven:

> 'Beethoven's answer to someone who asked questions about some music he had just played was to play it over again. This is, of course, the composer's true response about his own work.'

Else Stone and Kurt Stone, editors, *The Writings of Elliott Carter. An American Composer looks at Modern Music*, Bloomington, Indiana University Press, 1977, p. 310.

PABLO CASALS

The Spanish writer on music Josep M. Corredor interviewed his celebrated fellow countryman, the cellist Pablo Casals — widely acknowledged for elevating Bach's six Cello Studies to their rightful status following years of neglect. On the occasion in question, however, he sought Casals's opinion on the present-state (mid-1950s) of orchestral playing. He introduced the subject by recalling an entry in one of Beethoven's Conversation Books in which a friend had recorded how poorly the orchestra had played the Fifth Symphony. This prompted the friend to identify, with this disparaging observation, with his own rejoinder: 'It looks as if these crimes were the order of the day then as well as now.' Casals responded:

> 'Neither the "purists" nor the "archaeologists" convince me. How do you imagine the orchestra sounded in the days of Mozart and Beethoven when all the wind instruments were "out of tune" ... And how did the orchestral players of those days care for proper intonation? And that's only one thing. You all know that one of the duties of the leading violinist of those days was to drag the rest of the orchestra along. And that is exactly what happened: the leader was always heard very slightly ahead of the other instruments. That was considered normal; today we laugh about it. If only we had some gramophone records of how Beethoven symphonies were played in those days! Many illusions would be destroyed ... And here is another point to consider: a masterpiece is something which is an actuality at all times. It is the opposite to a fossil, since it continues to move us — thanks to its greatness and richness;

we people of today should approach it with our own sensitiveness and conception of beauty.'

Josep M. Corredor, *Conversations with Casals*, London, Hutchinson, 1956, pp. 192–93.

ALFREDO CASELLA

The Italian composer, pianist, and conductor Alfredo Casella came from a family that included many musicians — his grandfather was a friend of Niccolò Paganini — and from an early age he learned piano from his mother. In *Music in My Time*, he describes the advent of concert music in his hometown:

'In 1872 the first regular, permanent series of symphonic concerts in the peninsular was begun in Turin. The city thus laid the first stone in the vast edifice of instrumental revival which had arisen in Italy in the last fifty years. These concerts were directed for the first ten years by Carlo Pedrotti, a very talented conductor who gave them from the first a serious character and a decisively modern tone. In fact, Wagner appeared on the programmes before Beethoven. As early as 1872 — the prelude to *Lohengrin* and the overture to *Tannhäusser* were included, the latter being received with frenetic enthusiasm to which were opposed angry howls of "Outside with the barbarians!" The following year Beethoven's First Symphony was heard, followed by the Second in 1877, by the Fifth in 1880, and by the others in later years.'

The programmes to the Turin concert series for the period 1872–1913, to which Casella makes reference, reveal that the music of Wagner triumphed with 193 performances and Beethoven with a creditable 115.

Spence Norton, editor and translator, *Music in My Time: The Memoirs of Alfredo Casella*, Norman, University of Oklahoma Press, 1955, pp. 5–6.

CARLOS CHÁVEZ

Carlos Chávez was a Mexican composer, conductor, music theorist, and founder-director of the Mexican Symphony Orchestra. From 1958–59, he was the Charles Eliot Norton professor at Harvard University and the public lectures he gave there were published as *Musical Thought*. In lecture IV (Chapter IV) he discussed musical construction, making reference to Beethoven who he considered to be 'the universal master, whose influence is felt even by the most advanced masters of our day'. Of musical construction Chávez writes:

> 'We may perhaps say that, from the standpoint of form and construction, a piece of music is not a solid block but an aggregate of parts that constitute a unity. The intrinsic value of each part and the degree of cohesion existing between all the parts are the ultimate measure of the actual merit or artistic value of the piece.'

He describes the constituents of music — the 'building blocks' — in the following terms:

> '[There] are parts which compose the whole, and parts which compose the parts, and parts which

compose the parts of the parts, and so forth and so on. There are parts of differing sizes and varied importance and meaning: a well-grounded hierarchy of parts which begins with the smallest group of notes makes sense by itself and ends with a large architectural unit. The smallest group of notes is called the *motive* and should consist of two or more notes. The motive has a rhythmical pattern on the same or different melodic intervals. Anybody can remember the remarkable two-note motive of Beethoven's Ninth Symphony ... on intervals of alternating fifths and fourths.'

Carlos Chávez, *Musical Thought*, Cambridge, Harvard University Press, 1961, p. 55.

EDWARD T. CONE

The American composer, music-theorist, and pianist Edward T. Cone gave the Enrst Bloch Lectures in 1972. In his discourse *Perception and Identification*, he suggested we have perhaps heard Beethoven's symphonies too often and need to give renewed consideration as to how we listen to, and appreciate, his music:

'We have followed every Beethoven symphony every step of the way so often that we can no longer summon up the excitement or suspense in response to one more repetition. We have exhausted them as compositions — ironically enough, without ever really getting to know them, for the exhaustion is usually the result of a surfeit of superficial hearings. True, we still listen, but no longer to the music. We hear only performances of an abstraction called *The Score*, performances that we constantly measure against one another or against a hypothetical ideal. As a result, we do not really experience even the performances: we criticise them — failing to realize the futility of all criticism that is not based on vivid experience of both performance and composition.'

Cone was not overly enamoured of our formulating an impression of Beethoven through the medium of recordings:

'Recordings, too, encourage the attitude that what one is hearing is religiously fixed — in this case, the reading as well as the text. As a result, it is not uncommon to find a standard recording accepted by many as *the* composition, from which all other interpretations are considered to some extent deviant.'

Combining his views on musical perception with his outlook on the contemporary appreciation of music, Cone expressed the regret:

'This unhealthy state of affairs reflects the fact that our contemporary musical culture is more interested in the preservation of the past than in the development of the present. But only a culture that takes a lively and genuine interest in the art of its own day can preserve the art of it past in more than ritualistic fashion.'

Edward T. Cone, *The Composer's Voice*, Berkeley, London, University of California Press, 1974, pp. 126–27.

BARRY COOPER WITH **NICHOLAS MARSTON**

The British musicologist Barry Cooper is internationally recognised for his scholarly studies of the life and work of Beethoven. In addition, Beethovenians have him to thank for his reconstruction of a performing edition of the composer's Tenth Symphony — from the many surviving sketches that were left incomplete at the time of the composer's death. Pianists are no less in debt to Cooper for his recently released edition of the Piano Sonatas for The Associated Board of the Royal Schools of Music (ABRSM). This incorporates Beethoven's three youthful *Kurfürstensonaten* (WoO 47) — dedicated to the Elector (Kurfürst) Maximillian Fredrick — that Cooper is known to believe are unjustly neglected. At the conclusion of his *Beethoven*, Cooper writes:

> 'It was the end of an era — the "Age of Beethoven" as it is sometimes known. Never since, and probably never before, has one composer been so dominant for such a long period; and his successors, though often using his ideas, had to find new paths, since he had traced his to its limits. Beethoven is still in many ways the central figure in western music, the culmination of the Classical period and an archetype for the Romantic concept of a genius — heroic, individualistic, eccentric, single-minded, and visionary. His art ranged over the whole gamut of human emotion, from the ecstatic joy of the Ninth Symphony to the profound suffering of the *Pathétique* Sonata, and from the deep mysticism of the *Missa Solemnis* to the playful humour of his many scherzos. And his compositional technique far surpasses that of most composers,

manipulating themes, pitches, intervals, registers keys, instruments, rhythms, phrases, and structural patterns in ways previously unimagined — halving note values in a triple-time fugue, for example, or creating a form that is simultaneously both a single movement and a multi-movement structure, or exploring the utmost extremes of the piano, or using timpani as a melody instrument. Yet a nobility and seriousness of purpose invariably underlie his music — a desire to "raise men to the level of gods" through his art.'

Barry Cooper, *Beethoven, The Master Musicians Series*, Oxford, Oxford University Press, 2000, pp. 349–50. See also: Barry Cooper, *Beethoven and the Creative Process*, Oxford: Clarendon Press, 1990 and Barry Cooper, in collaboration with Anne-Louise Coldicott, Nicholas Marston and William Drabin, *The Beethoven Compendium: A Guide to Beethoven's Life and Music*, London: Thames and Hudson, 1991.

In his contribution to Cooper's *The Beethoven Compendium*, Nicholas Marston opens his account of the composer's symphonies asserting:

'It would be difficult to exaggerate the importance of Beethoven's nine completed symphonies, either in relation to the rest of his output or in relation to the subsequent history of music. For many listeners the symphony represents the quintessential Beethoven; and although we should now shut the door firmly shut on Schindler's [see below] improbable claim about the knocking of fate in the Fifth Symphony, this work perhaps remains the quintessential symphony. Certainly, the nature of Beethoven's compositional thinking made it almost inevitable that he would excel in the genre and transform it radically.' (p. 214.)

MARTIN COOPER

In his study *Beethoven: The Last Decade, 1817–1827*, the music critic and author Martin Cooper considers what Beethoven means to the typical music lover:

'Beethoven's case is unique in the history of music: there is no other instance of a composer whose works, one hundred and fifty years after his death still form the staple basis of the repertory in the concert hall, in chamber music, and amongst pianists of all degrees, from the beginner to the greatest virtuoso, satisfying in different ways the simplest, most ignorant listener and the most intellectual, most exclusively "musical" professionals. The extraordinary position that he occupied in the imagination of his contemporaries — "one God in heaven and one Beethoven on earth", as a young English admirer put it — he has really never lost ... No reputable musician has seriously questioned the quality of Beethoven's music, though they may, like Stravinsky, have delighted in finding flaws in a popular idol, may have resented the domination of the repertory by often unintelligent, routine performances of his music and felt that the concept of the "Beethoven symphony" weighed like a dead hand on the further development of the art and must therefore be violently rejected. The ordinary music lover, on the other hand, has been unswervingly loyal to the great works by which he has known Beethoven — the symphonies and the concertos in the first place, perhaps a dozen of the thirty-two piano sonatas, half a dozen of the chamber works, *Fidelio* and its overtures ... These works of Beethoven "speak" to quite uncultivated human sensibilities and command their attention in a way that is literally unique.'

Cooper devotes an Appendix to the challenging question of Beethoven's metronome markings. Towards the end of his life Beethoven became familiar with the metronome of Johann Nepomuk Mälzel. Although he is credited with its invention, priority really belongs to the Dutch instrument maker Dietrich Nikolaus Winkel. In his enthusiasm for the metronome, Beethoven began to insert metronomic tempo indications into such late works as the *Hammerklavier* Piano Sonata and the Ninth Symphony. These have since been regarded with suspicion, resulting in them being adapted or even ignored. Beethoven himself appears to have had second thoughts and revised his own tempo indications. Moreover, Beethoven's metronome had a fine graduated scale that was difficult to read (Beethoven needed spectacles for close work) and, to add to his difficulties, it was sometimes not in full working order. As Cooper comments:

'The whole position with regard to Beethoven's metronome markings has been bedevilled by the composer himself, the shortcomings of whose mathematics made it hard for him in the first place to express his wishes with regard to tempo in the mechanical numerical formulae devised by Mälzel.'

Martin Cooper, *Beethoven: The Last Decade, 1817–1827*, London, Oxford University Press, 1970, pp. 4–5 and pp. 467–68.

In his study *Ideas and Music*, Cooper, considers Beethoven in 'Human Terms' and as 'Revolutionary'. With regard to Beethoven in human terms he observes:

> 'No hero has been more fantastically misrepresented, more assiduously idealised than Beethoven; and it is easy to understand why. The extreme disparity between an artist's work and his personal life is still a mystery to psychologists and a stumbling-block, even an offence, to simple people; and in no case is the disparity more extreme than in Beethoven's.'

With regard to Beethoven as revolutionary Cooper remarks:

> 'Beethoven-Prometheus hurls defiance and exalts like a giant ... Beethoven's centre lies in himself, he refuses to be dependent; almost he persuades himself — and has persuaded others — that he is creator, not creature.'

Cooper elaborates:

> 'Towards the three points of the trident which the French Revolution aimed at the heart of the old régime, Beethoven's attitude throughout his life was always unambiguous — though that is not to say that it was always the same, or that his understanding of Liberty, Equality and Fraternity was that of the politicians. For Beethoven was a

rebel, but not a revolutionary. He judged the laws and conventions of the society of his day by a wholly subjective standard, that of his own nature. His exuberant and powerful character would have found any system likely to win general acceptance with the rest of mankind and irksome and full of illogical anomalies. His passionate belief in Liberty never faltered, though it changed in character; but it was in the first instance a wholly natural, instinctive egoism, the emotional reaction of a high-spirited, hugely talented youth increasingly aware of his exceptional gifts and irritated by the difficulties and frustrations which lay in the way of their development.'

Martin Cooper, *Ideas and Music*, London, Barrie and Rockliff, 1965, p. 6, p. 45 and p. 51.

AARON COPLAND

The American composer and all-round musician Aaron Copland has been described by his peers and critics as 'the Dean of American Composers' and for many his harmonies epitomize the very sound of American music, evoking its vast landscape and the American pioneer spirit. He considered Beethoven to be a composer of 'the first rank', alongside Palestrina and Bach, singling out for mention the psychological depth of his music, its dramatic instincts, his dynamic forms and their 'sense of inevitability'. In response to the proposition 'What made Beethoven so compelling?' he responded:

'How can one not be compelled and not be moved by the moral fervour and conviction of such a man. His finest works are the enactment of a triumph — a triumph of affirmation in the face of the human condition. Beethoven is one of the great yea-sayers among creative artists; it is exhilarating to share his clear-eyed contemplation of the tragic sum of life. His music summons forth our better nature; in purely musical terms Beethoven seems to be exhorting us to be noble, be strong, be great in heart, yes, and be compassionate.'

Howard Pollack, *Aaron Copland: The Life and Work of an Uncommon Man*, New York: Henry Holt, 1999, p. 60.

Copland set out his views about music in an essay titled *What to Listen for in Music* (1939). In this he remarks:

'Don't get the idea that the value of music is commensurate with its sensuous appeal or that the loveliest sounding music is made by the greatest composer. If that were so, Ravel would be a greater creator than Beethoven. The point is that the sound element varies with each composer, that his usage of sound forms an integral part of his style and must be taken into account when listening.'

Copland addressed the challenge of attempting to pin down the 'meaning' that might be ascribed to a particular musical work:

'In the first place it is easier to pin a meaning-word on a Tchaikovsky piece than on a Beethoven one. Much easier. Moreover, with the Russian composer, every time you come back to a piece of his it almost always says the same things to you, whereas with Beethoven it is often quite difficult to put your finger right on what he is saying. And any musician will tell you that that is why Beethoven is the greater composer.'

Richard Kostelanetz, editor, *Aaron Copland: A Reader; Selected Writings 1923–1972*, New York, London, Routledge, 2003, pp. 4–5.

In 1958, Copland spent some time in London when he wrote occasional pieces for the *Sunday Times*. In his article *Interpreters and New Music*, he stated cryptically:

'To play or conduct Beethoven *scherzi* in a contemporary spirit, you must feel at home with Stravinskian rhythms. And I can even recommend familiarity with the rhythms of American jazz for those who want to play Couperin.'

Aaron Copland, *Copland on Music*, London, Deutsch, 1961, p. 264.

JOHN CRABBE

The British writer compares Beethoven's influence on Western culture with that of Shakespeare's:

'Apart from Shakespeare I can think of no other figure in Western culture who commands such supremacy and veneration in his own art, yet is known to a universal public. What is it that still confers on Beethoven, more than 150 years after his death, to the universal public? [Crabbe was writing in 1982]. What is it that still confers on Beethoven, more than 150 years after his death, the mantle of a prophet with a perennially vital message for each new generation? Why does his music radiate such energy that it shines right across the romantic age to probe even today, beyond the boundary of ordinary musical feelings?'

Of the Fifth Symphony he asks:

'Why, when elated by the Fifth Symphony's exaltation or absorbed in the questing mysteries of the late quartets or piano sonatas, do we feel the urge to wonder what Beethoven is saying or to ask what he means?'

More generally, Crabbe continues:

'Similar questions are sometimes asked of new composers whose musical aims and idioms seem obscure, but Beethoven has been dead for two whole lifetimes and ordinary music-lovers have been familiar with his idiom for almost as long. Yet still we sense an extra-musical "something" behind the notes, an intense individual person striving with all his might to direct our attention to things of great human concern, then — his last utterances — towards the transcendental. The very least that can be said is that he brought to music a passionate and visionary element, a sense of drama and struggle that was absolutely new. It has been emulated since, but never repeated on the same scale by ay one man.'

Crabbe extends his views:

'Paradoxically, I believe that Beethoven's very individuality contributes to his universal appeal: his craggy turbulence; his love of nature; his contempt for authority and etiquette; an assertive will contrasted with humility before his God; a careless disregard of physical surroundings; a passionate desire to beg, borrow or steal fire from the gods in order to benefit mankind with his art; and above all, strong feelings that we should direct our attention to higher things, beyond the hurly-burly and chaos of the world ... He believed that his music could in some fashion provide men with new liberties. He was a dreamer who ultimately might conquer the world, and if the poet Arthur O'Shaughnessy had lived and written at an earlier time, the words of his, which Elgar set as *The Music Makers*, would surely have been clothed with the music of Beethoven — "We are the music makers / And we are the dreamers of dreams." — Such sentiments are of Beethoven's very essence, an epitome of that spiritual empire in which his own dreams had an all-conquering power.'

John Crabbe, *Beethoven's Empire of the Mind*, Newbury: Lovell Baines, 1982. Crabbe's book title is derived from one of Beethoven's most cherished sayings: 'I much prefer the *empire of the mind*. I regard it as the highest of all spiritual and worldly monarchies.'

WILLIAM CROTCH

The composer and organist Dr. William Crotch was one of the first English musicologists to make reference to the music of Beethoven. Crotch was for a time organist at Christ Church College, Oxford where he later became Professor of music. In 1831 he published his *Substance of Several Courses of Lectures*. In these he considered the music of Haydn, Mozart, and Beethoven as being 'frequently magnificent but seldom sublime'; Crotch was clearly not easily pleased! However, he did consider the opera overtures (as he refers to them) of Beethoven, Cherubini, and Weber to be 'extremely fine' and 'deserving of study'. Indeed, he believed they demonstrated 'the improvement of instrumental music'.

Crotch regarded Mozart as 'the greatest of all modern composers' after hearing a performance of his *Requiem*. He acknowledged 'the novelty and gaiety' of the style of Haydn's symphonies, and conferred on Haydn the accolade 'the greatest of all instrumental composers'. He praised Beethoven's piano music for being 'original, masterly, and frequently sublime' though only 'when it does not abound with difficulties of execution'. Crotch honoured Beethoven's symphonies with the designation 'wonderful productions' but complained:

> 'That ... Beethoven has ever disregarded the rules of composition is to be regretted, and there does not seem to have been the least good obtained by it in any one instance.'

Jonathan Rennert, *William Crotch (1775—1847): Composer, Artist, Teacher*, Lavenham, Terence Dalton, 1975, p. 46. Crotch's lectures were originally published as: *Substance of Several Courses of Lectures on Music, read in the University of Oxford, and in the Metropolis*, A. & R. Spottiswoode, 1831.

LOUISE ELVIRA CUYLER

In her study *The Symphony*, the American musicologist Louise Elvira Cuyler positions Beethoven as a central figure in the history of music:

> 'Historians who advocate a strictly evolutionary view of music are confounded by the emergence of a Titan like Beethoven. He is an anomaly that defies categorising. His compositions were the catalyst for musical attitudes of the entire nineteenth century, yet the works themselves stand proudly detached — from their ancestors as from each other.
>
> 'Beethoven found in music the noblest means of enunciating the sublime, and he freed music for all time from necessary reliance on a text. When, in such late works as the finale of the Ninth Symphony and the *Missa Solemnis*, he made conspicuous use of voices, Beethoven used the vocal component as a resource for contrasting timbres and increased sonority; the integrity and articulateness of the music did not rely on the presence of words.'

Culer positions Beethoven the symphonist in the realm of the liberal arts:

> 'Beethoven was born, it would seem, to write symphonies. Although he had composed a considerable body of music — mostly chamber works and sonatas — before he undertook his first symphony, his whole musical style crystallised and became assured with the completion of that first work in 1800. Beethoven's nine symphonies have stood for more than a century and a half as ideals for others to emulate. There is neither an

uncertain composition nor a genre of work among the nine. Each is a confident, individual statement from an artist for whom music was the supremely expressive language. Beethoven restored music to the proud pinnacle it had occupied in earlier times when, along with arithmetic, geometry, and astronomy, it was included in the quadrivium of liberal arts. He proclaimed himself a *Tondichter* (tone poet). In so doing, he set himself apart from his craftsmen-forebears of the eighteenth century, and he placed his art on a par with literature, philosophy, and religion, as a means to uplift, instruct, and heal mankind.'

Louise Elvira Cuyler, *The Symphony*, New York, Harcourt Brace Jovanovich, 1973, pp. 48–49.

CARL CZERNY

The Austrian pianist, composer, and pedagogue Carl Czerny is remembered by generations of pianists, both amateur and professional, for the many technical exercises he wrote to encourage the acquisition of a secure pianoforte technique. Beethoven accepted Czerny as a pupil when he was just ten years old. At his audition he impressed Beethoven by playing his recently composed *Pathétique* Piano Sonata, prompting him to remark: 'The boy has talent, I will accept him as my pupil.' Thereby, he initiated a fruitful teacher-pupil relationship that lasted throughout the composer's lifetime. Czerny's letters and recollections of Beethoven (1842) provide a rich source of information about the composer.

Beethoven's orchestral compositions were in demand in four-hand, piano-transcription form, the undertaking of which, however, held little appeal for Beethoven. Carl Czerny made such transcriptions of the composer's symphonies that were published as, *Collection Complète des Sinfonies de L. van Beethoven, Arrangées pour le Pianoforte à Quatre Mains.* These have since been somewhat eclipsed by the similar arrangements by Franz Liszt – himself a pupil of Czerny – but they were well received at the time. This is evident from a review that appeared in the *Allgemeine musikalische Zeitung* on 1 January 1829:

> 'Every lover of music knows that *Beethoven* wrote magnificent symphonies; indeed, we would like to say that in regard to energy, fantasy, and impressive greatness, he wrote the most magnificent. Most fortepianists know as well that Herr *Carl Czerny* is quite suited to translate an orchestral piece in full harmony effectively, and in the most appropriate way for pianoforte for four hands. Therefore, we can cast the most favourable horoscope for this complete collection of *Beethoven's* symphonies, arranged by *C. Czerny.* This first volume justifies the favourable prejudice that we held for this work.'

Of related interest is that Czerny arranged Beethoven' symphonies, as he states, for 'our new fortepianos' – a reference to the keyboard instruments of the late 1820s that had both an extended range and greater sonority than those of earlier instruments.

Wayne M. Senner, Robin Wallace and William Meredith, editors, *The Critical Reception of Beethoven's Compositions by his German Contemporaries*, Lincoln: University of Nebraska Press, in association with the American Beethoven Society and the Ira F. Brilliant Center for

Beethoven Studies, San José State University, 1999, Vol. 1, p. 128.

CARL DAHLHAUS

The German musicologist Carl Dahlhaus outlined his views on the music of Beethoven in his *Ludwig van Beethoven: Approaches to His Music*. In considering the composer's legacy he makes the following generalizations:

> 'Beethoven overwhelmed the limits of Classical form in his sonata movements by blurring the demarcations between sections and theme-groups and in creating such gigantic structures as the first movements of the *Hammerklavier* Sonata and the Ninth Symphony ... No composer of the nineteenth century could wholly escape Beethoven's influence, for his musical activity was so universal that he must be regarded as the trunk of the tree of nineteenth-century music from which so many branches sprang ... Beethoven gave the strongest impetus, at least for music, to the idea that art was a substitute for, or at least as noble as, religion.'

Carl Dahlhaus, *Ludwig van Beethoven: Approaches to his Music*, Oxford, Clarendon Press, 1991.

In his study *Nineteenth-century Music*, Dahlhaus discusses what he describes as the Beethoven 'Myth and Legend' in the following terms:

> 'The Beethoven myth ... is separated from empirical biography by a chasm that represents

something more than a simple opposition of truth and falsehood. Still, it would be a gross oversimplification to claim that the myth of Beethoven is a direct imprint of his music. The mythical figure in the "romantic image of Beethoven", whether, sorcerer, or saint, cannot be conveniently equated with the persona behind his works, however close the connection between them. Just as the aesthetic subject that we sense in Beethoven's music bears little relation to the man we know from his biography, it is no less foolish to try to identify this subject with the Beethoven of myth and legend. First of all, the works on which the Beethoven myth thrives represents a narrow selection from his complete output: *Fidelio* and the music of *Egmont*; the Third, Fifth and Ninth Symphonies; and the *Pathétique* and *Appassionata* Sonatas. It is not a fact in support of the Beethoven myth that these works are "representative", but rather are one of the claims that make up the myth. To the same extent that the myth was abstracted from the music, the reception of the music was tempered by the myth. And if the myth, once it impinges on biography, transforms anecdotes into allegorical cyphers, it also creates an order that separates symbolic works from non-symbolic ones.'

Turning to a consideration of Beethoven's symphonies Dahlhaus contends:

'The history of the symphony ... looks almost like a history of the conclusions that composers were to draw from Beethoven's various models of the symphonic principle: from the Third and Seventh Symphonies in the case of Berlioz, the Sixth in the case of Mendelssohn, and the Ninth in the case of Bruckner. Yet the line of development breaks of in mid-century. Mendelssohn and Berlioz strangely rub shoulders in the history of the symphony immediately after Beethoven, and from the 1870s to the early years of our century the symphony experienced a "second life" But the quarter of a century between these two periods is a yawning chasm with [Niels] Gade, [Joachim] Raff, and [Anton] Rubinstein as stopgaps. And it was during this "dry period" of the symphony that the "symphonic poem", which Liszt developed from the concert overture, emerged as the epoch-making genre of orchestral music in the grand style.'

In his chapter *The Symphony after Beethoven*, Dahlhaus further reflects on the challenge Beethoven's symphonic achievement posed to composers of the nineteenth century:

'By and large, the task that composers faced in assimilating the Beethoven legacy had to do with a will to large-scale form. Beethoven had transformed the symphony into a monumental genre, just as his admired forebear Handel had done to the oratorio. Thereafter, a symphony manifested compositional ambitions of the highest order, the audience it addressed being no smaller than the whole of humanity.'

Carl Dahlhaus, *Nineteenth-Century Music*, Translated by

J. Bradford Robinson, Berkeley, London, University of California Press, 1989, p. 29, p. 32, pp. 75–78 and p. 152.

PETER MAXWELL DAVIES

The British composer Sir Peter Maxwell Davies reflects on the classical symphony and the challenge posed by Beethoven's symphonies to those composers, following after him, writing in the symphonic genre:

> 'The classical symphony, as perfected by Beethoven, cast a shadow that took a century to deal with and can still cause confusion. The attempts by very great composers to cope with its implications resulted in a protracted compositional problem every bit as real and as poignant as any in our own century. This is not to suggest that the attempt didn't produce some glorious pieces of music whose very contradictions are the source of their fascination. But it is important to realise that Beethoven's successors were fleeing both from and towards an inheritance that was too near to ignore and not far away enough to use.'

Davies examines the dilemma faced by Beethoven's successors in greater detail:

> 'The great 19th-century composers and some of their 20th-century successors ran aground because of their tendency to take the scenario of the Beethoven symphony too literally, particularly with regard to first movement sonata-discourse. Haydn, Mozart, and Beethoven knew about sonata discourse, whether they called it that or

not, but they looked on it as a reference-point *beneath the surface of the music* against which the specific and individual conflicts of a given work could be meaningfully displayed. The result was always three-dimensional and involved a tension between what was on the surface of a piece of music and what was beneath it.'

Davies concludes:

'The post-Beethoven composers misunderstood this, and turned a substructure into a social code of behaviour at a surface-level which any well-bred symphonic first movement will ignore at its peril. There resulted the paradox that classicism, with its implications of strictness and control, used sonata-discourse to liberate any number of individual solutions to the problems of making a new piece of music, whereas romanticism, with its aura of freedom and individualism, turned the discourse into a straight-jacket which it imposed with the force of an obsession.'

Peter Maxwell Davies, *Studies from two Decades*, selected and introduced by Stephen Pruslin, London, Boosey & Hawkes, 1979, p. 5.

COLLIN DAVIS
The English conductor Sir Colin Davis was interviewed by the American cultural historian Joseph Horowitz. Their subject was primarily the Chilean pianist Claudio Arrau — an acknowledged interpreter of Beethoven. In passing, Davis made some characteristically modest remarks:

'I'm reading this biography of Beethoven, by Maynard Solomon [*Beethoven*, New York: Schirmer, 1977]. I'm learning an awful lot of things from it, about Beethoven and about myself. Not that I think I'm in any way comparable; I'm unworthy to untie his shoes, I wasn't born into a professionally musical family, as Beethoven was. I wasn't a child prodigy, as he was; I didn't start studying an instrument until I was twelve. I don't have that kind of musical background. I am therefore full of reverence for those who do.'

Joseph Horowitz, *Conversations with Arrau*, London, Collins, 1982, p. 236.

The Greek-born author and biographer Helena Matheopoulos interviewed Colin Davis, who she describes as 'philosopher and psychoanalyst'. In his capacity as conductor, he outlined his approach to coming-to-terms with an orchestral composition:

'[You] have to understand the process of [the composer's] thoughts, read right though the symphony first and then break it into sections so as to get the structure right; otherwise you may trip up, thinking there might be another bar. Of course, there *could* be, and then you would have another version of the symphony — although there is no reason why there should be. It just *could* have gone another way ... The possibilities of music are never exhausted just by the score in front of you ... [A] good score should convince you that everything is inevitable, the *only* way the music could have gone, like Beethoven's usually do. Beethoven always worked by doing many sketches and hammering at them until they sounded right; and he expresses himself with such force that you cannot dislodge these versions anymore.'

Helena Matheopoulos, *Maestro: Encounters with Conductors of Today*, London, Hutchinson, 1982, pp. 155–56.

BASIL DEANE

The Irish musicologist and academic Basil Deane pays tribute to Beethoven's position in music and his symphonic achievement:

'The uniqueness of Beethoven's historical position, standing as he does between two ages and two philosophies, is nowhere more apparent than in his attitude towards the symphony. The symphony in the nineteenth century was essentially an aristocratic entertainment; to the Romantics it was a vehicle for self-confession on a grandiose scale. For Beethoven it was neither. It was a public work, not a private one. It did not reflect his immediate personal situation, nor did he use it to symbolize an immediate human relationship: the Second Symphony was written at the time of the *Heiligenstadt Testament*, and no woman was paid the compliment of receiving the dedication of a symphony or an overture. But Beethoven's public was mankind, and he was mankind's spokesman. In his symphonies and overtures he proclaimed his concepts about life, concepts which, he believed, are of universal application: love of nature, desire for peace, freedom and brotherhood, the reality of conflict, of defeat, of triumph. To achieve his aim, it was necessary for him to forge a new symphonic language, one direct in its impact, yet capable of a hitherto unexplored range of expression. The story of the symphonies is the story of his creation and extension of this language.'

Basil Deane, *The Symphonies and Overtures* in: Denis Arnold and Nigel Fortune editors, *The Beethoven Companion*, London, Faber and Faber, 1973, p. 281.

CLAUDE DEBUSSY

Claude Debussy's views about Beethoven oscillate between respect, on the one hand, and disdain on the other. The essence of this is captured in the recollections of some of those who met him. We offer the following selection:

The English composer and poet Cyril Scott met Debussy early on in his long life — he lived to be ninety-one — and left several recollections of the composer. He considered Debussy to be one of those Frenchmen who sacrificed politeness to sincerity: 'He was charming to those whom he liked but was the opposite to those he disliked.' Scott recalls Debussy's general dislike of Beethoven who he was given to describing as *le vieux sourd* — 'the old deaf [one]'.

The English writer and collector Simon Harcourt-Smith met Debussy at the period when his father was head of the British School at Athens. Harcourt-Smith was then still only a child but recalls the composer seizing him by the arm and saying: 'If you have any affection, my boy, for me, *never* play or even talk of Wagner or Beethoven to me, because it is like somebody dancing on my grave.'

The French writer on music Georges Jean-Aubrey was a staunch supporter of contemporary composers and met Debussy when he was in his forties. He remarks how the composer was then disposed to speak very little and when he did it was in brusque phrases that seemed to contain ill-restrained wrath and irony for those who did not understand him or who endeavoured to falsify his beliefs. Of composers he ridiculed Grieg, whose music he described as 'a pink bon-bon stuffed with snow' and of Saint-Saëns he exclaimed: 'I have a horror of sentimentality and I cannot forget that its name is Saint-Saëns!' Jean-Aubrey recalls Debussy expressed his liking for Mozart but Beethoven did not escape his critical censure:

> 'He believed Beethoven had terrifically profound things to say, but that he did not know how to say them, because he was imprisoned in a web of incessant restatement and of German aggressiveness.'

Roger Nichols, *Debussy Remembered*, London, Faber and Faber, 1992, p. 105, p. 120 and p.166.

The French writer and academician Georges Delaquys interviewed Debussy, the text of their conversation being subsequently published as an article in *Excellsior* on 18 January 1911. In this, Debussy affirmed his love of music and what it meant to him:

> 'I love music passionately, and through my love I have forced myself to break from certain sterile traditions with which it is encumbered. It is a free

art, a wellspring, an art of the open air, an art comparable to the elements — wind, the sea, and the sky!'

Debussy attempted to put the record straight concerning opinions that were being attributed to him:

'All kinds of attitudes toward the great masters have been attributed to me, and I have been quoted as saying things about Wagner and Beethoven that I never said. I admire Beethoven and Wagner, but I refuse to admire them uncritically just because people have told me that they are masters! Never! In our day, it seems to me that we adopt poses in regard to the masters more becoming to bitter old cleaning women; I wish to have the freedom to say that a boring page of music is annoying no matter who its author.'

In 1913 Debussy contributed an article on taste in the February issue of *SIM — Société Internationale de Musicology*. He considered the true meaning of the word 'taste' was in decline merely signifying a difference of opinion — usually settled, in Debussy's words 'with knuckle dusters'. Turning to taste in music, he remarks — with a dig at Beethoven:

'Geniuses can evidently do without taste: take the case of Beethoven, for example. But, on the other hand, there was Mozart to whose genius was added a measure of the most delicate "good taste." And if we look at the works of J.S. Bach — a benevolent God to whom all musicians should offer a prayer before commencing work, to defend themselves from mediocrity — on each new page of his innumerable works, we discover things we thought were born only yesterday.'

Richard Langham Smith, editor, *Debussy on Music: The Critical Writings of the Great French Composer Claude Debussy*, London, Secker & Warburg, 1977, p. 96, pp. 232–3, pp. 244–5 and p. 277.

In an article titled *M. Croche, Antidiltettante* that Debussy wrote in 1927, he reflected on the future of the symphony after Beethoven:

> 'A symphony is always received with enthusiasm. It seemed to me that after Beethoven the uselessness of the symphony was proved. Neither with Schumann nor Mendelssohn is it anything more than a respectful but already less forceful repetition of the same forms. Still, the "Ninth" is a model of genius, showing a magnificent desire to enlarge and liberate the accustomed forms by giving them the harmonious measurements of a fresco.
>
> 'The true lesson taught by Beethoven, then, was not to preserve the old forms, nor an obligation to set our feet in the imprints of his earliest footsteps. It was to look out of open windows upon the free heavens. But it seems to me that they have been shut forever: the few successes attained by men of genius with this species do little to excuse the studied and factitious exercises which are habitually described as symphonies.'

John L. Holmes, *Composers on Composers*, New York, Greenwood Press, 1990.

FREDERICK DELIUS

The English composer Frederick Delius outlined his views on composers in a letter to Peter Heseltine, better known as Peter Warlock:

> 'When I first heard Chopin as a little boy of six or seven, I thought heaven had been opened before me. When also as a little boy I first heard the *Humoresken* of Grieg a new world was opened to me again. When at the age of 23 I heard *Tristan* – I was perfectly overcome – also when I heard *Lohengrin* as a schoolboy. Beethoven always left me cold and reserved – Bach I always loved more – it seemed to me more spontaneous – Brahms I never liked much and never shall – it is philistine music – although some of the chamber music is good – But to have to get accustomed to music is a fearfully bad sign – The sort of people who get accustomed to music are the unmusical and when once accustomed to it they will hear no other.'

Lionel Carley, *Delius: A Life in Letters*, London: Scolar Press in association with the Delius Trust, 1988, pp. 91–2.

The English composer, conductor, and teacher Eric Fenby is perhaps best known for being Delius's amanuensis. He served the composer in this capacity for the period 1928–34 and, thereby, helped Delius realise several compositions that otherwise would not have been forthcoming. On one occasion, Fenby ventured to ask Delius his views of other composers. His question provoked Delius to respond: 'You needn't ask me to listen to the music of the Immortals. I can't abide them. I finished with them long ago!' Fenby recalls Delius adding: 'It takes a genius to write a movement like the slow movement of Schuman's Piano Quintet in E flat' and 'How much better Mendelssohn uses the orchestra than Beethoven.'

Eric Fenby, *Delius as I knew Him*, London, Quality Press, 1936, p. 195.

The composer Sir Granville Bantock, a former pillar of the British musical establishment, was a close friend of Delius. Delius briefly outlined his views on music to Bantock when he was Principal of the Birmingham and Midland Institute of Music:

> 'Do tell your students not to continue to write music or to imitate what they think is deep or severe music — England seems never to get over this sort of nonsense and the best result seems to rise to a weak imitation. Since Beethoven, the symphony has gradually become weaker and more meaningless — à travers Mendelssohn, Schumann, and Brahms. Tchaikovsky managed to put a spirited march or tune *Valse Lento* into it which gave new colour to it — but very slight, but somewhat more human.'

Christopher Redwood, editor: *A Delius Companion*, London, John Calder, 1976, p. 59.

DAVID B. DENNIS

David B. Dennis is an American professor of history with particular interests in the Western humanities, and modern European cultural and intellectual history. His *Beethoven in German Politics, 1870-1989* (Yale University Press, 1996) examines evocations and uses of Beethoven's biography and music by all of the major parties of 19th- and 20th-century German political culture. Dennis reworks many of his views, concerning the place of Beethoven in Western culture, in his essay *Beethoven at Large: Reception in Literature, the Arts, Philosophy, and Politics* as outlined in the *Cambridge Companion to Music*, editor Glenn Stanley, 2000, pp. 292–304. We cite the following from this text:

Dennis first considers what Beethoven means to the typical music lover:

> 'Amid the enormous collection of Beethoven-inspired lyric in the Beethoven-Haus archives of Bonn stands a thick folder overflowing with poems "on single sheets", in other words never published. Hand-written or carefully typed, these verses were submitted by their authors themselves, often after visits to the Geburtshausmuseum. Such amateur, but heartfelt, words remind us that the majority of artistic responses to Beethoven come from men and women whose names remain unfamiliar to the world of high letters; they might reveal more about how his music and life-story for general listeners than all "expert" disputations. Above all, the collection symbolizes a compulsion widely felt by persons who encounter this composer, his music, or simply memorabilia and places associated with him: Beethoven lovers tend to react to his art in active, often creative fashion, not passively. Such is the intense, ongoing influence that he and his works have on Western and even world cultures, both inside and outside musical life.'

Dennis adds:

'His triumphs over deafness and loneliness fixed his reputation as a paradigm of the "artist". Inspired by this heroic image and the élan of his most popular works, musicians, writers, visual artists, politicians, and a host of others have attempted to imitate aspects of his personality, and convince others to do likewise.'

Denis acknowledges:

'That Beethoven was a complex character, partly explains the diversity of ways listeners set him into their cultural and ideological horizons. Combing through records of his inconsistent, even volatile nature, interpreters have found evidence to support associating the composer and his music with almost every modern current thought and behaviour.'

In the context of Beethoven's own time Dennis states:

'Scholars generally agree that common perceptions of Beethoven were strikingly — and permanently — coloured by his young contemporaries; the Romantics E.T.A. Hoffmann and Bettina Brentano urged listeners to interact emotionally with music, Beethoven's in particular, seeking and expressing soulful responses instead of merely being entertained.'

Dennis quotes the following passage from a letter of Brentano to Goethe:

'I believe in a divine magic that is an element of spiritual nature; and this magic, Beethoven exercises in his art.'

In this context, Dennis continues:

'Romantics underscored Beethoven's self-description as a *Tondichter* or "poet of tones" [consider for example the *Pastoral Symphony*] in order to associate him with their own goal of synthesizing the arts. This epithet functioned as a beacon summoning interpreters to mine his music for poetical ideas.'

Franz Grillparzer (see below) had the honour of eulogizing Beethoven at his Vienna funeral. In Dennis's estimation:

'[He] portrayed the composer as outcast and ignored, doomed to suffer alone, but — like a fairy-tail wizard — in possession of magnificent powers.'

Dennis quotes the following lines from Grillparzer's oration:

'An enchanter, tired of the world and life / Sealed his magic in an impregnable chest / Threw the key into the sea, and died.'

In his all-embracing survey of the manner in which Beethoven has been absorbed into Western culture, Dennis quotes the following: Charles Baudelaire and his *La Musique* (1857), dedicated to Beethoven; Walt Whitman's lines: 'Hastings, urging, restless — no flagging, not even in the "thoughts" or meditations — to be perceived with the same perceptions that enjoys music — free and luxuriant — as in Beethoven's; and E. M. Forster's, *A Room with a View* (1908) and *Howard's End* (1910). We remind the reader that both of the latter provide instances when Lucy Honeychurch 'disturbs her friends by playing the Piano Sonata Op. 11 on a rainy day in Florence and when Helen Schlegel listens to "the most sublime noise that ever penetrated the ear of man".' These are illustrations, Dennis suggests, of the 'register [and] the ongoing influence of Romanticism on literary allusion to Beethoven'.

Continuing his survey of Beethoven, as instanced in Romantic literature, Dennis contributes the following further illustrations:

Of Victor Hugo, he notes that whilst he never made specific reference to the composer in his own novels, he considers he sketched the main lines of Beethoven's representation in such allusions to: ' "crippled body, flying soul", producing music like a "deep mirror in a cloud" that reflects everything his listeners desire: in it "the dreamer will recognize his dream, the sailor his storm ... and the wolf his forests".'

For Dennis, Romain Rolland presented the composer as 'a holy martyr who sublimated pain through creative acts'. He quotes Rolland's words: "Blessed is the misfortune that has come upon thee! Blessed the sealing of thine ears!" He interprets this as Rolland's recognition of the manner in which Beethoven overcame 'the terror of deafness' and was shown 'a path to self-redemption: "poor, sick, alone — and yet a victor!" ' Dennis places Rolland as a central figure in the popularization of Beethoven in France 'in spite of ... his hero's Germanic origins'. High in Dennis's estimation of Rolland's prose works is what he considers to be his masterwork *Jean Christophe* (1904–12), an epic concerning an artist whose youth was mirrored on Beethoven's especially in the sense of obstacles to be overcome. To this work of Rolland's we may add his: *Life of Beethoven* (1903); *Beethoven and Handel* (1917); *Beethoven the Creator* (1929); and *Goethe and Beethoven* (1930).

In the representational arts, Dennis's survey encompasses the manner in which Beethoven has been portrayed in sculpture, portraiture, illustration and indeed a wide variety of other media relating to the Western music tradition. Concerning these he notes:

> '[The] commercialisation of Beethoven's physiognomy ... overshadows a long tradition of fashioning his likeness for reasons other than marketing. Through every phase of modern history, painters and sculptors have conveyed their regard for this musician as a source of inspiration across artistic boundaries ... Portraits done during Beethoven's life, often in a Romantic vein, established a number of constants in the visual representation of this genius. Unruly hair, tensed brow, frowning mouth, gaze directed elsewhere'.

Dennis laments the later trivialisation of Beethoven's visual imagery as is often depicted in the least accomplished of Biedermeier, the term used to identify the sentiment that permeates much early to mid-nineteenth century illustrative work — watercolour, line drawing and the like. A typical example, from literally hundreds, is Johann Peter Lyser's depiction of Beethoven seated by the bank of a stream composing his *Pastoral* Symphony. The reader for whom such Beethoven iconography holds particular fascination is encouraged to consult the Beethoven Haus 'Digital Archives'.

Franz Klein's life mask of Beethoven, taken in 1812, provided the basis for numerous later depictions of the composer in sculptural form. More than any other work this study identified Beethoven with the characteristic expression of defiance we have come to associate with him. Alessandra Comini has devoted an extended essay on this very subject in her *The Visual Beethoven: Whence, Why, and Whither the Scowl?* See Scott G. Burnham and Michael P. Steinberg, editors, *Beethoven and his World*, Princeton, New Jersey; Oxford: Princeton University Press, 2000, pp. 287–312.

By the mid-nineteenth century, attempts began in earnest to capture Beethoven, the titan, in stone and bronze, and locations associated with the composer began to erect monuments in his honour. Dennis comments: 'Taken together, these monuments embody the conflicting motives of depicting the composer "as he really appeared" while simultaneously idealizing him.' He considers: 'One of the most successful placements of Beethoven on a pedestal to be Kaspar Clemens Zumbusch's Vienna monument (1880): 'Scowling downward, the composer is as imposing as Michelangelo's Moses.' Alongside this work, we may cite that of the German artist Max Klinger. He depicted Beethoven partly robed – Roman fashion – seated in a chariot and worked in an array of marble, alabaster, ivory, bronze, amber and semi-precious stones (now located in the Museum der bilden Künst, Leipzig).

Dennis makes reference to the French sculptor Antoine Bourdelle who created over forty-five versions of Beethoven. He left many of his busts with rough and ragged surfaces suggesting to Dennis 'primal forces in the composer's character: like Michelangelo's bound slaves, Bourdelle's Beethovens emerge from earth's stony veins.'

Dennis cites examples of artists seeking to liberate 'the earthbound and monumentalised image of Beethoven to a more spiritual level'. He comments:

'This is nowhere more true than in the friezes Gustav Klimt designed to compliment Klinger's sculpture [see above] at the 1902 Vienna Secession exhibition. Fashioned in Klimt's suggestive style intimating psycho-sexual drives then being postulated by Sigmund Freud, each of the three panels proposes psychological correlates for portions of Beethoven's *Ninth Symphony.*'

Among philosophers who discuss Beethoven and his music, Dennis cites Friedrich Nietzsche, Theodor Adorno, and Ernst Bloch. In his estimation, these writers and thinkers stand out:

'They genuinely incorporated ideas about the composer into their thought.' In particular, Dennis remarks how, as a young man, 'Nietzsche set forth in poetry the awe he felt before this sublime creator: "I look upon you mutely / Wishing to ask your eyes / Why, you miraculous man / Does my pulse beat stormily / When you pass through the forest of my soul?" ' Nietzsche clearly felt a strong affinity with Beethoven, recognizing that, like himself, he both suffered and gained from solitude: 'It was only with Beethoven', in Nietzsche's view, that music:

> 'began to discover the language of pathos, of passionate desire, of the dramatic events which take place in the depths of man ... Beethoven was the first to let music speak a new language, the hitherto forbidden language of passion'.

Of Adorno, Dennis remarks: 'Adorno advanced a musical sociology in which the "inner syntax" of musical language correlates with social conditions and cultural patterns.'

Of Bloch, Dennis quotes: "How elated we feel when at the thought of you, infinite one! ... Our soul bubbles up to the stars in the initial rough, tempestuous, eloquent sea of this music. Beethoven is Lucifer's benign offspring, the eloquent, the demon that leads to the ultimate things." Dennis also quotes Bloch's admiration of Beethoven's opera: "Every future storming of the Bastille is implicitly expressed in *Fidelio* ... Here and nowhere else ... music becomes a rosy dawn, militant-religious, the dawning of a new day so audible that it seems more than simply a hope." Dennis cites the universal popularity of the Ninth Symphony:

> 'Since the Second World War it has become [the] tradition to perform [the Ninth Symphony] every December throughout the country.' He cites performances with a chorus of ten thousand given in Japan. Beethoven's Ninth Symphony has also been adopted as a symbol of peace by the United Nations.'

Dennis concludes his majestic survey of Beethoven's influence: 'This Western composer's life and music have clearly become touchstones in world culture.'

David B. Dennis, *Beethoven in German Politics, 1870-1989,* Yale University Press, 1996. *passim.*

DOMENICO DRAGONETTI

The Italian double-bass virtuoso Domenico Dragonetti met Beethoven in 1799. The encounter had far-reaching consequences for Beethoven's awareness of the potential of the double bass and his subsequent writing for it. The composer's biographer Alexander Wheelock Thayer describes Dragonetti as 'the greatest contrabassist known to history and writes: 'Dragonetti was not more remarkable for his astounding execution than for the deep, genuine musical feeling which elevated and ennobled it.' (Thayer, 1967, p. 208) It was hearing Dragonetti play that appears to have emboldened Beethoven to write for the double bass in a more challenging fashion. Dragonetti was known for his formidable strength and stamina which, combined with large hands and strong fingers, enabled him to coax from his double bass, music written for the cello.

Following his meeting with Beethoven, Dragonetti took up residence in London where he remained for the rest of his life. In 1816 he established a relationship with the Philharmonic Society and in the same year took part in the English première of Beethoven's Fifth Symphony. As remarked, it was Dragonetti's virtuosity that disposed Beethoven to extend his writing for the double bass far beyond the then orthodox treatment of merely doubling up the cello line. Such, indeed, were his innovations that, upon hearing the double bass passage that occurs at the close of the first movement of the Seventh Symphony, Weber is said to have exclaimed: 'Our Beethoven is now fit for the madhouse!'

Fiona Palmer has written of the challenges posed by Beethoven's writing for the double bass. She states:

> 'There can be little doubt that performances of the double bass part must have varied widely from player to player and country to country. Transposition and simplification were key to performance for most players. It seems unlikely that Dragonetti found it necessary to do the latter.'

Fiona M. Palmer, *Domenico Dragonetti in England (1794–1846): The Career of a Bouble Bass Virtuoso*, Oxford, Clarendon, 1997, p. 73.

ANTONÍN DVORÁK

Otakar Dvorák, writing about her composer-father, relates:

'Some critics have not taken my father seriously as a composer because he did not have much of an education ... But father's self-education and, of course, his talent gave him more than any music conservatory could have. He said to me, "How much time I spent learning the rich forms of Beethoven's sonatas!" ' Recalling a later occasion she adds: 'Father adored Mozart and Beethoven. A very small bust of Mozart's head stood on Father's desk, and next to that a small picture of the gloomy face of Beethoven. Once, after a concert, Father received a wreath inscribed with the words, "To the greatest genius ever." Father took this wreath home and draped the ribbon over the picture of Beethoven.'

Otakar Dvorák, *Antonín Dvorák, My Father*, Spillville, Iowa, Czech Historical Research Center, 1993. p. 91 and p. 109.

ALFRED EINSTEIN

The German-American musicologist Alfred Einstein is best known for his studies of the music of Mozart and in particular of his revisions of the Köchel Catalogue of his compositions. In his *Mozart*, Einstein opens his account of the symphony in the following terms:

'Mozart wrote more than fifty symphonies ... When one compares this number with the nine symphonies of Beethoven or the four of Brahms it becomes clear that the word "symphony" did not quite have the same meaning for Mozart that it had for Beethoven and Brahms. In Beethoven's sense of the word — an orchestral work addressed, above and beyond any occasion for its composition, to an ideal public, to humanity ... Beethoven's conception of the monumental symphony found its greatest historical and spiritual stimulus in Mozart's "Prague" Symphony and the three great symphonies of 1788. The art of the great symphony is the achievement of both Mozart and Haydn, and their share in it is difficult to apportion, for neither one would have made the decisive step towards monumentality without the influence of the other.'

Alfred Einstein, *Mozart: His Character, His Work*, London, Cassell and Company Ltd., 1946, p. 215.

FREDERICK FREEDMAN

The American musicologist Frederick Freedman has undertaken a study of the early publication of the symphonies of Haydn, Mozart, and Beethoven by the London-based publishers Cianchettini and Sperati. The following is derived from his account.

Francesco Cianchettini and P. Sperati established a publishing house and music shop in London in 1805 where they became known as 'Importers of Classical Music'; none other than the Prince of Wales was their Patron. In May 1807, they announced their intention to publish '*A Compleat Collection of Haydn, Mozart, and Beethoven's Symphonies*'. Haydn was then still alive and was recognized as the greatest living composer. The symphonies of Mozart were beginning to be published posthumously. As for Beethoven, as Freedman remarks: '[Then] only thirty-seven years old, [he] was looked upon by most critics as an eccentric composer who antagonized performers and listeners alike by his lengthy, difficult, and "dissonant" music.' With this in mind, the inclusion of Beethoven by Cianchettini and Sperati in their publication venture is all the more enterprising.

At the period in question, and for many years later, it was the custom to issue symphonic works in separate orchestral parts. The London partners' proposal is all the more remarkable since, as they announced in their prospectus, they planned to publish the symphonies, by subscription, *in full score*. The enterprise started well and included eighteen symphonies by Haydn (1807 and 1809), four by Mozart — including K. 550 and K. 551 (1808), and Beethoven's symphonies One, Two, and Three (1809). Regrettably, with only sixty-two subscribers Cianchettini's and Sperati's pioneering venture founded. Their achievements, however, did not pass unrecognised. The correspondent to *The Harmonicon*, the leading London music journal of the day, observed:

> 'That, under such circumstances, Mr. Cianchettini should have withdrawn without completing his design, no longer excites us to wonder; we are only surprised that he proceeded so far, and brought out his work in so neat and correct a manner.'

Freedman himself concludes:

> '[It] should be observed that Cianchettini and Sperati merely reissued material that was already available, and while their editions claimed neither

approval nor authenticity ... they performed, nevertheless, a useful service in being the first to make some of these great works available to the British public — and the world at large — in full score. This alone should ensure them an honourable place among the music publishers of their time'.

Frederick Freedman, *First, Second and Third Symphonies by Ludwig van Beethoven*, Detroit reprints in music, 1975.

WILHELM FURTWÄNGLER

The universally recognised interpreter of Beethoven, Wilhelm Furtwängler, was fulsome in his praise of the composer:

'Scarcely any other German name has been accorded such veneration through the entire world as that of Beethoven. If it is not in the same sense national as the creations of Wagner or Schubert, Beethoven's work yet possesses a spiritual power that Germany does not possess elsewhere in the art of music. Through no one else is the force and greatness of German perception and being brought to such penetrating expression.'

Originally published in: Walter Riezler, *Beethoven,* Zurich, 1936, translated, G.D.H Pidcock, New York: Vienna House, 1972, p. 9. Quoted in: John L. Holmes, *Composers on Composers*, New York, Greenwood Press, 1990, p. 52.

For the years 1924–54, Furtwängler kept a notebook in

which he recorded his thoughts about music. From these we cite the following extracts:

> 'What makes Beethoven and Goethe so great, so compelling? The fact that they had *both*, the natural strength of the earth, breadth and stature, "sublimation". Both in such a proportion that the one was able to *grow* out of the other. The liberal world, the intellectuals, need to be told repeatedly that sublimation alone is not enough, and our contemporaries need to be told that folk-art and breadth alone are not enough ... In judging an artist, one should differentiate between the intellectual superstructure that is pervasive and individual to him, and the substance itself. In Beethoven this superstructure is very small, the substance enormous, In Bruckner the discrepancy is even greater. In today's artist it is generally the other way around. A great "intellectual" attitude and great intellectual abilities can mask quite a weak and false substance (and generally do so) ... The pernicious inheritance of Romanticism is the "art of inspiration". Overcoming it is a task that has been taken up anew by every individual artist since Beethoven.'

In writing about Wagner (1939) Furtwängler makes reference to Beethoven:

> '*Eroica*! Exaggeration of the early style, sometimes almost abstract (first movement). For all its greatness a unique work, i.e. a work of transition. Even the Fourth is freer and, consequently, greater. A sign that any style, even the most natural, can rigidify,

indeed rigidifies immediately upon, ceasing to be a completely natural expression. And it is always only this for one moment. The difference between Beethoven's early and middle styles, particularly in the transition periods, are not so tangible as that which we now call Beethoven's style. There is no "development" of harmony or rhythm, but only of the soul, which makes use of the musical space to a higher degree than before. The soul expresses more freely; that is the whole thing.'

Later, Furtwängler asks the question 'What is style?' and answers:

'Style can be productive, that is, a part of production, if it serves the "poetic" idea of the work. As in Wagner, as in Beethoven, in Bruckner, where it is the "world" of the individual work. (The epic attitude of the *Eroica*, the drama of the Fifth, the idyll of the Sixth, the humanism of the Eighth Symphony). But the general thing, the style of the age, which the young Beethoven was given, for example, was the initial premise on which he built something taken for granted rather than something meritorious. But one never attains major achievements when — as today — self-evident things have to be turned into virtues.'

Michael Tanner, editor, *Notebooks, 1924–1954: Wilhelm Furtwängler*, London, Quartet Books, 1989, p. 97, pp. 103–5, and pp. 150–1.

In his essay *Beethoven, a World Force*, Furtwängler wrote:

'What is most evident in respect of Beethoven, and exerts more influence than anything from other composers, is what I would term the "Law". He strives like no one else after the natural law, and after what is definitive, as a consequence of which we have the extraordinary clarity that distinguishes his music. The kind of simplicity that prevails therein is not the simplicity of naïveté, nor is it a calculated effect like that, for instance, of a modern popular number. Yet at no time was music written that confronts the listener so directly, so openly and — one might say — so nakedly! We know from Beethoven's life that he never found his work as an artist easy, that the monumental and simple qualities of his themes did not simply fall into his lap. On the contrary: each of his works shows a concentrated essence of a whole world, and — from a limitless, chaotic life and experience — is given order, form, and clarity by means of the iron will of the artist. This particular kind of clarity signifies nevertheless the renunciation of all means — which exist in art as in life — of placing the subject in an advantageous light so that through kinds of colouring and through refinement it may appear as more profound and greater than it really is.'

This preceding quotation is derived from the writings of Santeri Levas who was the personal secretary to Jean Sibelius for twenty years. He considered the words quoted to be also appropriate to his master and the manner in which he evolved his own creations.

Santeri Levas, *Sibelius: A Personal Portrait*, London, J. M. Dent, 1972, p. 62.

Furtwängler wrote at length about Beethoven in his *Vermächtnis Nachgelassene* – 'Legacy Writings' (1956). In these, he acknowledged the pioneering value of Wagner's writings about Beethoven. He conceded: 'Some of these may strike us [today] as overly rhetorical in parts, but we must not overlook the sense of necessity that he felt to communicate his knowledge.' Quoting Wagner: "One cannot discuss the essence of Beethoven's music other than in a mood of ecstasy". Of Wagner's role in shaping our understanding of Beethoven in performance, Furtwängler states:

> 'One achievement will always remain to Wagner's credit. Through his writings, and even more through his performances, he was the first, investing his whole passionate nature, to reveal what Beethoven really is. He demonstrated that a merely "correct", that is, mediocre performance – the kind no less the norm than it is today – is a bad performance, the more so in the case of Beethoven than any other composer, because it ignores what lies between the lines – and it is precisely there that the essence of the music resides.'

Furtwängler considered the 'organic' nature of Beethoven's orchestral music:

> 'Wagner was the first to point to the practical implication of [the] organic experience of the structure of Beethoven's works. Foremost among them is the use of rubato, that almost imperceptible yet constant variation of tempo which turns a piece of music into what it really is – an experience of conception and growth, of a living organic process.'

Describing Beethoven's working method, Furtwängler indulges in some Wagner-style rhetoric:

> '[Held] in the grip of raging passion, he retains his steely control, his singularity of purpose, his unshakable determination to shape and master his material down to the very last detail with a self-discipline unparalleled in the history of art. Never has an artist, driven by an irresistible creative force, felt so intensely the "law" that underlies artistic creation, and submitted to it with such humility.'

With regard to the sensory — sound-world experience — of Beethoven's symphonic writing, Furtwängler avers:

> 'There are *fortissimi* which, though scored for ridiculously few instruments, have an inner drive and power which completely overshadow the explosive outbursts of a modern symphony orchestra. This reveals itself in performance. Confronted with the inner stresses and tensions of this music, all our genteel, refined striving after artistry and euphony proves useless. Beethoven lies beyond the limits of what people call *Beauty*. The smouldering heat within his works consumes all who perform it, singers and instrumentalists alike. To change the metaphor — every work has to be wrenched from the consciousness of whoever performs it ... The music owes far less than that of other composers to specific sensory qualities — that is to say, when working out his ideas, Beethoven does not proceed primarily

from the nature of the instruments or the voices through which he conveys these ideas ... He captures the fundamental ethos of a symphony or a quartet but rarely exploits the acoustic potential of the medium in question — the wealth of timbres achievable by the orchestra, for instance. He adapts himself to the instruments he uses but never surrenders to their power. They are vehicles for ideas that go far beyond the realm of sense perception.'

On the interpretation of Beethoven, Furtwängler, the pre-eminent Beethovenian, asserts:

'The powerful tensions in Beethoven's music make it necessary to observe a clarity and strictness of formal build-up ... If the performer does not re-experience and re-live the music each time anew, these formal elements will thrust themselves into the foreground, giving an impression of regulation and prescription, of hackneyed repetition, while draining the work of its energy, the vitality of its spiritual freedom and giving the impression that it is the form that matters most.'

Of Beethoven's enduring legacy, Furtwängler is pithily succinct: '[Beethoven] represents for us an art of the present, and art relevant to our day and age, not an art of the past.'

Wilhelm Furtwängler, originally published in, *Vermächtnis Nachgelassene Schriften* and quoted in: Robert Taylor, editor, *Furtwängler on Music: Essays and Addresses*, Aldershot: Scolar Press, 1991, pp. 34–37.

HANS GAL

In his survey of *The Golden Age of Vienna*, the Austrian-British composer and author Hans Gal reserves a special position for Beethoven who he describes as *The Master Builder*. He adds:

> 'Beethoven is the first representative of the modern intellectual type, whose range of interests is not confined to his art. Wherever one looks into his letters, subjects of general interest are touched. Though his scanty education is pathetically obvious in certain limitations of style and difficulties of spelling, a great mind, a wide, comprehensive conception assert themselves everywhere.'

Gal considers Beethoven's early achievements in composition:

> 'Beethoven was twenty-one when he became Haydn's pupil, and the most remarkable composition he brought with him, a Cantata on the death of Joseph II, already gives the impression of a fully asserted personality. But his technique as a composer was inadequate, more superficially acquired that systematically built up, the outcome of irregular studies with indifferent teachers, who obviously did their best, but could not give more than they had themselves. His Op.1, published three years later and with the unmistakable intention of discarding everything he had done before — the most remarkable first work a composer has ever published — shows him as a master of his art.'

*

The Cantata to which Gal refers was written when Beethoven was just twenty years old but was never performed in his lifetime — the Bonn orchestra available to him found the parts too taxing. It was only premiered in 1884, fifty-seven years after his death. However, echoes of the work can be heard in the composer's opera *Leonore, or The Triumph of Marital Love* — later reworked as *Fidelio*.

Gal reaffirms his view as Beethoven being an architect-like constructor:

> 'The fact is that no great master has ever regarded form as more than a principle, based on the common sense of musical construction, adapted to the peculiarities of the actual material and idea in every single instance. This is what Beethoven, the most clear-sighted architect of music who ever lived, seems to demonstrate in every single work. The main difference between his conception and his predecessors' is not the actual form but, so to speak, the voltage, the degree of tension between the component musical characters or ideas.'

Gal reasons the *Eroica* Symphony was transformational for Beethoven and marked an epochal event in the history of music:

> 'The first work in which [Beethoven] fully realised his own vision of a monumental conception, *Sinfonia Eroica*, was probably the most staggering novelty in the history of music. There is not only a new style, a new sound, a new greatness of form and design, but a completely new attitude to the world of the artistic person-

ality. No obedient servant of his liege-lord had ever been able to conceive such music. Here, the artist feels himself an equal to the greatness of this world. It is not unlikely that the title of the symphony, still more its dedication to the Consul Bonaparte, was an afterthought. It would have been an odd compliment, anyway, to glorify a living hero with his own funeral celebration.

'When shortly after completion of the score the hero proclaimed himself Emperor of France, and thus made a parody of himself to the idealistic republican, Beethoven, in fit of rage, he tore the idol down from the pedestal he had erected for him. The story is well known and borne out by the crumpled and torn Title Page of a manuscript copy of the Symphony, on which the half-erased traces of Beethoven's hand-written dedication are still visible. His furious outburst betrays his self-reproach: he could not forgive himself for having debased his ideal by linking it to an individual, though the greatest of his time, and his human weakness. In its personal grandeur, *Sinfonia Eroica* stands out as the noblest monument of heroism as a pure idea, higher and loftier than its realisation by any mortal hero.'

Gal concludes:

'Beethoven — like Michelangelo, who offers the most obvious parallel among the great artists — is the prototype of such a living volcano. Like Michelangelo, he had the titanic power of moulding the eruptive material, of imposing on it his creative will. It is the most demoniac of all elements: Chaos, both the eternal source and eternal contradiction of Cosmos, the ordered world.'

Hans Gal, *The Golden Age of Vienna*, London, Max Parrish & Co. Limited, 1948, pp. 44—46 and pp. 51—52.

CHARLES GOUNOD

Charles Gounod was born in Paris to a musical and artistic family. His mother Victoire was a talented pianist and his father François was a painter and successful architect. Gounod's own musical gifts earned for him, in due course, the Grand Prix de Rome. It was Victoire who encouraged Gounod's musical development. He recalls the occasion when she took him to a performance of Mozart's *Don Giovanni*. It proved to be the formative musical influence at that time in his life — he was fourteen at the time. He describes the effect the opening chords had on him:

> 'The first notes of the Overture, with the solemn and majestic chords out of the Commendatore's final scene, seemed to lift me into a new world. I was chilled by a sensation of actual terror; but when I heard that terrible threatening roll of ascending and descending scales, stern and implacable as a death warrant, I was seized with such shuddering fear, that my head fell upon my mother's shoulder.'

Later, Gounod heard Beethoven's *Pastoral* and *Choral* Symphonies at the Conservatoire that he describes as adding 'fresh impulse to my musical ardour'. He closes this episode in his youthful recollections remarking: 'Something told me that these two great talents, each so peerless in its way, came of a common stock, and professed the same musical dogma'.

Marie Anne de Bovet, *Charles Gounod: His Life and His Works*, London, S. Low, Marston, Searle & Rivington, Ltd., 1891, pp. 38—41.

PERCY GRAINGER

The Australian pianist, composer and arranger of folk music Percy Grainger gave his first public recital in Melbourne at the age of twelve — including works by Beethoven. In 1903, Grainger studied with the eminent pianist Ferruccio Busoni. Later, when performing in London, *The Times* critic reported Grainger's playing 'revealed rare intelligence and a good deal of artistic insight'. In a letter written in 1909 to Karen Holten, one of his pupils, Grainger — notwithstanding his success — seems to have been in a despondent mood disposing him to invoke the circumstances of other composers including Beethoven:

> 'Few folk have so little calamity happen to them as I, and few can afford to digest *inner* soul-sorrow more soundly than I. Most men of my talents have more "push" or yearning for activity and *realization* than I. Wagner with his schemes, his wars, his whole forcefulness was an army continually on the move. Beethoven too with his despair & bubbling joyousness had not the calm for clear cold *onlooking* sadness that I have. Men who have died young like Keats, Schubert, A. Beardsley, Dowson seem often to have been as publicly inactive as I.'

Kay Dreyfus, *The Farthest North of Humanness: Letters of*

Percy Grainger, 1901–1914, South Melbourne; Basingstoke: Macmillan, 1985, p. 289.

During his stay in London (1915–21) Grainger wrote pieces for the *Musical Quarterly*. In the opening issue of 1915, he briefly outlined responses to sound in nature:

> 'Out ... in nature men have long known how to enjoy discordant combinations. A telegraph wire humming B flat, a bird piping a flat B natural, and a factory whistle chiming in with notes resembling D and F sharp; the mournful appeal of such accidental ensembles has frequently awakened emotional response.'

With these considerations in mind, Grainger directed his thoughts to Beethoven:

> 'Probably Beethoven was one of the first of the "moderns" to find such suggestions in everyday sounds. The trumpet behind the stage in the third *Leonora* seems an instance of this, while the premature entry of the horn in the first movement of the *Eroica* and the belated notes of the bassoon in the scherzo of the *Pastoral* shows his readiness to perpetuate in his scores hints derived from the mistakes of the rehearsal room and the happy-go-lucky ensemble of tavern "Musikanten".'

Malcolm Gillies and Bruce Clunies Ross, editors, *Grainger on Music*, Oxford, New York: Oxford University Press, 1999, pp. 58–59.

FRANZ GRILLPARZER

The Austrian writer, poet and dramatist Franz Grillparzer became acquainted with Beethoven when he was about seventeen years of age. At this time (the summer of 1808) he was living with his mother in rooms close by those occupied by Beethoven in a house in Heiligenstadt. Thayer reports:

> 'Mme. Grillparzer, mother of the poet, was a lady of great taste and culture, and was fond of music. She used to stand outside her door in order to enjoy Beethoven's playing [improvising], as she did not then know of his aversion to listeners. One day Beethoven, springing from his piano to the door to see if anyone were listening, unfortunately discovered her there. Despite her messages to him through his servant that her door into the common passageway would remain locked, and that her family would use another, Beethoven played no more.'

In 1823, Grillparzer discussed the possibility with Beethoven of collaborating with him in an operatic project on the fable of the fresh-water spirit *Melusine* but, like many other of the composer's putative operatic ventures, it came to nothing.

Elliot Forbes, editor: *Thayer's Life of Beethoven*, Princeton, New Jersey, Princeton University Press, 1967, pp. 441–2 and pp. 843–4.

Grillparzer is perhaps best remembered in Beethoven musicology for his Funeral Oration that was read at the composer's graveside, from which we cite the following passage:

'Standing by the grave of him who has passed away, we are in a manner the representatives of an entire nation, of the whole German people, mourning the loss of the one highly acclaimed half of the fatherland's full spiritual bloom. There yet lives — and may his life be long! — the hero of verse in German speech and tongue; but the last master of tuneful song ... the organ of soulful concord, the heir and amplifier of Handel and Bach's of Haydn and Mozart's immortal fame is now no more, and we stand weeping over the riven strings of the harp that is hushed.'

A number of versions of Grillparzer's text exist. We have quoted from the following source: Gerhard von Breuning, Oscar George Theodore Sonneck, *Beethoven: Impressions of Contemporaries*, London, Oxford University Press, 1927, pp. 229–30.

GEORGE GROVE

The name Grove is familiar to generations of music lovers through association with *Grove's Dictionary of Music and Musicians* of which Grove was the inspiration and source. Sir George Grove, however, did not receive a formal education in music and trained as a structural engineer, being admitted as a graduate of the Institution of Civil Engineers. He worked in this capacity for the first thirty years of his life and it was while he was engaged on the Britannia Bridge that he became known to such luminaries of the age as Robert Stephenson, Isambard Kingdom Brunel and Sir Charles Barry.

Through their influence, Grove made a change of career and was appointed in 1849 to the Secretaryship of the

Society of Arts — at the period of gestation of the Great Exhibition of 1851. When the exhibition relocated to Sydenham, in the guise of The Crystal Palace, it was as a result of the actions of Grove that the German-born August Manns was appointed, first as bandmaster and later as the conductor of a full-size orchestra. Manns presided over regular concerts for more than forty years, Grove providing numerous programme notes that later formed the basis for his *Dictionary*.

Many of Beethoven's works were performed at The Crystal Palace under the direction of August Manns including overtures, concertos, symphonies and choral works. *Fidelio* received a concert performance in 1859 and in 1866 the resident orchestra had to be augmented for a rendering of the *Eroica* Symphony that was billed as 'a special event'. The occasion of Queen Victoria's Diamond Jubilee in 1894 offered *The Musical Times* the chance to review some of the significant musical activities that had taken place at The Crystal Palace in its preceding forty-or-so years of concert life. Sir George Grove was singled out for being a 'very natural exhibitor' and for promoting the works of Beethoven amongst others including Mendelsohn and Schubert.

The following year was the 125th anniversary of Beethoven's birth, an event that was commemorated in a special concert devoted entirely to works by the composer, namely: Overture *Prometheus*; First Symphony, slow movement; *Emperor* Piano Concerto; *Ah! Perfido*; *Eroica* Symphony; a selection of songs; and to conclude the Overture *Leonora* No. 3. A detailed inventory of the works of Beethoven performed at The Crystal Palace, and the role played by Sir George Grove, will be found in: Michael Musgrave, *The Musical Life of the Crystal Palace*, Cambridge: Cambridge University Press, 1995.

In 1896, Grove published *Beethoven and his Nine*

Symphonies — republished, in near facsimile, by Dover *Books on Music* (1998). Grove based his study on the many programme notes he had written for the orchestral concerts held at the Crystal Palace. His text incorporates more than 400 musical quotations combined with extracts from his correspondence.

In his capacity as music critic for *The Saturday Review*, George Bernhard Shaw reviewed Grove's undertaking. In doing so, he, characteristically, expressed his own opinions about Beethoven and his music:

> '[I] knew Beethoven's symphonies from the opening bar of the first to the final chord of the Ninth and yet made new discoveries about them at every fresh performance ... Beethoven was the first man who used music with absolute integrity as the expression of his own emotional life. Others had shown how it could be done — had done it themselves as a curiosity of their art in rare, self-indulgent, *unprofessional* moments — but Beethoven made this, and nothing else, his business ... Haydn really came nearer to Beethoven, for he is neither the praiser of God nor the dramatist, but, always within the limits of good manners and of his primary function as a purveyor of formal decorative music; a man of moods. This is how he created the symphony and put it readymade into Beethoven's hands ... The revolutionary giant at once seized it, and throwing supernatural religion, conventional good manners, dramatic fiction, and all external standards and objects into the lumber room, took his own humanity as the material of his music, and expressed it all without compromise from his

roughest jocularity to his holiest aspiration after that purely human reign of intense life — of "Freude — Alle Menschen werder Brüdeer / Wo dein sanfter Flügel welt" [Choral Finale on Schiller's *Ode to Joy*, Symphony No. 9 in D minor, Op. 125] ... He seeks always for the mood, and is not only delighted at every step by the result of his search, but escapes quite easily and unconsciously from the boggling and blundering of the men who are always wondering why Beethoven did not do what any professor would have done. He is always joyous, always successful, always busy and interesting, never tedious even when he is superfluous (not that the adepts ever found him so), and always as pleased as Punch when he is not too deeply touched.'

Shaw concludes his review of Grove's pioneering study of Beethoven:

'It is delightful to have all the old programmes bound into a volume, with the quotations from score all complete, and the information brought up to date, and largely supplemented. It is altogether the right sort of book about the symphonies, made for practical use in the concert room under the stimulus of a heartfelt need for bringing the public to Beethoven.'

Dan H. Laurence, editor, *Shaw's Music: The Complete Musical Criticism in Three Volumes*, London: Max Reinhardt, the Bodley Head, 1981, Vol. 3, pp. 382–87.

FRANÇOIS-ANTIONE HABENECK

François-Antione Habeneck is recognised today for his pioneering achievement in introducing Beethoven's symphonies to France and for his founding of the *Société des Concerts du Conservatoire* in Paris. In 1804, he joined the Orchestra of the *Opéra Comique* but later found his vocation as an orchestral conductor — perhaps it was in his blood since his father had been the leader of a military band. In 1807, Habeneck directed the first performance of Beethoven's First Symphony with the Second Symphony following shortly afterwards. It is believed he gave the Paris première of the *Eroica* Symphony in 1811. At the *Opéra* he conducted the *Allegretto* of the Seventh Symphony and in 1826 he returned once more to the *Eroica* Symphony. At this time Habeneck introduced French audiences to the Fifth Symphony and the *Choral* Symphony in 1831. In the years 1828–37, Beethoven's symphonies were performed on no fewer than sixty-eight occasions.

Hector Berlioz was uncharacteristically curmudgeonly in his estimation of Habeneck's style of conducting, but he did acknowledge the rendering he achieved with the string section of his orchestra. Anton Schindler (see below) also remained somewhat aloof in his estimation of Habeneck's interpretation of Beethoven's symphonies — until 1841. It was then that he heard the Conservatoire Orchestra under Habeneck and acknowledged him to be a supreme interpreter of his former master's music. Wagner had no qualms in recognising Habeneck's command of the orchestra and of his familiarity with Beethoven's scores — that Habeneck had committed to memory. In 1839 Wagner attended a rehearsal of the Ninth Symphony, the experience and impact of which were immediate. He enthused:

'The scales fell from my eyes. I came to understand the value of *correct* execution and the secret of a good performance. The orchestra had learned to look for Beethoven's *melody* in every bar — that melody which the worthy Leipzig musicians had failed to discover, and the orchestra *sang* that melody. *This was the secret.* Habeneck who solved the difficulty, and to whom the great credit of this performance is due, was not a conductor of special genius. While rehearsing the Symphony during an entire winter season, he had felt it to be incomprehensible and ineffective (would German conductors have confessed as much?), but he persisted throughout a second and third season until Beethoven's new *melos* was understood and correctly rendered by every member of the orchestra. Habeneck was a conductor of the old school; *he was* the master, and everybody obeyed him. I cannot attempt to describe the beauty of this performance.'

The New Grove, A Dictionary of Music and Musicians, Oxford University Press, 1980, Vol. 10, p. 634; Adam von Ahn Carse, *The Orchestra from Beethoven to Berlioz: A History of the Orchestra in the First Half of the 19th Century, and of the Development of Orchestral Baton-Conducting,* Cambridge, W. Heffer, 1948, pp. 90–92; and Harold C. Schonberg, *The Great Conductors*, The New York Times, 1967, pp. 102–03.

WILLIAM HENRY HADOW

In June 1917 the educational reformer and musicologist,

Sir William Henry Hadow was invited by the British Academy to give its *Annual Master-Mind Lecture*. Hadow took Beethoven as his subject. He made reference to the manner of his composing and of its self-imposed challenges:

> 'In the study he beat his music out in a sort of physical agony, turning it again and again on the anvil, and forcing it by titanic energy into the shape that he desired. The sketchbooks, which he always carried with him, are a complete musical autobiography: they show the thought from its first germinal inception to the ultimate form which alone could satisfy him: sometimes there are as many as twelve versions of the same theme — each one exhibiting some advance, some felicitous turn of phrase, some further revelation of meaning, until the melody bursts into full blossom, more vivid and spontaneous for the successive stages that have brought it to birth.'

Hadow reflected on the so-called 'three periods' of Beethoven's compositions, as originally propounded by Wilhelm von Lenz in his influential study of the composer, *Beethoven et Ses Trois Styles* (1855):

> 'Historians have customarily distinguished [Beethoven's] music into three periods, a division which is really valuable if we do not insist too closely on lines of demarcation. They cannot be chronologically determined, partly because he did not master all his media simultaneously, partly because, like all great artists, he occasionally threw back to an earlier idiom or method.

Still, allowing for some looseness and elasticity in the use of terms, the distinctions are not only intelligible but also illuminating. There can be no doubt that the first two symphonies are essentially different from the *Eroica*, the first six string quartets from the *Rasoumoffskys* [sic]: the three piano sonatas, published as Op. 31, are described by Beethoven himself as "written in a new Style". An equally unmistakable frontier is crossed by the last pianoforte trio, the last violin sonata, and the F-minor Quartet, precursor and herald of the greatest achievements in all chamber music. It may be observed that the succession corresponds closely to the natural growth and development of Beethoven's character.'

Hadow quoted from an article that had just appeared in *The Times Literary Supplement* (14 June 1917) that he considered supported his thesis:

'The value of art lies in the fact that it communicates the experience and the experiencing power of one man to many. When we hear a symphony of Beethoven we are for the moment Beethoven, and we ourselves are enriched forever by the fact that we have for the moment been Beethoven.'

Hadow endorsed these thoughts with additional words of his own:

'This seems to me essentially and profoundly true, and its truth is nowhere more evident than in the sense of mastery which is communicated to us by great music. The effort to produce may actually have been toilsome — we know with Beethoven it often was so; in the finished work all trace of effort has disappeared, and the phrase a dozen times reconsidered sounds as spontaneous as an impromptu. It is the pleasure of sharing this victory over a medium always difficult and often rebellious which gives at least a part of our delight as listeners, and this pleasure is enhanced and intensified by the assurance that such a victory is certain.'

Hadow concluded:

'[Beethoven's] music is not only a joy of beautiful sound and emotion nobly felt and nobly communicated: it is also a marvel of intellectual power and of deep spiritual insight; nor is it only a master of melody, but in very truth as a *Maestro di color che sanno* ['the colour master who knows' — Aristotle], that I ask you to place him among the master-minds of all humanity.'

William Henry Hadow, *Collected Essays*, London, H. Milford at the Oxford University Press, 1928, pp. 107–23.

CHARLES HALLÉ

Sir Charles Hallé was of German extraction and in his early years was renowned as a child prodigy — at the age of four, for example, he performed a sonatina in public. In his student days, in Paris, he associated with Frédéric Chopin and Franz Liszt. He moved to England in 1848, changing his name from Karl Halle to Charles Hallé, and became a favourite of the musical salons and a pioneer in the promotion of Beethoven's piano sonatas. Hallé was the first pianist in England to perform the complete series of the composer's piano sonatas, initially in recitals held at his own house and later in the St. James Concert Hall, Piccadilly. It has been said that it was due in great measure to Hallé's recitals 'that a knowledge of Beethoven's pianoforte sonatas became general in English society'.

As he recalls in his *Autobiography*, Hallé was eager in his student days to widen his musical experience. This is evident in a letter he wrote to his parents from Darmstadt on 6 July 1836; Hallé was then seventeen and was preparing for a career as a concert pianist. He writes of having made the acquaintance of Carl Mangold, Kapellmeister of the Court Theatre, who had invited him to attend one of his rehearsals. Of this he recounts:

> 'I went this morning, and my joy was quite indescribable. The orchestra consists of more than sixty members: they play like angels. I have never heard anything like it, and I must describe it more closely another time. Today they played Beethoven's *Eroica* Symphony — that is, indeed, a mighty composition — at times a cold shiver ran through me, but more of this later.'

Hallé was in Paris during the winter of 1838—39 and became friends with the Hungarian pianist Stephen Heller. The two played piano duets including four-hand transcriptions of Schubert's and Beethoven's symphonies. Of this experience, Hallé writes:

> 'It was during these *séances* in my humble lodgings in the Rue Notre Dame de Lorette that we made acquaintance with and revelled in the beauties of

Schubert's Great C major Symphony, then recently discovered and published as a pianoforte duet. [Mendelssohn had conducted the first performance at Leipzig in March 1839] It was a revelation to us, and we were never tired of playing it through. But the same was the case with all the great compositions for orchestra, or orchestra with chorus, arranged in a similar form. How often we played Beethoven symphonies it is impossible to tell, and how we enjoyed them! All the more as the opportunities of hearing them performed by the orchestra were then rare, the Concerts du Conservatoire only bringing forward two or three during a season, so that certain of them, for instance, Nos. 4, 7, and 9, were heard perhaps once in three or four years. In 1839 neither Heller nor I heard the *Choral* Symphony performed, and were all the more eager to study it closely.'

Michael Kennedy, editor, *The Autobiography of Charles Hallé; With Correspondence and Diaries*, London, Paul Elek, 1972, pp. 77–78. See also: C. E. Hallé, *Life and Letters of Sir Charles Hallé: Being an Autobiography (1819–1860) with Correspondence and Diaries*, London, Smith, Elder & Co., 1896, pp. 52–54.

Hallé moved to Manchester in 1853 to direct the City's *Gentleman's Concerts*. His reputation as an orchestral conductor was elevated when, in May 1857, he was invited to create a small orchestra to play for the musically inclined Prince of Wales at the opening ceremony of the *Art Treasures of Great Britain* Exhibition. The group so-formed became in due course the Hallé Orchestra, the name of which Hallé is today associated. In the concert season of

1870, to commemorate Beethoven's Birth Centenary, the Hallé Orchestra performed all his symphonies under Hallé's direction.

Furthermore, in fulfilment of a personal resolution, Hallé gave a performance of the composer's C sharp minor Piano Sonata; the concert in question did not finish until 11. 00 p.m. As a tribute to Hallé's love of Beethoven, in the concert season of 1907–08, the Hallé Orchestra once more played all of the composer's nine symphonies in chronological order.

Michael Kennedy, *Hallé Tradition: A Century of Music*, Manchester, Manchester University Press, 1960, p. 163.

HAMILTON HARTY

Sir Herbert Hamilton Harty was an Irish composer, conductor, and pianist. Notwithstanding his gifts as a solo pianist, *The Musical Times* described Harty as 'the prince of accompanists'. In 1920 he established a career as a conductor. In this role he conducted the London Symphony Orchestra, the Liverpool Philharmonic Orchestra, and was later appointed the permanent conductor to the Hallé Orchestra. In this role he earned the approval of Samuel Langford, the respected music critic of *The Manchester Guardian*. On hearing a performance of Harty's, and comparing Harty with others who had conducted the Hallé Orchestra, he wrote (March 1919): 'Mr. Harty has latterly achieved far more immediate control over the orchestra, and his spirit, judgement, and control were ... equally admirable.' Perhaps Harty is best remembered today for his orchestral arrangements of Handel's *Water Music* and *Music for the Royal Fireworks*.

In 1927, *The Musical Times* invited Harty to contribute to its *Special Issue* published to commemorate Beethoven's

Death Centenary. He did so in an article titled *Beethoven's Orchestra: A Conductor's Reflections.* He makes the following general remarks concerning Beethoven's orchestration:

> 'Beethoven's general habit and manner in orchestration is fully exemplified in his symphonies, and it is not necessary to go further afield, even if, in other works, he makes use of some instrument which does not appear in his scores. If we take the nine symphonies and regard them from a merely technical point of view, they reveal, to an impartial eye, that the strings are always used with the greatest fullness and resource, the bassoons and drums with a special originality. And the flutes, oboes, clarinets, horns, trumpets, and trombones in a way we might expect (and that we get) from any well-equipped typical musician of those days. There are obscurities and miscalculations in certain places, some of which appear to be due to the impatience and brusqueness which were part of the composer's character, others which are undoubtedly the result of simple errors in questions of balance. Instances of both will occur to the minds of those familiar with the scores.'

Harty next considered the detrimental changes he considered some orchestral instruments had undergone since Beethoven's time:

> '[Nowadays] we use a very much larger body of strings than was the general custom in Beethoven's lifetime [and] there is no doubt that many of the wind instruments have undergone

since then a considerable change, and have gained in ease of manipulation at the expense of beauty of tone. The flute, for instance, must have frequently possessed a much sweeter and more characteristic tone before it was furnished with the ingenious mechanism in use today, and there is no doubt that the horn has also suffered in this respect by the addition of valves, and the trumpet, probably for the same reason. The oboe and bassoon, on the other hand, were rougher and coarser in quality, and the timpani less accurate and shallower in tone. It is likely that the trombone is the only wind instrument which has not altered in timbre, for there has been no change in its mechanism. Keeping these considerations in mind, it is interesting to imagine how Beethoven's symphonies may have sounded to his audiences, and, at the same time, it may give some justification for the readjustments it is felt necessary to make in modern performances.'

Harty suggested modern-day alterations to Beethoven's orchestration should take into consideration the inherent character of the music:

'The symphonies seem to fall into two main categories. In one we might place the more idyllic works — the First, Second, Fourth, Sixth, and Eighth; in the other, those immense dramatic conceptions — the Third, Fifth, Seventh, and Ninth, in which Beethoven breaks completely with former tradition and enters his own absolute kingdom. It is in these that the technical problems of readjustment become more acute. The other symphonies (with the exception, perhaps, of part of the Sixth – the *Pastoral*) require, certainly, a carefully balanced performance in order to make their full effect, but in the main the orchestration can be left untouched and unstrengthened.'

Harty was adamant that no 'real' musician would ever contemplate touching the orchestral details of Beethoven's 'mighty works' unless he were convinced some revision would help to fulfil the composer's intentions. Reflecting on the recent past, Harty acknowledged composer-musicians of the standing of Wagner had given thought to such considerations as, indeed, Harty believed every conductor should. With this in mind he cited, as being worthy of study – though circumspectly – Felix Weingartner's treatise *On the Performance of Beethoven's Symphonies*. Regarding Beethoven's 'grandest manner', Harty averred, 'are not power and urgency the dominant characteristics?' and therefore call for 'force and passion' rather than for 'grace and sensuous beauty of tone'. He elaborated: 'Refinement and delicacy are not the essential features of Beethoven that they are in composers like Mozart, and even in his softer moments it is unwise to overemphasise them.'

Harty considered Beethoven's slow movements and scherzi were the most deserving of individual expression. He was even prepared to sanction the use of additional instruments on occasions: 'Without some radical change, either by reduction of the strings or by an increase of wind instruments, it is impossible to give performances which are really satisfactory.' He suggested, for example, the Funeral March in the *Eroica* Symphony could be 'reinforced' by the incorporation of wind instruments. That said, he cautioned: 'It is impossible to lay down hard and fast rules where everything must be left to individual taste and conviction, but occasionally one sees "improvements" suggested which show an entire misconception of the questions at issue.'

Certain 'improvements' to Beethoven's scoring earned Harty's censure: 'It is no improvement, but a horrible atrocity, to introduce trombones into scores of Beethoven where they do not already exist, or to add extra passages for the timpani merely because modern tuning is possible.' He maintained: 'It should never be a question of introducing a new colour, but merely the deepening or restoration of one now faded, and the process is not that of adding fresh tints to a picture but of allowing some which are obscured to be more clearly seen.' Harty concluded his essay:

> 'It is worthwhile to consider whether over-caution is in the best interest of these bold and unconventional masterpieces, or whether, in reality, it does not cripple freedom and candour of interpretation. What Beethoven would have said to our modern methods of preforming his works it is impossible to tell. Wagner was not above taking the advice of Richter, nor Brahms of a Joachim, and, on the whole, it seems probable that Beethoven, great autocrat as he was, would not have rejected without consideration any suggestions made to him by a qualified craftsman who revered his music, and who disclaimed any wish or intention to interfere with essentials ... In the end, this is all that anyone entitled to the name of good musician has ever proposed, or ever will propose in connection with the music of Beethoven — "To amend the letter so that the spirit may shine forth more brightly".'

Hamilton Harty, *Beethoven's Orchestra: A Conductor's*

Reflections in: *Beethoven*. London, Special Number, *Music & Letters*, 1927, pp. 172–77.

CHRISTOPHER HEADINGTON

The English composer and musicologist Christopher Headington affirms:

> 'No history of music can offer a simple answer. But it can draw attention to Beethoven, a composer whose work attracts experts and public alike. In this, his art resembles that of Shakespeare. Beethoven believed in the message of the choral finale of his last symphony, "Be embraced, ye millions!" For him, all men were brothers under God.'

Headington places Beethoven alongside Tchaikovsky:

> 'But when we think of Beethoven's Fifth Symphony beside Tchaikovsky's work we immediately sense a profound difference between these two composers. Beethoven reaches out beyond himself to a universal ideal: he speaks to mankind at large, even to God. Music was for him "a higher revelation than all wisdom and philosophy", offering entrance to a spiritual world. He saw his work, quite consciously, as a humanitarian vocation in a religious sense. This is perhaps why he has been called "too great an artist to be left to the musicians".'

Christopher Headington, *The Bodley Head History of Western Music*, London, The Bodley Head, 1974, pp. 155–6.

E. T. A. HOFFMAN

Ernst Theodor Amadeus Hoffman was celebrated in his day for being a pioneering author of romantic tales alongside his gifts in jurisprudence, music, music criticism and art illustration. From about 1810 he became an ardent admirer of Beethoven's music to which he gave expression in newspaper articles and contributions to the music journal *Allgemeine musikalische Zeitung* (see above). Writing in the style and spirit of the day, Hoffman described Beethoven's music in the following vivid terms:

> '[Beethoven's] instrumental music opens to us the realm of the colossal and the immeasurable. Glowing beams of light shoot through the deep night of this realm and we perceive giant shadows surging back and forth, closer and closer around us, destroying everything in us except the pain of that endless longing in which each that had risen in jubilant tones sinks back and perishes; and it is in this pain which consumes love, hope, and happiness without destroying them, in this pain which seeks to break our breast with the chords of all passions that we live on and become enchanted visionaries!
>
> 'Haydn conceived the human element of this life romantically; he is more commensurable, more comprehensible for the majority. Mozart is concerned with the superhuman, the miraculous element that inhabits the inmost soul.
>
> 'Beethoven's music moves the lever of fear, of terror, of pain, and awakens just that infinite longing which is the essence of romanticism.'

Hoffman recognised the correct interpretation of Beethoven's music posed challenges to the would-be performer of his works:

> 'Now, as regards difficulty, the correct and proper performance of a work by Beethoven demands nothing more than that one should understand him, that one should enter deep into his being, that, aware of one's own consecrated nature, one should dare to step into the circle of the magical phenomenon evoked by his powerful spell.'

S. R. Murray Chafer, *E.T.A. Hoffmann and Music*, Toronto, University of Toronto Press, 1975, p. 84 and p. 89.

Hoffman's enthusiasm and support for Beethoven's music subsequently came to his attention. It must have been a pleasant surprise to him, accustomed as he was for having his music subject to vituperative criticism in the press and for himself being castigated as a discordant and uncompromising modernist. It disposed Beethoven to write to Hoffman in terms of warmth and respect — a rare document in the composer's extensive correspondence that is free from his typical irony and disdain:

> 'I am taking the opportunity ... of making myself known to such a gifted person as you are — Moreover, you have written about my humble self. Herr Starke [a musician friend of Beethoven's] showed me his album of a few lines of yours about me. So, I am bound to think that you must take some interest in me. Allow me to

tell you that this interest on the part of a man like you who, endowed with such excellent qualities, is very gratifying to me. I send you me best wishes and remain, Sir, with kindest regards, your most devoted BEETHOVEN.'

Emily Anderson editor and translator, *The Letters of Beethoven*, London: Macmillan, 3 vols.,1961, Vol. 2, Letter No. 1014, pp. 884–85.

GUSTAV HOLST

The English composer and educationalist Gustav Holst is known best for his orchestral suite *The Planets* and for being Director of Music at St. Paul's School for Girls. He also held other teaching posts at Morely College and was Lecturer in Composition at The University of Reading. For a period, he collaborated with his life-long friend Vaughn Williams teaching composition at The Royal College of Music, London – their *alma mater*. Edmund Rubbra was a pupil of Holst and has left the following account:

> 'His period at the Royal College of Music, all too short as it was, exercised a remarkable influence. His own vision was wide-eyed, and his own sincerity so unequivocal, that to have been in contact with him was an experience one would not willingly have missed, and it is a tribute to his teaching to say that none of his composition pupils have turned out works that might have been "chips from the master's workshop".

Being aware of the irregular occurrence of seemingly barren periods in any creator's life, Holst never insisted that any pupil should bring fresh work at each lesson. The pupil was, therefore, freed from the strain and anxiety of forcing out unfelt ideas. If no original work was forthcoming, then a lesson could be spent in any number of delightful and profitable ways, for Holst was never at a loss to show how surprise and delight could be mingled in a lesson. There might be a score to read through, either a Beethoven symphony (how he enjoyed uttering unorthodox opinions about the scoring of Beethoven!), a Brahms' orchestral work (he used to say that the scoring of the Brahms-Haydn Variations was perfect in aptness) or a modern work.'

Edmund Rubbra, *Holst the Teacher* in: Gustav Holst, *Collected Essays*, London, Triad Press, 1974, pp. 42–43.

ARTHUR HONEGGER

The French organist and musicologist Bernard Gavoty put a number of questions to the Swiss Composer Arthur Honegger. He first invited him to express his views on the nature of music and composition. The following are extracts from his extended response: 'Absolute originality does not exist.'

Honegger argued that each generation builds on what has gone before but acknowledged that the works of a powerful genius have revolutionary power. To the lay mind, Honegger believed 'the act of composing music remains an incomprehensible thing'. He identified with Beethoven's manner of working, stating 'musical construction must first be done in the mind, then be noted on paper ... Composing is a mental operation which takes place in the brain of the composer'. Honegger qualified this observation, and, in so doing, further identified with Beethoven's own way of working: 'However, I don't claim that to check certain passages at the piano is not useful, if only as an aid or guide in the linking of certain passages.'

Honneger's remark runs close to Anton Schindler's description of Beethoven testing at the keyboard what he had written, particularly in the case of the piano sonatas. Honegger's next passage could almost be a description of Beethoven when at the height of his powers as a virtuoso: 'Searching at the piano can be fruitful, especially when the composer is a skilful instrumentalist who gives himself to improvisation ... Thus, chance becomes inspiration.'

Honegger turned his attention directly to Beethoven:

> 'What has always astounded people is the existence of the deaf composer. It is not improbable that a great part of the admiration bestowed on Beethoven stems from his infirmity. Actually, apart from the tragic aspect of this situation, the fact that a creator can never hear the *execution* of his work should remove great technical restriction for him. Beethoven had gradually forgotten the purely aural qualities of certain combinations of tones. We discover this in the vocal writing of the *Missa Solemnis* and the *Ninth Symphony*. We also observe it in the great interval between the right hand and the left in his piano writing and especially in the paradoxical harmonization of up-beats. However, this had no influence whatsoever on the essence of his thought. I should be tempted to say that his deafness, which immured him in himself, helped him in the concentration of his genius and detached him from the tastelessness and banalities of his time.'

John L. Holmes, *Composers on Composers*, New York, Greenwood Press, 1990, pp. 466–9. Honegger's responses to the questions put to him were initially published as *Je Suis*

Compositeur. See also: Sam Morgenstern, editor, *Composers on Music: An Anthology of Composers' Writings,* London, Faber & Faber, 1956, pp. 468—9.

ANTHONY HOPKINS

Anthony Hopkins was recognised for his many musical attainments being variously a composer, pianist, conductor, writer and broadcaster. It is in the latter capacity that he became known to a wide audience captivated by his authoritative discourses on musical analysis. These were broadcast by the BBC, on the Third Programme (later Radio 3) from 1954 for almost forty years, as *Talking About Music.* Writing about Beethoven he opens his account:

> 'Speculation about who is the greatest composer is a fairly fruitless exercise but it is undeniable that Beethoven was one of the most significant; he it was who extended and developed such major musical forms as the sonata, symphony, string quartet, and concerto; he it was who liberated music from Classical restraints and opened the way for the Romantic Movement in which composers expressed emotions in personal terms rather than as abstractions. Early Beethoven works take over from Haydn, late Beethoven leads towards Schumann, Brahms and even (in the slow movement of the Ninth Symphony) towards Mahler. To accomplish such a revolution in musical taste required an immensely powerful creative personality; to accomplish it, despite the handicap of deafness, needed exceptional moral courage.'

Anthony Hopkins, *The Concertgoer's Companion*, London, J.M. Dent & Sons Ltd., 1984, p. 59.

PETER LE HURAY AND JAMES DAY

The authors give their estimation of the character of Beethoven's orchestral music:

'Beethoven's music is tense with expectation; so much is pregnant with significance; magnificent themes emerge like beautiful shapes out of slowly dissolving clouds. The pauses on individual chords, the sheer luxuriance of sound, the very melodic ideas which would have been condemned as boring in a previous age, all proved to be just right at that time when people were plumbing the depths of nature's profoundest secrets. Interest in the miraculous supplanted a previous concern to achieve a balance between intellect and emotion. Yet a third romantic element manifested itself in between Beethoven's music humour. This spiritual quality which is so often confused with wit — whimsicality or a sense of fun — is effectively an amalgam of the two states of pleasure and pain. It springs from the realisation that nothing in the world, however sublime it may be, is wholly without fault, and that ironically enough, nothing, however terrifying it may be, is free from the temporal limitations of this earthly existence. This Shakespearian characteristic lends Beethoven's music its particular significance. In his symphonies, Beethoven frequently plays like a child with the sublimest ideas in the midst of the most earth-shattering events. The juxtaposition of the sharply contrasting moods most distinguishes Beethoven from his predecessor the witty and ingenious Haydn.'

Peter Le Huray and James Day editors, *Music and Aesthetics in the Eighteenth and Early-Nineteenth Centuries*, Cambridge, Cambridge University Press, 1988, p. 562.

VINCENT D'INDY

The French composer and teacher Vincent d'Indy was considered to be a child prodigy. At the Paris Conservatoire, he became a devoted student of César Franck and later in life returned to the Conservatoire where he taught until his death in 1931. An ardent admirer of Beethoven, d'Indy published a biography about him in 1911 that was translated into English and published as *Beethoven: A Critical Biography*. Boston Music Company, 1913. Writing of the composer he states:

'Beethoven, the noble outcome of classic force, who began by writing purely formal symphonic works, before he won the place of a genius in the upward progress of his art, marked out by the works of his third period (1815—1827) a new road, and although he himself did not travel far along it, he left it open for such of his successors as were endowed with a sufficiently robust temperament to force their way along it, knowing also how to avoid the dangers they might encounter.'

D'Indy considered Beethoven had transformed the very concept of sonata form — what he described as 'that admirable basis of all symphonic art which had been accepted by all musicians from the seventeenth century onward by virtue of its harmonious logic'. D'Indy was aware that Hector Berlioz was a passionate admirer of Beethoven but remarked:

> 'It would be difficult to find two artists more completely at the opposite poles of creative thought than the creator of the *Symphonie Fantastique* or *La Damnation de Faust* and the mind which planned the *Missa Solemnis* and the Twelfth Quartet [E-flat major, Op. 127].'

D'Indy writes of the prejudices that composers of orchestral music had to overcome in the late nineteenth century. The view prevailing in the minds of many was that, with Beethoven, the symphony had virtually reached its highest peak of development. D'Indy cites an incident in February 1889 when César Franck's Symphony in D minor was performed at a concert given by the Société des Concerts du Conservatoire. Apparently, this was contrary to the wishes of most of the members of the orchestra who, together with the subscribers to the Société, 'could make neither head nor tail of it'. D'Indy sought the opinion of a professor at the Conservatoire regarding what he considered of Franck's composition. The professor retorted:

> 'That, a symphony? But my dear Sir, who ever heard of writing for the cor anglais in a symphony? Just imagine a single symphony by Haydn or Beethoven introducing the cor anglais?

'That', remarks d'Indy, 'was the attitude of the Conservatoire in the year of grace 1889'.

Vincent D' Indy, writing in: *César Franck*, New York, Dover Publications, 1965, p. 54, pp. 84—5, and p. 87.

DAVID WYN JONES
David Wyn Jones is a British musicologist and a recognised authority on the music of the Classical period, with particular regard to the works of Haydn and Beethoven. Concerning the latter, he offers the following summary-outline of several of the composer's symphonies in relation to their performance-context:

> 'As a youth Beethoven's entire experience of the symphony was as a private work performed at Court, in Bonn, and had the French Revolution not taken its course he would have returned to this environment in the 1790s. The First and Second Symphonies were always intended for public performance, staple works in the benefit concerts at the Burgtheater in 1800 and the Theater an der Wien in 1805. The *Eroica*, Fifth and Sixth Symphonies were also destined for public performance but were first performed in private at the Lobkowitz Court. Following a visit to the estate of Count Franz Oppersdorff in Oberglogau (Glogów), Silesia, Beethoven was commissioned to write a symphony for the Count's orchestra, No. 4, subsequently dedicated to him. Nos. 7 and 8 again were first performed as public works, in the hall of the University [of Vienna] in 1813 and in the Grosser Redoutensaal in 1814 respectively; there were no preliminary performances in private.'

Jones considers the symphonies of Beethoven in relation to programme music.

'Beethoven's three programme symphonies are spread evenly across his symphonic output from 1799 to 1813, the *Eroica* in 1803, the *Pastoral* Symphony five years later in 1808, and *Wellington's Victory* a further five years later in 1813. Their subject matter, individual and universal heroism, followed by the escapist, purely secular world of the pastoral, and, finally, the graphic evocation of battle and victory, were familiar ones to Beethoven's audiences and, as Richard Will has demonstrated [*The Characteristic Symphony in the Age of Haydn and Beethoven*, 2002 and 2010] constitutes a continuation and a culmination of practices in the classical symphony that go back decades ... In the 1790s and early 1800s it was the symphonies of the Wranitzky brothers [Anton and Paul] that most frequently provided the context for Beethoven's three programme symphonies.

'At one stage Beethoven wanted to give the title *Bonaparte* to the Third Symphony and dedicate it to the eponymous hero, an outlook that was in keeping with the mood of contemporary politics in Austria; Beethoven's well-known change of mind coincided with a shift in the diplomatic position of Austria, when it entered into a definitive alliance with Russia against France ... Between them, the *Eroica* Symphony and *Wellington's Victory* denote the range of musical experience covered by the term *programme symphony* [italics added],from a work that takes the extra-musical as a point of departure in order to explore it in heightened abstraction to a work in which the extra-musical controls rather than liberates the composition.'

David Wyn Jones, *The Symphony in Beethoven's Vienna*, Cambridge: Cambridge University Press, 2006, pp. 174–6 and p. 178,

KARL AUGUST KAHLERT

In May 1864, the German historian and aesthetician Karl August Kahlert contributed an influential essay to the magazine *Allgemeine musikalische Zeitung* ('General music Newspaper') — which was founded at about the same time that Beethoven was becoming established in Vienna (1798). Kahlert's article is recognized for being among the first to define classicism and romanticism in music, in terms that are generally accepted today. The essay contains the following passage:

> 'Beethoven's music is tense with expectation; so much is pregnant with significance; magnificent themes emerge like beautiful chords, the sheer luxuriance of sound, the very melodic ideas which would have been condemned as boring in a previous age all proved to be just right at that time when people were plumbing the depths of nature's profoundest secrets. Interest in the miraculous supplanted a previous concern to achieve a balance between intellect and emotion. Yet a third romantic element manifested itself in Beethoven's music: humour.'

Karl August Kahlert in: Peter Le Hurray and James Day, editors: *Music and Aesthetics in the Eighteenth and Early-Nineteenth Centuries*, Cambridge, Cambridge University Press, 1988, p. 560.

WILLIAM KINDERMAN

The American pianist and musicologist cites the British philosopher Isaiah Berlin's writings on early Romantic aesthetics together with his own reference to Beethoven:

> 'All creation is in some sense creation out of nothing. It is the only fully autonomous activity of man. It is self-liberation from causal laws, the mechanism of the external world, from tyrants, or environmental influences, or the passions, which govern me — factors in relation to which I am as much an object in nature as trees, or stones, or animals [Isaiah Berlin].'

Kinderman adds:

> 'Beethoven, a pivotal figure in this reassessment of artistic creation as original, autonomous activity, left an incomparable documentary record of the process itself, in the form of thousands of pages of sketches and drafts for his musical works.'

William Kinderman, *Contrast and Continuity in Beethoven's Creative Process*. In: Scott G. Burnham and Michael P. Steinberg, editors: *Beethoven and his World*. Princeton, New Jersey, Oxford, Princeton University Press, 2000. p. 193. Kinderman also gives expression to his views about Beethoven in the following: William Kinderman,

Beethoven, Oxford, Oxford University Press, 1997; William Kinderman, *Beethoven's Diabelli Variations*, Oxford, Clarendon Press; New York, Oxford University Press, 1987; and William Kinderman editor: *The String Quartets of Beethoven*, Urbana, Ilinois, University of Illinois Press, 2005.

OTTO KLEMPERER

As a young man the widely acclaimed German-born conductor Otto Klemperer studied piano in Berlin with the intention of becoming a concert pianist. When age twenty he gave a performance of the *Hammerklavier* Sonata that his fellow student Ilse Fromm praised for what she described as Klemperer's 'sense of musical equilibrium'. In 1905, Klemperer entered the Anton Rubinstein piano competition held that year in Paris. The winner was the twenty-one years old Wilhelm Backhaus, but opinions amongst the judges were apparently divided. A month later, Klemperer entered for the coveted Mendelssohn Prize in Berlin, then the foremost music competition in Germany. On that occasion he was commended by a jury, which included the violinist Joseph Joachim — again for his performance of the *Hammerklavier* Sonata. Although this mighty work was judged to be in keeping with Klemperer's own physical stature — he was 1.96m tall (six feet five inches), a later meeting with Gustav Mahler determined the young Klemperer's career as an orchestral conductor.

Peter Heyworth, *Otto Klemperer, His Life and Times*, 1983–1996, 2 Vols., derived from Vol. 1, pp. 16–17.

Years later, Klemperer reflected on his relationship with Beethoven in his role as an orchestral conductor:

> 'I have very often conducted Beethoven cycles in the course of my long life: Los Angeles in 1933, La Scala, Milan, in 1935, Strasbourg in 1936, Budapest in 1947, Amsterdam in 1949, London in 1957, and Vienna in 1960 (with the Philharmonia). The result was that, as time went by, I found myself wearing a sort of dog collar marked "Beethoven specialist".
>
> 'Things were very different in my earlier days. Having been engaged to direct the state-subsidised Staatstheater in Berlin (the Kroll Opera), I was able to present a great deal that was new and even experimental. In those days, therefore, I was called a "modern conductor".'

Klemperer expressed his views about Beethoven and his symphonies:

> 'Most people think of Beethoven as a melancholy, tragic, gloomy character, but this is a crude distortion. He was, particularly in his youthful years, a happy-natured, cheerful person. The language of the First and Second Symphonies is unmistakable, and even the Fourth conveys a mood of exaltation ... It was not until the Sixth Symphony that the clouds began to gather. His hearing deteriorated progressively, but he put up a stout fight: "I shall seize fate by the throat. It will never humble me utterly".' [Beethoven's defiant utterance as expressed in the *Heiligenstadt Testament*]

Regarding Beethoven's later musical style, Klemperer states:

'Beethoven's musical language attained ever greater heights with the passage of the years, becoming more and more difficult and idiosyncratic. At the end of his *Grosse Fuge* (Op. 133) Beethoven wrote "tantôt libre, tantôt recherché". These words might equally be applied to the last movement of the Ninth Symphony, with its formal dissolution and absence of sonata movement, rondo and fugue — yet from this chrysalis there emerged something new, a sort of euphoria.'

Klemperer briefly expressed his thoughts on the controversial subject of departing from Beethoven's score:

'Much has been said about the instrumental retouching of Beethoven and the conflict between fidelity to the original and the reverse. Both schools of thought are right and wrong. Mahler once said at a rehearsal of his own Eighth Symphony that, after his death, anyone would be welcome to alter anything in his work which sounded wrong. Both Richard Wagner and Mahler subjected Beethoven to extensive retouching. Today we feel this to be unnecessary. Besides: "Let each man see his own, see where he stands and, when he stands, see that he does not fall".' [Quoted from Goethe's *Beherzigung*]

Otto Klemperer, originally published in 1961 in an essay to accompany his complete recording of the Beethoven symphonies, and reproduced in: Martin Anderson, editor, *Klemperer on Music: Shavings from a Musician's Workbench*, London, Toccata Press, 1986, pp. 97–99.

RAYMOND KNAPP

The American musicologist Raymond Knapp has written on the challenge Johannes Brahms had to confront, in the genre of symphonic composition, in the context of Beethoven's inheritance. Regarding the latter, Knapp maintains:

> '[The] symphony ... after Beethoven had come to represent, to both its champions and detractors, the pinnacle of absolute music. Beethoven's symphonies were, for the nineteenth century, his most important and vital legacy, demonstrating more than any other body of work both the power and, for doubters, the limitations of "pure" discourse. The symphonies themselves provided ample justification for either perspective, with a funeral march, bird calls, a storm, and an eventual recourse to words testifying to Beethoven's own discontent with pure musical expression on the one hand, countered on the other by a fervent conviction that such intrusions were overwhelmed by and absorbed into the larger musical argument; thus, with the Ninth Symphony, it is not the words that mattered, but the *musical* result of voices joined in song.'

Raymond Knapp, *Brahms and the Challenge of the Symphony*, Stuyvesant, N.Y., Pendragon Press, c.1997, pp. 195–96.

NIKOLAI RIMSKY-KORSAKOV

The Russian composer Rimsky-Korsakov was a member

of the so-called *Mighty Handful* of the New Russian School of composers who were prominent in the late nineteenth century; others in the group included Balakirev, Borodin and Mussorgsky. Rimsky's friend and associate V.V. Yastrebtsev was in regular contact with him during the last years of his life and kept a record, in diary form, of his meetings with the composer and his circle of friends. An entry for 19 January 1897 reveals Rimsky's estimation of Beethoven:

> 'You can't imagine how I envy Beethoven that he could say to his friend Stephan Breuning, a few hours before he died, "I did have talent, didn't I." These days, I'm coming more and more to love the classics: Bach, Beethoven, Haydn, and the others, whose music is still so fresh and full of life.'

Rimsky continued:

> 'You may not believe this but Beethoven had such inexhaustible resources when it came to form and modulation that, in this regard, alongside of him all other composers are pygmies.'

V.V. Yastrebtsev, edited and translated by Florence Jonas, **Reminiscences of Rimsky-Korsakov**, New York, Columbia University Press, 1985, p. 32 and pp. 173–4.

Rimsky-Korsakov recalled his Saturday evening visits to see Mily Balakirev:

> 'As far as I recall, Balakirev was then composing a piano concerto, excerpts from which he would

play for us. Often, he explained to me instrumentation and forms of composition. From him I heard opinions that were entirely new to me. The tastes of the circle leaned towards Glinka, Schumann, and Beethoven's last quartets. Eight symphonies of Beethoven found comparatively little favour with the circle.'

Reflecting more widely on the musical tastes of his distinguished circle of friends, Rimsky-Korsakov adds:

'[Under] the influence of Schumann's compositions, melodic gifts were then looked upon with disfavour. The majority of melodies and themes were regarded as the weaker part of music ... Nearly all the fundamental ideas of Beethoven's symphonies were thought weak; Chopin's melodies were considered sweet and womanish; Mendelssohn's, sour and bourgeois.'

Carl van Vechten, editor, *Nikolay Rimsky-Korsakov: My Musical Life*, London, Martin Secker & Warburg Ltd., 1942, p. 20 and p. 28.

SIEGFRIED KROSS

In a similar manner to that of Raymond Knapp (see above), the German musicologist Siegfried Kross has considered the influence of Beethoven's symphonic writing on that of Brahms. He opens his account:

'How closely the music of the young Brahms imitated the style of Beethoven's middle period has often been noted. This orientation was in accordance not only with his education in a classical tradition, under the tutelage of Eduard Marxen [German pianist and teacher], but also with the rather strongly romanticized image of Beethoven then prevalent. At the time, this was thought to be progressive. More conservative musicians were oriented towards Mozart, who, however, was also romanticized.'

Kross discusses Brahms's musical structures and his emancipation from Beethoven:

'With the Fourth Symphony, Brahms must have realized that he had not only exhausted the possibilities for shaping musical forms from ongoing thematic processes, but also reached the limits for shaping pieces formally based upon concentrated thematic material deployed horizontally and vertically. Indeed, the principle of stratification of thirds was the only possibility within traditional tonality for utilizing the same material horizontally and vertically. In both genres for which Beethoven had set the standards for his successors — the symphony and the string quartet — Brahms had found solutions to formal problems which proved able to sustain his conception of form, without being dependent on Beethoven. From this point of view, one must hold that Ludwig Speidel's characterization of Brahms as "the greatest living follower" of Beethoven and other Classical masters misses the mark.' [Ludwig Speidel: German writer and Viennese music critic]

Siegfried Kross, *Thematic Structure and Formal Processes in Brahms's Sonata Movements*, in: George S. Bozarth editor, *Brahms Studies: Analytical and Historical Perspectives*, Papers delivered at the International Brahms Conference, Washington, D C, 5–8 May 1983, Oxford, Clarendon Press, 1990, pp. 442–43.

CONSTANT LAMBERT

The British composer, conductor, and author Constant Lambert outlined his views on music in his 1930s publication *Music Ho*, to which he gave the subtitle *A Study of Music in Decline*. He makes reference to the Romantic Movement, to its having run its course, and how such composers as Claude Debussy sought new directions in music and a new harmonic language. Of Beethoven, and his challenging legacy, he wrote:

> 'However perfect we may consider the symphonies of Mozart to be, we must admit the first movements of the Third and Ninth Symphonies of Beethoven — to mention only two instances — represent a new scale of thought. Mozart may be more temperamentally sympathetic to us, but it is the standard set by the greatest creations of Beethoven that any succeeding symphony must be judged. Standing at the threshold of the Romantic Movement, yet imbued with all the traditions of a classical upbringing, Beethoven gave to the symphony a new richness of expression and yet achieved a balance between expression and form that has, except in one instance [see later], never been equalled since.

'But his symphonies carry with them the seeds of destruction. By giving his themes a greater emotional content and a more contrasted individuality, than we find in the symphonies of the eighteenth century, he raised the problem — always present in the symphony but never stated so acutely before — of the clash between emotional and formal balance.'

Lambert outlined what he considered to be the decline of the symphony after Beethoven:

'The classical symphony in the nineteenth century, far from marking a development of the Beethoven tradition, marks a definite decline. On the credit side, there are Borodin's symphonies, genial works which continue the Haydn rather than the Beethoven tradition, and the symphonies of Brahms, which, though entirely lacking in the germinating vitality of Beethoven, command at least our respect. But for the typical nineteenth-century symphony, as represented by Tchaikovsky's No. 5, Dvořak's *From the New World*, and César Frank's in D minor, there is frankly nothing to be said; their mingling of academic procedure with undigested nationalism or maudlin sentiment, or both, produces a chimerical monster, a musical Minotaur that fortunately has no progeny.

'The decline of the symphony from 1820 to 1900 is more spectacular than its advance from 1800 to 1820.'

Lambert did not think highly of the symphonies of his contemporaries:

> 'The symphonies of Bax, though technically speaking of our day, belong spiritually to the nineteenth century and suffer from the same inherent disadvantage as the romantic symphonies. It is doubtful whether future critics will consider them as important as his symphonic poems, any more than they will place Elgar No. 1 beside *Falstaff* and the *Enigma Variations* or Vaughan Williams' *London Symphony* beside *Flos Campii* and *Job*.
>
> 'The great revolutionary figures of before the [Great War], Debussy, Stravinsky, Schönberg, and Bartók, turned their back on the symphony and all that it stood for, and a post-war critic, ignorant of Sibelius' work, might have pardonably have thought that the symphony was as outmoded and antediluvian as the horse bus.'

Lambert championed the symphonic achievement of Jean Sibelius:

> 'In Sibelius however, we have the first great composer after Beethoven whose mind thinks naturally in terms of symphonic form. Coming at the end of the Romantic Movement, he is as far removed from the apex of the romantic past as Beethoven was from the future. His symphonies, then, though subjective in mood, are free from the tautological emotional repetitions of romantic music cast in the classical mould.'

Constant Lambert, *Music Ho!: A Study of Music in Decline*, London, Faber and Faber, Ltd. 1934, pp. 312—18.

PAUL HENRY LANG

The Hungarian-American musicologist and music critic considers Beethoven's originality:

> 'Beethoven was the first among the great masters to divorce the creative from the performing artist, the first to whom composing was a bitterly relentless affair, "perhaps the only language of his soul," as [Adolph Bernhard] Marx says in his early biography. And the Beethoven of his last period attains to that degree of universality in which tendencies and forms lose their significance, melting into a vision that encompasses all that is human. Those who in the early nineteenth century heard his agitated and yearning themes, who were struck by the irresistible propulsive force of the allegros, the majesty of the adagios, the menacing humour of the scherzos, and the wild rhythms of the finales, recognized that this music, compared to that of his predecessors, is somewhat raw, gnarled, even unfinished. There were some who were repelled, among them such able composers as Spohr and Weber; but many more, despite or perhaps because of these qualities, found Beethoven's music to be warmer, more intense, and more fulfilling that any other they had known.'

Lang considers Beethoven in the context of the emerging school of Romanticism:

'The new movement could not defend itself against Beethoven's invincible art; all its instincts of self-preservation ceased when confronted with him, for there was everything in this music that the Romantics desired and valued. "Terrible!" exclaimed the enervated Pope Leo X at the sight of Michelangelo's murals; it is this *terribilità* that the romantics saw in the *Sonata Appassionata* and the Fifth Symphony. But they saw only the means in this music, not its essence; they saw how Beethoven demolished the boundaries but did not see that he demolished only to force the unbounded into severe and logical unity.'

Lang reminds us that Beethoven reaches out in his music with both heart and mind:

'We tend to think that in Beethoven it is exclusively the heart that speaks to us, for we know about his deep interest in freedom and brotherly love, and our predecessors have already proclaimed him the liberator of music, or, as a book popular a generation ago was entitled, *The Man who Freed Music* [Robert Haven, 1929]. Even much earlier, he was regarded as the first great composer who in his music withheld nothing of himself, and so was the first true romantic. And yet the voice of the intellect is never absent in Beethoven, even when he is rebellious, because he immediately proceeds to rebuild what he demolishes; he does not deny, he only contradicts. It was romantic anti-intellectualism in the arts that created the fashion of banishing from music logic of construction and procedure as inimical to poetry, thus creating the greatest impediment to true appreciation of Beethoven.'

Lang reflects on Beethoven's working method:

'Looking at the famous sketchbooks, one's first impression is that they are haphazard and sporadic; we also see that while Beethoven's imagination and inventiveness are inexhaustible he often struggles with his material, notably with his themes, and there is constant and ever-growing need to set things right, "order from disorder sprung" [quoting John Milton]. The approach is always analytical and synthetic; he raises questions and then answers them, often years later. He neither gives way to the impatience that characterizes the romantic, nor allows his expression to fail for want of craftsmanship. It seems as if the germ of every idea has been there in his soul from the beginning, growing slowly as Beethoven returns again and again, attempting to prune it down or extend it to the shape he desired. Indeed, the sketchbooks disclose the triumph of the *ars combinatoria* of old, or as [Wilhelm von] Lenz so engagingly says about the *Waldstein* Sonata: "In the development section Beethoven makes a nest from torn feathers".'

Lang concludes:

'The world needs rebels in order to be able to move and preserve its rhythm. Beethoven does not represent the highest heroism precisely because the revolutionary character of his music is kept powerfully within bounds; the mind of the classically schooled craftsman is always in command, ordering and organizing.'

Paul Henry Lang, *Musicology and Performance*, New Haven, Yale University Press, 1997, pp. 89–90, p. 93 and p. 98. Originally published in: *The Creative World of Beethoven*, New York, W.W. Norton, 1971.

ERNEST MARKHAM LEE

In his *The Story of the Symphony* (1916), the English composer, pianist, organist, lecturer, and author Ernest Markham Lee writes about Beethoven in the 'grand manner':

'It is acknowledged on every hand that in Beethoven the greatest and mightiest form of instrumental music found its greatest and mightiest exponent.

'It is worthwhile enquiring why it is that Beethoven has won the proud position that has been assigned to him as *facile princeps* amongst symphonic writers. The reasons are various. First and foremost, he was born at the right time. The experimental work on the symphony had been done by Haydn and Mozart: its form was settled, and completely understood; the principles of orchestration, and the inclusion of certain instruments, were matters that had been determined quite satisfactorily; the great composers who preceded Beethoven had actually gone some distance upon the road towards introducing a certain amount of emotional material into their music. When, therefore, the great genius arrived, the time was ripe for him and the path had been opened by pioneers who had cleared all obstacles from his progress. Consequently, Beethoven was able to take the symphonic form for granted; he was able to experiment in the enlargement of its boundaries without any danger of being misunderstood; he was able to concentrate his thoughts upon the emotional contents of his music, to pour out his wealth of beautiful ideas with glorious effects of harmonic richness and orchestral colour, and to expand his movements until all stiffness and angularity of form had disappeared.'

Ernest Markham Lee, *The Story of the Symphony*, London, Scott Publishing Co., 1916, pp. 42–45.

RAYMOND LEPPARD

In 1992 the composer Mark Grant interviewed the English conductor and harpsichordist Raymond Leppard. He asked him: 'Do you think what makes greatness in a composer is the ability of his or her music to withstand the greatest number of differing interpretations?' Leppard responded:

'I think what matters is what we conceive of as being great now. Nevertheless, it certainly is true that someone like Beethoven has survived since ... he seems to have been such a towering person mentally that whatever he said in music, whatever the vitality he put into his music, has seemed apposite to every generation ever since, for 200 years now. And that's — I mean — I think that's jolly good. I wouldn't say it's more than that, but it is rather wonderful.'

Of Beethoven and his achievements he added:

'He was a towering mind and it served as an example, sometimes even as a threat to most composers who came after him in the nineteenth century, just as Shakespeare did to his successors. But at this distance and at this very point in time it seems important to stress that he was not, some would have us believe, writers and performers alike, the inventor of Brahms who, fifty years later, composed in a completely different style; nor was he the bedfellow of Mendelssohn, Schubert, Weber or Schuman and certainly not the musical progenitor of Siegfried, whose author claimed that he was.'

Leppard continues:

'Beethoven's compositions have never left the music scene and each generation, as with Shakespeare, has interpreted them differently. Lately he was seen as a sort of musical Zeus on an Olympian high altar before which all must kneel respectfully and slowly. Now we are coming to see his genius through the eyes of his own time finding him no less wonderful, no less Olympian but dressed differently, revealing his greatness from within the musical style he inherited and made his own ... The middle years show this most clearly. It was a time of great achievement.'

Raymond Leppard, *On Music: An Anthology of Critical and Personal Writings*, Thomas P. Lewis, editor, White Plains, N.Y., Pro/Am Music Resources, 1993, p. 367 and pp. 282–5.

FRANZ LISZT

As an interpreter of Beethoven's piano music, Franz Liszt may be regarded as being a direct descendant of the composer. He had been a pupil of Carl Czerny, who, in turn, as we have remarked (see above), learned Beethoven's pianos sonatas directly from the master. We know from Liszt's father Adam that his son begged him to be taught the piano from an early age and how he subsequently made astonishing progress. It is to Adam's credit that he taught his son how to read musical notation, to sight-read and to improvise. He also introduced the young Franz to a wide range of keyboard repertoire that included the works of Bach, Hummel and early Beethoven. Liszt soon became so proficient as to perform in public, revealing a special affinity for Beethoven. Liszt's biographer Alan Walker relates: 'Whenever Liszt was asked as a boy what he wanted to be when he grew up, he pointed to the wall where a portrait of Beethoven was hanging [and remarked]: "Ein solcher" – "Like him".' Liszt confided his enthusiasm for the piano in a letter to the writer of romances the Countess Marie d'Agout. As he reveals, for him it was a veritable orchestra:

> 'Perhaps I am deceived by this kind of mysterious feeling which attaches me to the piano, yet I consider its importance very great. It has, it seems to me, the leading place in the hierarchy of instruments. It is the most generally cultivated,

the most popular of all; and this importance and this popularity it owes to the harmonic power which it alone possesses; and, as a consequence of this power, to the faculty of summarizing and concentrating within itself the whole of the art of music. In the span of seven octaves it embraces the range of an orchestra; and the ten fingers of one man suffice to render the harmonies produced by the concourse of more than a hundred instruments playing together.'

Through the medium of his keyboard transcriptions, Liszt made a great deal of orchestral music accessible to both audience and performer. The transcriptions he made of the Beethoven Symphonies have been described as 'arguably the greatest work of transcription ever completed in the history of music'. (Alan Walker) When he was still only twenty-six, Liszt appears to have made progress with the Beethoven transcriptions. In September 1837 he wrote to his Geneva friend Adolpe Pictet de Rochemont — described as 'a gifted polymath':

'The serious study of [Beethoven's] works, a profound feeling for their virtually infinite beauty and for the piano's resources, which have become familiar to me through constant practice, have perhaps made me less unfit than anyone for this laborious task. The first four symphonies are already transcribed, and the others will be completed shortly.'

Liszt's anticipation of completing the cycle of all nine Beethoven symphonies proved to be overly optimistic. The following year, Liszt received an invitation to make transcriptions of the symphonies for Beethoven's former Leipzig-based publisher Breitkopf & Härtell. He responded:

> '[I] have undertaken the *arrangement*, or, more correctly speaking, the pianoforte score. To tell the truth, this work has, nevertheless, cost me some trouble; whether I am right or wrong, I think it sufficiently *different* from, not to say superior to, those of the same kind which have hitherto appeared ... I also intend to *finger* them carefully, which, in addition to the indication of the different instruments (which is important in this kind of work), will most certainly make this edition much more complete ... It will be a pleasure to me to conclude this little business with you, at the rate of *eight francs per page.*'

As Liszt intimates, others before him had made two- and four-hand arrangements of the Beethoven symphonies, including his former teacher Carl Czerny and Beethoven himself made a partial transcription of the A major Symphony, No. 7. Liszt suggested he should concentrate his efforts initially on the *Eroica*, C minor, *Pastoral*, and A major Symphonies that were, in his opinion, 'the ones which are most effective on the piano'. Almost twenty years elapsed before Liszt completed work on the entire cycle of nine symphonies. This was published by Breitkopf & Härtell in 1865, bearing Liszt's dedication to the virtuoso pianist and conductor Han von Bülow — his most favoured pupil and son-in-law. In commending the edition to the publisher, Liszt remarked:

> '[I] have tried not to neglect to take into consideration the relative facility of execution while

maintaining an exact fidelity to the original. Such as this arrangement of Beethoven's Symphonies actually is, the pupils of the first class in the Conservatoires will be able to play them off fairly well on *reading them at sight*, save and except that they will succeed better in them by working at them, which is always advisable.'

Alan Walker, *Franz Liszt, The Virtuoso Years: 1811–1847*, New York, Alfred A. Knopf, 1983, Vol. 1, pp. 59–60. Adrian Williams, *Portrait of Liszt: by Himself and his Contemporaries*, Oxford, Clarendon Press, 1990, pp. 92–93. Franz Liszt, *An Artist's Journey: Lettres d'un Bachelier ès Musique*, 1835–41. Chicago, University of Chicago Press, 1989, pp. 46–47. (La) Mara [pseudonym], *Letters of Franz Liszt, London*, H. Grevel & Co., Vol. 2, 1894, pp. 22–23.

EDWARD MACDOWELL

Edward MacDowell is primarily remembered today as a composer but he was also a pianist of considerably powers. He studied at the Paris Conservatory and was known to Clara Schuman and Franz Liszt. He once wrote:

'Beethoven is the first one who built a poem and brought poetic thoughts to a logical conclusion. His music expresses ideal things, not actual things, as previous music did.'

Notwithstanding this tribute, as MacDowell's biographer records, he also had reservations about Beethoven's music:

'Certain outwardly, and popularly regarded,

peaks of Beethoven's opus were actually not paramount in MacDowell's mind as to the true genius of the man. The "Ode to Joy" from the Ninth Symphony, for example, MacDowell found "essentially obvious and commonplace, so that nothing could be done with it". The late sonatas and string quartets were "a matter for despair, penetrating to such subtleties and intricacies of the spirit that it was difficult to follow them".'

His biographer continues:

'MacDowell did not see this [the preceding remarks] as Beethoven's failure. To some extent the failure lay with limitations among listeners. But mostly it was indicative of how the spirit of genius could range to levels that need not but often do bypass those of others.'

Alan Howard Levy, *Edward MacDowell, An American Master*, Lanham, Md. & London, Scarecrow Press, 1998, p. 196.

In his own scholarly writings, MacDowell wrote an essay titled *The Development of Pianoforte Music*. In this he discussed Beethoven's pivotal role and also gave expression to a wider consideration — not entirely favourable — of his orchestral music:

'It is, perhaps, needless to say that the vastly enlarged possibilities, both technical and tonal, of the newly invented *fortepiano* were largely the outcome of seeking for colour in music ... [It] remained for Beethoven to weld these new ... and strange colours into poems, which, notwithstanding the many barnacles hanging to them (fragments of a past of timid adhesion to forms and fashions), are, in truth, the first lofty and dignified musical utterances with an object which we possess.

'We find that Beethoven was the first exponent of our modern art. Every revolution is bound to bring with it a reaction which seeks to consolidate and put in safe-keeping, as it were, results attained by it. Certainly, Beethoven alone can hardly be said to have furthered this end; for his revolt led him into still more remote and involved trains of thought, as in his later sonatas and quartets. Even the Ninth Symphony, hampered as it is by actual words for which declamation and a more-or-less well-defined form of musical speech are necessary, suffers from the same involved utterance that characterises his last period.'

Edward MacDowell, *Critical and Historical Essays: Lectures delivered at Columbia University*, edited by W. J. Baltzell, London, Elkin, Boston, A.P. Schmidt, 1912, pp. 201–02.

CHARLES MACKERRAS

The Australian conductor Sir Charles Mackerras expressed his opinion of Wagner's editing of Beethoven's symphonies:

'Wagner suggested, with uncharacteristic modesty, that certain parts of the Beethoven symphonies should be re-orchestrated, so that the important melodies could be heard clearly. Although Wagner's suggestions have been taken up by many conductors in the past, the present tendency is to stick to Beethoven's original orchestration.'

Helena Matheopoulos, *Maestro: Encounters with Conductors of Today*, London, Hutchinson, 1982, p. 334. See: Richard Wagner.

JOHN B. MCEWAN.

Sir John Blackwood McEwen was a Scottish classical composer and educator. He was professor of harmony and composition at the Royal Academy of Music, London, from 1898 to 1924, and Principal from 1924 to 1936. It was probably for reasons of his acknowledged musicological standing that he was invited to contribute to the *Special Issue* of *The Musical Times* that was published in 1927 to commemorate Beethoven's Death Centenary. He structures his account along the lines of the so-called 'three periods' into which Beethoven's creative achievements are considered to fall. He wrote:

'In the first, which terminates about the thirtieth year of his age, Beethoven is regarded as imitating, more or less consciously, the methods and works of his predecessors. In the second, which lasted until his forty-fifth year, having consolidated his powers and perfected his equipment, he produces a series of works in which, while still conforming, more or less, to the methods of Haydn and Mozart, he adds to and modifies these methods and reaches a style which is really individual and personal. In his last period, however, having exhausted the old methods and idioms, he develops new ways of expression in a series of compositions, which when originally produced, not only appeared strange, bizarre and impracticable, but were regarded by some of his contemporaries as the product of a mind which had reached decadence.'

McEwan posed the questions:

'What then, is the real significance of Beethoven's latest works? How are they to be regarded, both from the point of view of his artistic development and from that of the general progress of art?'

In response McEwan remarked:

'Naturally, Beethoven's first works, based as they were on the example of his predecessors, approximate to that example both in manner and intention: but even in these first works there are intentions eloquent of a new outlook and objective. With regard to technical processes of composition, Beethoven's attitude was fundamentally different from that of his predecessors, and this difference illustrated both his methods and in the results of these methods. He seems always to have composed with difficulty — not because he was less able to manipulate structure and design than the other musicians, but because he could not regard design as an end in itself. His methods were laborious because he was unable to content himself with the unessential and the insignificant, and the search for the right and final expression of his thought did not proceed too easily. Lacking neither fluency nor facility, wisely he distrusted both.'

John B. McEwan, *The Significance of Beethoven's "Third Period"*, *Music & Letters*. *Beethoven*: Special Number. London, *Music & Letters*, 1927, pp. 156–62.

WILLIAM MCNAUGHT

William McNaught contributed a biographical preface to Gordon Jacob's notes to Beethoven's Symphony No. 1 in C, Op. 21. His opening remarks provide a context to the collection of writings in this Anthology:

'In the story of Beethoven's life the background is of special importance, for the political and social changes that occurred in his time affected the lives of all men, musicians not excepted. During the eighteenth century almost the only openings for a musical career, above the level of the playing-rank, lay in the service under an aristocratic patron or the church. In the German confederation, or Empire, there were many rulers great and small who kept up musical establishments, often called *Kapelle* because they centred in a chapel; and the posts of *Kapellmeister* were the prizes of the profession. Haydn, in service to Prince Esterhazy for thirty years, is the leading example of a Kapellmeister who was a great composer. When the French Revolution sent its armies into Germany, the political confederation crumbled, its princedoms disappeared, and the aristocratic rule that had done so much for music lost its resources and power.

'Beethoven began his career at Bonn under this system of patronage, and at Vienna he owed much of his advancement to aristocratic friendship and aid. But in later years he had to fend for himself; and since his deafness prevented him from playing and teaching he had to live entirely by selling his compositions. It was a precarious trade, for the market was not organised then as it is now. Had international copyright, the royalty system and legal protection been in their present state, Beethoven would have made a good living; and so would Mozart and Schubert, who threw a similar challenge to life and lost the fight. Beethoven, fighting against odds, made a hard success of it. Thus, he stands at the turning-point in the history of composers and their material circumstances: before him, the salaried official in his small orbit; after him, the public concert, the impresario and travelling virtuoso. In the difficult time between these epochs the imposing figure of Beethoven stands like a symbol of the changes that were going on in a far wider field than that of a musician's livelihood.'

William McNaught, Biographical preface to: *Beethoven, Symphony No. 1 in C, Op. 21*, Miniature score, with an Introduction by Gordon Jacob, Penguin Books, Harmondworth, (undated).

GUSTAV MAHLER

During a conversation about Beethoven, Mahler is reported to have said:

'In order to understand and appreciate Beethoven fully, we should not only accept him for what he means to us today, but must realize what a tremendous revolutionary advance he represents in comparison with his forerunners. Only when we understand what a difference there is between Mozart's G minor Symphony and the Ninth can we properly evaluate Beethoven's achievement. Of geniuses like Beethoven, of such sublime and most universal kind, there are only two or three among millions. Among poets and composers of more recent times we can, perhaps, name but three: Shakespeare, Beethoven, and Wagner.'

When on a walk with a friend, Mahler once remarked:

'You ask me whether they understand Beethoven today? What an idea! Because they have grown up with his works, because he is "recognized", they listen to him, play him, and perhaps even love him — but not because they are able to follow him in his flight. With their bleary eyes, they will *never* be able to look the sun in the face.'

Natalie Bauer-Lechner, *Recollections of Gustav Mahler*, London: Faber Music, 1980, pp. 29–30, p. 149 and p.174.

When she was a mere eight or nine years old Gisella Tolney-Witt — known later in life as the musicologist Gisella Seldon-Goth — wrote to Mahler to ask 'why such a large apparatus as an orchestra should be necessary in order to express a great thought'. Mahler, by his own admission, was reluctant to enter into correspondence, but on this occasion he must have been motivated to respond by the musical insight implicit in the young fräulein's question. Mahler's reply is long, discursive and full of interest. We give a brief outline of its salient points — that eventually lead us to Beethoven.

He first invited his young correspondent to think back to earlier times — he cites Bach in particular. Then, he explained, composers left questions of interpretation largely to the performer regarding, for example, determining the tempo of the music. He makes a distinction between the kind of orchestra Haydn required for the performance of his symphonies and the extended forces Beethoven demands in his *Choral* Symphony. Mahler then cites how chamber music, conceived to be played in a small space before a small audience, typically expresses feelings of joy or sadness. He adds:

> 'The musicians were confident that they knew their business, they moved within a familiar field of ideas and on the grounds of clearly delimited skill, well-grounded within these limits ... It was taken for granted that everything would be rightly seen, felt and heard.'

Turning to the heart of the question he had been set, Mahler next remarked on the complexity of later music and the corresponding need, on the part of the composer, to give greater care in its presentation to ensure its correct interpretation. He explains:

> 'So a great system of sign-language gradually evolved, which — like the heads of notes indicating pitch — provided a definite reference for duration or volume. Together with this, moreover, came the *appropriation of new elements of*

feeling as objects of imitation in sounds — i.e., the composer began to relate ever deeper and more complex aspects of his emotional life to the area of his creativeness — until with Beethoven the *new era* of music began: from now on the *fundamentals* are no longer mood — that is to say, mere sadness, etc. — but also the transition from one to the other — conflicts - physical nature and its effect on us — humour and poetic ideas — all these become objects of musical imitation.'

Mahler continues by explaining the need to enlarge the orchestra as music became more 'common property', with listeners and players becoming ever more numerous and the recital chamber being replaced by the concert hall:

'We moderns need such a great apparatus [orchestra] to express *our* ideas, whether they be great or small. First ... to distribute the various colours of our rainbow over various palettes; secondly, because our eye is learning to distinguish more and more colours of the rainbow ... thirdly, because in order to be heard by many in our over-large concert halls and opera houses we have to make a loud noise!

'With best wishes, Gustav Mahler.'

Knud Martner, editor, *Selected Letters of Gusta Mahler*, London; Boston: Faber and Faber, 1979, pp. 147–9.

Mahler reasoned that since concert halls had undergone such transformations since Beethoven's time — regarding their size and acoustics – the scoring of his symphonies required 'retouching' to help redress the balance. So, for example, to introduce greater sonority and a more vibrant sound, he adapted the *Eroica* Symphony with the addition of two flutes, two oboes, two clarinets, two bassoons, two trumpets, five horns, and two E flat clarinets; in the case of the Ninth Symphony he employs eight horns and four trumpets. At a performance of the latter work in Hamburg in 1895, utilizing Mahler's re-scoring, a music critic exclaimed: C'est magnifique, Monsieur Mahler, mais ce n'est pas Beethoven!'

> 'In March 1897, Mahler directed two 'trial' concerts in Munich in the hope of securing the position of resident conductor. He wrote to his sister Justi:
>
> 'Today I'm conducting *my* C minor again (Beethoven), and will be most interested to see whether I fall victim once more to my loyal old friends, *the critics.*' [Mahler's italics]

Herta Blaukopf, *Mahler's Unknown Letters*, London, Gollancz, 1986, pp. 109–10.

Mahler complained of he poor standard of the musicians:

> 'You see, people just can't observe the printed signs, and so they sin against the sacred laws of dynamics as well as against the inner rhythm that lies at the heart of any work. As soon as they see a *crescendo*, they immediately play loudly and get faster; for a *diminuendo*, they immediately play softly and hold back the tempo. In vain may you seek for the finer

nuances of *mezzo-forte, fortissimo*, of *piano, pianissimo, pianississimo*. Much less do *sforzando, fortepiano*, or any shortening or lengthening of notes ever register. And if you go so far as to do something that isn't in the score ... you are lost with any orchestra.'

After much rehearsal, Mahler persuaded the players to play Beethoven's C minor Symphony *his* way, but they rejected it for being 'extremely unclassical and arbitrary'. He lamented:

'Beethoven's First, Second, and Fourth Symphonies can still be performed by modern orchestras and conductors. All the rest, however, are quite beyond their powers. Only Richard Wagner (who can incidentally be called the discoverer of all Beethoven's symphonies) and in recent times I myself have done these works justice. And even I can manage it only by terrorizing the players; by forcing each individual to transcend his little self and rise above his own powers.'

The result of the trial concerts was that Mahler was not offered the post of Munich's resident conductor.

Natalie Bauer-Lechner, *Recollections of Gustav Mahler*, London, Faber Music, 1980, pp. 78–79 and pp. 139–40.

The American music critic Harold C. Schonberg places Mahler's approach to his editing of orchestral works in its contemporary context:

'Like every musician of the time, Mahler heavily edited the music he was conducting. "Of course the works of Beethoven need some editing", he said. Note the "of course". Bruno Walter, who idolized Mahler, attempted to explain his attitude. If Mahler did make changes in classical works, it was directed "against the letter and toward the spirit" of the composer. Mahler never hesitated to retouch, and was under constant attack for some particularly heavy modifications, as in the Schumann and Beethoven Symphonies. Mahler answered his critics with the old — even in his day — if Beethoven were alive argument. "The fanatical obedience to the score", Walter writes, "did not blind him to any contradiction existing between its instructions and the composer's actual intentions".'

Harold C. Schonberg, *The Great Conductors*, Simon & Schuster, 1967, p. 23.

NICHOLAS MARSTON
Nicholas Marston is Professor of Music Theory and Analysis in the Faculty of Music at the University of Cambridge. In his introduction to Beethoven's symphonies he writes:

'It would be difficult to exaggerate the importance of Beethoven's nine completed symphonies, either in relation to the rest of his output or in relation to the subsequent history of music. For many listeners, the symphonies represent the quintessential Beethoven; and although we should now shut the door firmly on Schindler's improbable claim about the knocking of fate in the Fifth Symphony, this work perhaps remains the quintessential symphony. Certainly, the nature of Beethoven's compositional thinking made it almost inevitable that he would excel in the genre and transform it radically.'

Nicholas Marston, [*The*] *Symphonies* in: Barry Cooper, *The Beethoven Compendium: A Guide to Beethoven's Life and Music*, London, Thames and Hudson, 1991, p. 214.

DENIS MATTHEWS

Denis Matthews is remembered today primarily for being a concert pianist with a particular liking for the music of the first Viennese school — notably that of Haydn, Mozart, Beethoven and Schubert. His many writings on music, however, reveal his knowledge of, and affinity for, the keyboard music of their contemporaries such as Hummel and Clementi. Matthews outlined his thoughts about music in his Autobiography *In Pursuit of Music* (1968) and reached a wide audience in his study of Beethoven, published in *The Master Musicians* series (1985). In his role as Professor of Music at the University of Newcastle (1971–81) Matthews wrote extensively about Beethoven, inspiring a younger generation thereby. Writing of the greatness of Beethoven he remarks:

'Beethoven sought, above all, independence: his greatest teacher was to be his own experience. It taught him early on that enduring art must satisfy in opposite, complementary ways. There is the emotional impact of music — "from the heart to the heart" — but there is also the desire to satisfy the mind and to arrange ideas in their most potent form. Call it, if you like, the architectural quality of music. Even the unskilled listener senses when a piece is well made, because the composer's struggle with form forces him to channel and to crystallize his thoughts.'

Denis Matthews, *Beethoven Piano Sonatas*, London, British Broadcasting Corporation, 1967, p. 11.

Matthews gives his interpretation of Beethoven's first venture into the genre of symphonic composition:

'Beethoven did not leap fearlessly into the world of the symphony like the child Mozart on his visit to London, or slip into it as an extension of the quartet or divertimento as Haydn had done. By the 1790s the symphony, like the quartet, was a force to be reckoned with, and he did not enter the field until the turn of the century. He had naturally contemplated the form before this. There is a very early sketch in C minor labelled *sinfonia*, and there are extensive ones for the C minor Symphony dating from his mid-twenties.

'His eventual First Symphony (1800) owed its key and the scalic opening of the finale to this unfulfilled work. As public music, it displayed none of the profound emotions expressed, for example, in the slow movement of the Piano Sonatas Op. 7 and Op. 10, No. 3; nor did it emulate the storm and stress, and indeed the smouldering orchestral effects, of the more recent *Pathétique*. It has its surprises — the misleading opening "out of key", the precipitous minuet that is really a scherzo, and the playful introduction to the finale — but its moods are neutral, even conventional, as though Beethoven had decided to test his powers on safe ground before venturing into uncharted territory.'

Denis Matthews, *Beethoven, The Master Musicians*, London, J. M. Dent, 1985, p. 152.

WILFRID MELLERS

The English musicologist and composer Wilfrid Mellers places Beethoven as a figure in history and one who made history:

'No work of art can be "explained" by reference to its historical connotations. Every artist self-evidently "reflects" the values and beliefs of his time ... At the same time, any truly creative artist is also making those beliefs. It is true that we cannot fully understand Beethoven without understanding the impulses behind the French Revolution. It is equally true that we cannot fully understand the French Revolution without some insight into Beethoven's music. We can see in his music those elements which are conditioned by his time (for they could not be otherwise) and yet are beyond the topical and local. Beethoven is a point at which the growth of the mind shows itself. He is a part of history: and also of the human spirit making history.'

Wilfrid Howard Mellers and Alec Harman, *Man and his Music*, London, Barrie and Jenkins, 1988, pp. 575–6.

Of Beethoven the revolutionary, Mellers writes:

'There *is* a connection between Beethoven's music and the French revolution, since even in so strikingly personal a work as the Fifth Symphony, he was directly influenced by French revolutionary music.'

He adds:

'[If] Haydn and Mozart were incipiently revolutionary composers, Beethoven is overtly so. The Fifth Symphony revolutionises the then accepted notion of symphonic form, and its technical revolution is inseparable from the fact that it conveys in musical terms a message — a new approach to human experience.'

Mellers considers Beethoven disturbed what he calls the 'equilibrium' of music:

'[From] the start, Beethoven desired change. He wanted to build a new world; and he thought of his music as a means to that end. Mozart's art, as we can see most readily from his operas, is based on acceptance, tolerance, and understanding. This does not preclude stringent criticism; but he has no ethical intentions. Beethoven was probably the first composer to be consciously animated by the desire to do good.'

In support of this contention, Mellers quotes words that Beethoven inscribed in a friend's album: 'To help wherever one can / Love liberty above all things / Never deny the truth / Even at the foot of the throne.'

In a summary passage, Mellers concludes:

'[Beethoven] was born into a great musical tradition which he respected; for with his disrespect towards people and things he considered unworthy, he had the true humility of the great. So, the subversive tendencies of his music are not immediately evident. He accepts the conventions which he inherited from Haydn and Mozart: but emphasises the revolutionary at the expense of the traditional features.'

Wilfrid Howard Mellers, *The Sonata Principle (from c. 1750)*, London, Rockliff, 1957, pp. 53–6.

FELIX MENDELSSOHN

In the autumn of 1825, Felix Mendelssohn completed work on his Octet in E-flat major, Op. 20 — he was just sixteen years old at the time. Conrad Wilson, writing of this achievement (2003) — that was remarkable even by Mozartian standards — remarks: 'Its youthful verve, brilliance and perfection make it one of the miracles of nineteenth-century music.' Four years later, Mendelssohn paid homage to Beethoven, albeit indirectly, in his first string quartet that is also written in the same key of E-flat major.

For Mendelssohn's views about Beethoven and his music, we are indebted to the reminiscences of the composer and music theorist Johann Christian Lobe. He recalls a walk one day with the composer that provided him with the opportunity to seek his opinions concerning 'originality' in Beethoven's music. Mendelssohn was cautious in conceding what was innovatory in music. For him, breaking new ground consisted of producing creations that obeyed 'newly discovered' and 'more sublime laws'. He was of the opinion:

> 'Never, in fact, did an artist break new ground. In the best case he did things imperceptibly better than his immediate predecessors.'

Mendelssohn accepted Beethoven had opened up new ground but questioned if his early orchestral music departed so greatly from that of Mozart and Haydn He questioned:

> 'Do Beethoven's symphonies proceed down completely new paths? No, I say. Between the first symphony of Beethoven and the last of Mozart I find no extraordinary [leap in] artistic value, and no more than ordinary effect. The one pleases me and the other pleases me.'

Lobe asked Mendelssohn about his views on the music of Beethoven's final period including his last string quartets, the Ninth Symphony and the *Missa Solemnis.* 'Here', Lobe reasoned, 'one cannot speak of a comparability with Mozart, or any other artist before him?' Mendelssohn responded:

> 'That may be, in a certain sense ... [Beethoven's] forms are wider and broader, the style is more polyphonic, more artificial, the ideas for the most part darker, more melancholy, even when they want to be cheerful; the instrumentation is fuller, and *he went somewhat farther along the path he had already embarked on, but he did not clear a new one*. And let us be honest; where did he lead us? To regions that are really *more beautiful?*' [Mendelssohn's emphasis]

*

Mendelssohn summarized his views about Beethoven with the observation:

> 'The fact that Beethoven's genius took the shape it did is a consequence of the sequence in which it appeared. In Handel's time he would not have become our Beethoven. Haydn and Mozart would have been different people if they had come after Beethoven. And all this would most certainly have come about no matter how the world might have looked from a political or religious viewpoint.'

Roger Nichols, *Mendelssohn Remembered*, London, Faber and Faber, 1997, pp. 99–103 and p. 108.

In 1821 Johann Wolfgang von Goethe, then in his 70s, met the twelve-year old Mendelssohn. He was astounded at his ability to improvise and play from sight, disposing him to compare his facility with that of the youthful Mozart. Goethe maintained his friendship with Mendelssohn who played for him on several occasions. In 1830 Goethe commissioned an artist to make a portrait of the young composer – a black crayon sketch. He described the occasion in a letter to his sister Fanny:

> 'In the forenoon [Goethe] likes me to play for him the compositions of the various masters in chronological order, for an hour, and also to tell him the progress they have made, while he sits in a corner, like a Jupiter Tonans, his old eyes flashing at me. Hi did not wish to hear anything of Beethoven's, but I did tell him that I could not

let him off, and played the first part of the Symphony in C minor. It seemed to have a singular effect on him; at first he said, "This causes no emotion nothing but astonishment; it is only *grandiose*". He continued grumbling in this way, and after a long pause he began again, "It is very noble, wild; it makes one fear that the house is about to fall down; and what must it be when played by a number of men together!" '

Felix Mendelssohn in a letter to Fanny Mendelssohn (25 May 1830), reproduced in: *Letters from Italy and Switzerland*, London, Longman, Green, Longman, and Roberts, 1862, pp. 7–8. See also: M. E. Glehn, *Goethe and Mendelssohn: (1821–1831)*, London, Macmillan, 1874, pp. 60–61, and Hans Gal, *The Musician's World: Great Composers in their Letters*, London, Thames and Hudson, 1965, pp. 156–57.

Mendelssohn was in demand as a conductor, even when he and his wife Cécile were on their honeymoon in 1837. In a letter to Cécile's mother, Mendelssohn describes how he was obliged to conduct Beethoven's C minor Symphony:

'I had to conduct ... the C minor Symphony and the trombones and tympani exerted themselves so much that I admit I felt somewhat worn out at the end of the concert.'

The occasion was, however, propitious since Mendelssohn received the Diploma of the Gesellschaft der Musikfreunde making him an Honorary Member.

Peter Ward editor and translator, *The Mendelssohns on Honeymoon: The 1837 Diary of Felix and Cécile*

Mendelssohn Bartholdy, together with Letters to their Families, Oxford, Clarendon Press, 1997, p. 198.

A contemporary account provides an indication of Mendelssohn's style of conducting:

> 'Mendelssohn possessed the finest sense of rhythm. The slightest wavering was admonished with the call: "Tempo, tempo, gentlemen!" In a tutti no fault escaped him, nor any wrong note and he adhered with great strictness and punctilious observation of the performance instructions that the composer had written down. His manner of preparing a piece for performance was wholly to the point. First, he let it be played through, after which he went through the particular passages that required improvement ... By means of this proceeding ... he was able to achieve a great deal in a comparatively short time.

Another eye-witness writes:

> 'He directed the Gewandhaus Concerts in the spirit of joyful delight at the beauty of serious art and its pursuit, and through their excellent achievements raised them to one of the best and most high-ranking of all musical institutions.'

Clive Brown, *A Portrait of Mendelssohn*, Yale University Press, 2003, p. 251.

When the youthful Mendelssohn was resident in Paris, he had occasion to write on 14 February 1832 to his former music teacher Carl Friedrich Zelter. His remarks provide insights into the state of musical performance in Paris and of the reception of Beethoven's symphonies:

> '[It] is the Paris Conservatoire that gives the concerts; but more than that, it is the most perfect performance to be heard anywhere ... The general arrangements, too, are very appropriate and sensible ... Moreover, the hall is a little one, so that for one thing the music makes twice the effect and we hear every detail twice as clearly and for another thing the audience is small, very select, and yet seems a large gathering.'

Beethoven's orchestral music was finding favour:

> 'The musicians themselves delight in Beethoven's great symphonies; they have made themselves thoroughly familiar with them, and are happy to have mastered the difficulties. Some of them, including Habeneck himself, undoubtedly have a perfectly genuine love of Beethoven; but as for the others, who are the loudest in their enthusiasm, I do not believe a word they say about it; for they make this an excuse for decrying the other masters – declaring Haydn was merely a fashionable composer, Mozart an ordinary sort of fellow; and such narrow-minded enthusiasm cannot be sincere. If they really felt what Beethoven meant, they would also realize what Haydn was, and feel small; but not a bit of it, they go briskly ahead with their criticism. Beethoven is uncommonly popular with the concert public, as well, because they believe that only the connoisseur can

appreciate him; but only a small minority really enjoy him, and I cannot abide the disdainful attitude towards Haydn and Mozart; it infuriates me.'

François Habeneck, the French violinist and conductor to whom Mendelssohn makes reference, was the first conductor to introduce French audiences to the Symphonies of Beethoven in the late 1820's. A few weeks later, Mendelssohn attended a rehearsal of Beethoven's *Pastoral* Symphony and found himself unexpectedly the centre of attention. The rehearsal over, he left his seat to greet some friends. To his pleasure and surprise the full orchestra exclaimed 'There is Mendelssohn'. He wrote to his father: 'I shall never forget that, for it meant more to me than any distinction.'

Hans Gal, *The Musician's World: Great Composers in their Letters*, London, Thames and Hudson, 1965, pp. 163–5.

YEHUDI MENUHIN

Although Yehudi Menuhin will be forever associated with the legendary recording he made of the Elgar Violin Concerto (HMV 1932), performed at the age of sixteen. It is for many, though, that his lasting fame endures with his association of Beethoven's Violin Concerto. One of his first teachers, Louis Persinger – first violin of the San Francisco Symphony Orchestra, – recalls that at the age of eight the young Yehudi begged to be allowed to work on the D major concerto. Later in his career, Beethoven's Violin Concerto came to be something of a talisman for Menuhin. For example, in 1947, in the wake of the Holocaust, he returned to Germany to play concerto concerts including the

Beethoven Concerto with the Berlin Philharmonic Orchestra under Wilhelm Furtwängler.

Menuhin saw this as an act of reconciliation, remarking to his Jewish critics that 'he wanted to rehabilitate Germany's music and spirit'. Similarly, the present writer recall's Menuhin's response to the events subsequent to the emergence of the so-called 'Prague Spring' when the reformist Alexander Dubček was elected First Secretary of the Communist Party of Czechoslovakia. Following its ruthless suppression, later in the year by the Soviet Union, Menuhin, then taking part in the Edinburgh International Festival, dedicated his performance of the Beethoven Violin Concerto "to the oppressed people of Prague".

Menuhin was more than a violinist of course. He has been described as a philosopher, visionary, humanist, music's ambassador to the world — he was nominated 'UNESCO Ambassador of Goodwill, 1992' — and, amongst his numerous other awards, he was the recipient of more than twenty honorary doctorates. Perhaps the most significant tribute paid to Menuhin was the estimation of him as:

> 'An artist who believed the music he played to be, quite literally, a form of human healing, out of which we might make peace with ourselves.'

The spirit of the preceding remarks pervades much of Menuhin's recorded conversation and writing about music, of which the following is a selection of texts.

When in conversation with the author and writer on music Robin Daniels, Menuhin outlined his views about music, making occasional references to Beethoven:

> 'Music can penetrate all one's defences. The combination of music and an especially poignant

occasion can be unbelievably potent ... We all have joys and tragedies, ecstasies and struggles, but we may not have enough experience of life to draw the full measure of emotional depth or rational analysis or philosophical meaning from what has happened to us. We need elucidation, and so we go to the great creative artists whom we can trust, such as Bach or Beethoven or Shakespeare. The experience of the most evolved people — whether artists or religious leaders or people from any profession or background — opens our eyes, broadens and matures us, and unlocks our repressed feelings, giving them shape, sound, form, and meaning. A great work of art *re-presents* human beings to themselves ... Music, unlike the visual arts, lives in time. The music of Bach or Beethoven captures our vibrations, compels co-living. I am prepared, without reservation, to live through Beethoven and his depth of experience, but what I cannot accept is the almost total subservience that cheap entertainment demands. I want to be informed, enlightened, enhanced, by art; I am not willing to be presented with the crudest sensations — fear, cruelty, bizarre behaviour.'

Menuhin reflected briefly on Beethoven's symphonic achievement:

'[When] Beethoven tackled the Fifth Symphony, he set himself the task in the realm of form greater than any he had previously attempted. He not only changed what had been accepted as material for a symphony, he sought to unify the themes of all the movements so that their development would reflect a total unity as the work progressed. In fact, the scherzo continues without a break, an unheard-of liberty, straight into the striding sunburst finale where Beethoven, always a deft orchestrator, brings in the opera-house trombones for the first time in this score in the history of the concert orchestra. It is a masterstroke a shaft of light whose noble theme is a transformation of those found in both the slow movement and the scherzo,'

Menuhin positions Beethoven and Schubert as protagonists of the Romantic era:

'At the emergence of the Romantic era, Beethoven was one pillar of Western music; the other was Franz Schubert. He was as modest and humble as Beethoven was overbearing and arrogant, as intuitive as Beethoven was philosophical, as true to man's subjective inner turmoil, passions, even nightmares, as Beethoven was true to man's social and personal struggle. Like Beethoven, he never heard many of his greatest works performed — Beethoven because of his deafness and Schubert because his greatest works were largely ignored. Yet the phenomenon of Schubert lies in the fact that he marks one of those apparently inevitable milestones along man's path toward self-realization, a conscience answerable to itself rather than to some higher power. The voice of Schubert is suddenly the voice of Everyman. Beethoven is cataclysmic, speaking to a million, while Schubert speaks one-to-one to the individual human heart.'

Robin Daniels, *Conversations with Menuhin*, London, Macdonald General Books, 1979, p. 65 and p. 154.

Menuhin collaborated with the television producer Curtis W. Davis in a television series called *The Music of Man*. In their resulting publication Menuhin writes of Beethoven's struggle to achieve perfection — in the context of similar creative efforts made by contemporary composers:

> 'The emerging doctrine of egocentric, personal self-realization [at the opening of the nineteenth century] could not have found a more vigorous expression than it did in Beethoven, which may be due in part to his eventual deafness and isolation. This tendency has continued to our day when every literate composer feels obliged to invent a new style, rather than simply evolve a distinctive personality. The result has been a great number of disappointments and blind alleys. No composer has ever refined his raw material to the degree of purity Beethoven achieved. Wrestling with it until he transformed it into a concentrated statement of intense meaning, he focused his fire in the process. Today, when composers so often begin with their raw material already in an advanced state of abstraction, there can be no such process of distillation, of self-immolation, in the creative act. In Beethoven, more than in almost any other creative artist, we are allowed to witness the struggle for the ideal of beauty, purpose and truth.'

Menuhin directed his attention to more personal aspects of Beethoven:

'Beethoven's tragedy has been compared to blindness in a painter. That is only a half-truth; the blind painter may no longer be able to paint, but blind musicians compose and perform, like Cabezon in Spain. And while the deaf performer cannot play, the deaf composer can still write, creating by a process of inner conception, drawing on aural images etched onto his mind and heart; for music is finally an inner experience, a happening occurring within ourselves. Beethoven needed only his eyes and his hand, and they continued to serve him well. And yet, how are we to assess the depth of tragedy in the monumental despair of this colossus, facing so fateful and shattering a curse? It was as if Beethoven were Prometheus, who stole fire from the gods and gave it to man; then, like Prometheus, the gods punished him by chaining him to a rock, the rock of his deafness.'

Menuhin discusses Beethoven in the wider context of mankind's musical heritage:

'By nature man is an explorer, one of the most consistent characteristics of the human race. Beethoven is an explorer in search of first causes. His nature was not an accepting one, but challenging, defiant and questioning. Indeed, his incomparable stretches of utmost serenity were very dearly bought, and so often were followed by bucolic festivity, as the celebration of inner creative struggle leads to serenity, thanksgiving and celebration. Nowhere in his volcanic temperament can we see this more clearly than in his sketchbooks, of which hundreds survive. These are like the sketchbooks of Leonardo da Vinci, only without their neatness and precision. Beethoven was too impatient, struggling constantly to reinvent music itself, working under pressure, to make form emerge from recalcitrant material. Beethoven started as a disciple of Haydn and Mozart, but soon he no longer quoted others, as a scientist like Darwin might quote ideas and techniques learned in the course of setting forth an argument. In the final analysis, Beethoven is like Moses, an intermediary between Divine Will and human recalcitrance, leading us out of bondage into the Promised Land, a mortal become immortal, no longer quoting others. God perhaps said it first and Beethoven was content to quote God.'

Menuhin concludes:

'Beethoven's greatness of soul transcends craft while illuminating it. As he became increasingly locked inside his deafness, he devised elaborate hearing aids so that he could pick up vibrations from his piano directly, applying a stick against the sounding board and pressing the other end directly against the side of his head. Beethoven's isolation emphasizes something new in Western music: the separation between composer and performer that had begun at the turn of the nineteenth century ... Beethoven's achievement is that universality of utterance which partakes alike of the rigors of mathematical equation and the emotions of human experience.'

Yehudi Menuhin and Curtis W. Davis, *The Music of Man*, London: Macdonald and Janes, 1979, p. 147 and pp. 150–4.

OLIVIER MESSIAEN

The French composer, organist and ornithologist Olivier Messiaen is known for his exploration of sound-worlds and sonorities inspired by bird song. Aware of this, fellow Frenchmen and composer Claude Samuel, in conversation with Messiaen in the early 1990s, put to him the question: 'Western music is played regularly in the concert halls of Tokyo. How does a Japanese person experience a Beethoven symphony?' To which Messiaen replied:

> 'I'll answer you with an anecdote. My pupil, Gerald Levinson [American composer of contemporary classical music], who lived in Bali to learn the technique of the gamelan, one day played two European pieces for his Balinese teacher: an excerpt from Mozart's Symphony No. 40 in G minor and a fragment of my *Transfiguration*. Now, it was my music that the Balinese musician appreciated more readily, doubtless because he recognized the sound of tam-tams and gongs, which reminded him of his metallophones. The music of Mozart left him indifferent. I think the Japanese find reminders of their own music in certain Western works, but Beethoven naturally is very far removed from their sensibility.'

Samuel invited Messiaen to give his views on rhythm:

'With Beethoven, the rhythms and themes have a masculine pace, a single burst and no special accenting; this is probably due to his strong-willed personality. Clearly, there's less rhythmic investigation in Beethoven than Mozart — the focus is on a different plane — but we'll note an interesting element all the same: development by elimination, which is a blueprint for the rhythmic characters in *The Rite of Spring*.'

Samuel asked Messiaen if he had 'made a clean sweep of classical forms' and on which 'formal frameworks' did he rely. He first responded:

'[One] can now no longer write a Mozartian opera with arias and recitatives, it's impossible to write, like Beethoven, the first movement of a symphony with an opening theme that says, "I am the theme". And that returns after the development affirming, "Here I am again, I'm the theme, do you recognize me?" '

Messiaen elaborated:

'I haven't abandoned the eternal principle of development because that would be inconceivable, nor that of the variation which is also timeless. I've used forms that, if not classical in the eighteenth-century sense, were nevertheless so in a distant past, like the Greek triad: strophe, antistrophe, epode, for example.'

Olivier Messiaen, *Music and Color: Conversations with*

Claude Samuel, Portland, Oregon, Amadeus, 1994, pp.69–70, pp. 102–3, and p. 117.

In an essay, primarily in defence of Igor Stravinsky, Messiaen opened his account with the question: 'What did Beethoven do to be the greatest of all?' And his response: 'He loved, he suffered, and his music speaks from the heart.'

Peter Hill, *The Messiaen Companion*, London, Faber and Faber, 1995, p. 154.

PAUL MIES

The German musicologist and pedagogue Paul Mies is acknowledged in Beethoven musicology for being a pioneering modern-day authority on the composer's sketch sources (***Beethoven's Sketches: An Analysis of his Style based on a Study of his Sketchbooks***, German text 1925, English text 1929 – reprint 1969). In his more general writings about the composer he reflects on his uniqueness:

> 'It is remarkable that even the names of the symphony-composers of Beethoven's time are hardly remembered today and that their works have almost disappeared. To a greater extent that at any other time one composer — Beethoven — overshadowed all his contemporaries ... To a certain extent this was true even in Beethoven's own day. When a critic, writing of the performance of the Fourth Symphony at the *Niederreinisches Musikfest* in 1828, declared that "nothing more magnificent of this kind has probably ever been written, nor ever will be written". That was not an isolated judgement but one constantly

reaffirmed by Beethoven's contemporaries. If not all his works were fully valued at once, if contemporaries were for a while placed by his side, he was in his own day already regarded as the greatest living composer.'

Mies remarks on Beethoven's relatively late venture into the symphonic genre:

> 'It was not until he was thirty that Beethoven appeared before the public with his First Symphony. For the eighteenth century this was a late beginning; Haydn wrote his first symphony in his twenty-seventh year, Mozart as early as his eighth. In the next century, Brahms waited to the age of forty-three, Bruckner to thirty-nine. Thus, reluctance to put such demanding works before the public had grown in the intervening time. Just as Haydn's and Mozart's symphonies impelled Beethoven to severe self-criticism, his own works had the same effect on his successors.'

Regarding Beethoven's patrons, Mies suggests:

> '[Beethoven] stands, at least superficially, still in the eighteen-century relationship of the composer to his patrons. His patrons were, to begin with, the Electoral Court in Bonn; Count Waldstein for his journey to Vienna; and subsequently the noble families of that city, in whose houses he gave concerts and lessons and also found friends. Mozart had gained his freedom from princely commissions only at the cost of his livelihood — not to the detriment of his genius but to that of

his personal existence. The ageing Haydn owed his social equality to the benevolence of Prince Esterhazy. But Beethoven attained his by force — not only for himself but for the whole profession. He was convinced that the artist was the equal of the most eminent, and he gained his point.'

Paul Mies, *The Orchestral Music of Beethoven's Contemporaries* in: Philip Radcliffe, *The Age of Beethoven, The New Oxford History of Music*, Vol. VIII, Gerald Abraham, editor, 1988, p. 120, p. 124, and p. 158.

DARIUS MILHAUD

In the early 1920s, the French composer Darius Milhaud undertook to write articles of music criticism for the Paris Journal *Courrier musical*. Reporting on the Sunday concerts held in Paris at this time, he likened them 'to the display of *old masters* to be seen at the Louvre's *Salon Carré*. Regarding Beethoven and Wagner, Milhaud considered it was possible to have too much of a good thing:

'The Sunday concerts were a sort of musical *Salon Carré,* an exhibition of the masters of past centuries. I loved classical music, but protested in my articles against the excessive number of Beethoven-Wagner and Wagner-Beethoven programmes. It was very tiresome. Every Sunday, the *Fifth*, the *Third*, the *Leonora Overture*. And Wagner every Sunday ... Apart from one or two of his overtures, his works should never be performed in the concert hall.'

Mihaud turned his criticism to music festivals that he considered also to be over-representative of the works of Beethoven and Wagner. He concedes, in a final outburst — and not without a sense of humour — that these are inevitable:

> '[Our] criticisms are wasted, and we shall always have to put up with festivals of this kind, I may say I am prepared to shout, "Long live Beethoven!" even after the hundred-thousandth performance of the *Fifth*, but — oh, yes! Certainly — always to cry, "Down with Wagner!" '

Darius Milhaud, *My Happy Life*, London, Boyars, 1995, p. 95.

IGNAZ MOSCHELES

Following a series of European concert tours, the Bohemian composer and virtuoso pianist Ignaz Moscheles settled in London where he soon became part of the music establishment. In 1822 he was conferred an honorary membership of the London Academy of Music (Later The Royal Academy of Music) and secured the friendship of Muzio Clementi and Johann Baptiste Cramer. He wrote in his Diary: 'I feel more at home in England.' He was an early enthusiast of Beethoven's (then revolutionary) piano music and absorbed something of its spirit into his own piano compositions. Moreover, it was Moscheles who conducted the first British (English) performance of the *Missa Solemnis* that took place in 1882.

Sir Henry Rowley Bishop was another pillar of the musical establishment, being variously a founder member of the (Royal) Philharmonic Society, Music Director at Covent Garden, and Professor of Music at the University of Oxford.

Now long forgotten, save for his two songs *Home Sweet Home* and *Lo! Hear the Gentle Lark*, he was a close associate of Moscheles and shared the direction of the Philharmonic Society's concerts with him. From this time we have the following recollections of his style of conducting and that of Beethoven:

> '[At] the rehearsal [Moscheles] addressed the band to the following effect: "Gentlemen, as we are here assembled together, I should like to compare your performance with the fingers of an admirably trained pianoforte player's hand. [Moscheles studied piano with Clementi] Now, will you allow me to be the hand which sets these fingers in motion, and imparts life to them? May I try to convey to you all the inspirations I feel when I hear the works of the great masters? Thus, may we achieve excellence".'

Bishop recalls Moscheles' description of Beethoven conducting:

> '[When] a Beethoven Symphony was to be played, [Moscheles] told the band how he heard this and the other great works of Beethoven when they first came out, and how he has kept the tradition of the *tempi*, which at that time were given by Beethoven himself. [He amused] his hearers exceedingly by imitating Beethoven's movements as a conductor; his stooping down more and more until he almost disappeared at the *piano* passages, the gradual rising up at the *crescendo*, and standing on tiptoe and bounding up at the *fortissimo*.'

*

Bishop closed this part of his recollections of Moscheles on a more respectful note:

> 'Moscheles did not forget to add: "Inasmuch, however, as I cannot emulate the great man in his works, I abstain from copying him in his attitudes; with him it was all originality, with me it would be caricature".'

A. D. Coleridige, *Life of Moscheles, with Selections from his Diaries and Correspondence by his Wife*, London, Hurst & Blackett, 1873, pp. 139–40.

CHARLES MÜNCH

In his *Je Suis Chef d'Orchestre* (1954) the French conductor Charles Munch outlined his thought on conducting and the role of the orchestral conductor. Regarding the planning of a concert he remarked:

> 'There are many ... burdens on your conscience at the moment of fixing on a programme. Must you play contemporary music? I agree with this aphorism of Saint-Saëns: "The two kinds of music are not the contemporary and the other kind, but the good and the other." Of course, the knowledge that Beethoven's symphonies are good does not require you to measure all others by his. But having accepted the principle, when you find good contemporary music, can you play it without risk?'

Munch answered his own question with characteristic optimism:

'This is really no problem. It is proper to play some at every concert but with moderation, lest the public be discouraged. Nothing does modern music a greater disservice than dissociating it from the rest of the repertoire.'

Munch considered the legitimacy of changing Beethoven's orchestration:

'For three hundred years the orchestra has been changing. When Beethoven used the horns in his symphonies, he did so with discretion and often with regret, we think now that he could not give them an even greater role to play. In his time the horns had certain mechanical limitations that no longer exist. You can sense these limitations when you come upon holes in the orchestration, places where Beethoven had to take the horns out — even in the middle of a phrase. The gaps are easy to fill. The benefits derived from this small license are obvious, but Beethoven did not leave us word that should the day come when horns could play chromatically he would be happy to have them do so in his works. When I take it upon myself to make modifications of this kind, I feel that I do not betray Beethoven but remain faithful to his spirit. It is a burden on my conscience nevertheless.'

Charles Munch, *I Am a Conductor*, New York, Oxford University Press, 1955, pp. 40–41 and pp. 52–53.

MODESTE MUSORGSKY (MUSSORGSKY, MUSORSKY)

For a period Musorgsky studied with fellow Russian composer Mily Balakirev. To assist his pupil with his studies, Balakirev obtained a piano that subsequently provided the opportunity for a four-hand Beethoven musical celebration. On 17 December 1857, Musorgsky wrote enthusiastically to his teacher:

> 'I am a thousand times grateful to you for the excellent choice. *La machine est perfaitement solide*... The tone is excellent the bass very good, and I am entirely satisfied with the instrument. I've stored away Beethoven's Second Symphony for the inauguration on Thursday. Thank you again. Modeste Musorgsky.'

Jay Leyda and Sergi Bertensson, *The Musorgsky Reader: A Life of Modeste Petrovich Musorgsky in Letters and Documents,* New York, W.W. Norton, 1947, pp. 3–4.

BRIAN NEWBOULD

In his prefatory remarks to *Schubert and the Symphony*, Brian Newbould discusses the relationship between the two contemporaneous symphonists [Schubert and Beethoven] as 'the younger one [who] chose to strive for mastery in the still bubbling wake of the older composer'. He continues:

> 'The symphonies of Haydn and Mozart were the natural models for Beethoven and Schubert. But Schubert could learn from another potential model — Beethoven himself, who had begun to

blaze the trail of the nineteenth-century symphony eleven years before Schubert took his first tentative steps at the age of fourteen.'

Newbould compares Schubert and Beethoven the symphonists:

'Schubert's period of symphonic activity, in the same city as Beethoven's, can be chronologically located about a dozen years after Beethoven's by comparing the dates of their first symphonies (1800, 1813) and their eighth (1812, 1822). This is a convenient simplification, of course, and one of the facts it conceals is that Schubert was in truth more prolific a symphonist than Beethoven. Beethoven's nine symphonies amount to 13,162 bars of music (bars are a crude measure but reasonably valid over so large a sample). Schubert's seven-and-a-half finished symphonies contain 10,241 bars, but whereas Beethoven's total represents the accumulated *oeuvre* of a 54-year old (to take the date of completion of No.9), Schubert's is the product of a 29-year-old. The resultant ration of productivity is Beethoven, 234 bars per annum; Schubert's 321 bars per annum. This figure excludes the 3,421 bars additionally sketched by Schubert. Schubert was, indeed, by this measure not only more prolific than Beethoven but more productive than any of the well-known nineteenth-century symphonists, including Bruckner and Dvořak.'

Brian Newbould, *Schubert and the Symphony: a New*

Perspective, Surbiton, Toccata Press, 1992, pp. 18–19, and p. 29.

The Mexican composer, music theorist, and educator Carlos Chávez made reference to Beethoven's productivity in one of his Charles Eliot Norton Lectures (1960). What he has to say relates to Professor Brian Newbould's observations:

> 'We are used to thinking of quantity in a pejorative sense — quantity as opposed to quality — but this notion needs clarification. A pilot's mastery is measured in terms of the quantity of hours flight: so too can Beethoven's mastery be measured. If he had written three symphonies instead of nine — a pure matter of quantity — he would not have reached the ever-increasing mastery of the other six symphonies. If he had not worked consistently, the supreme mastery of the Ninth would have never been achieved. As the flyer's mastery is measured in terms of quantity of flying hours, so Beethoven's can be measured in terms of composing hours.'

Carlos Chávez, *Musical Thought*, Cambridge, Harvard University Press, 1961, p. 32.

ERNEST NEWMAN

The English music critic and musicologist Ernest Newman has been described as 'the most celebrated British music critic in the first half of the 20th century' (*Grove's Dictionary of Music and Musicians*). He was Music Critic for the Sunday Times for almost forty years. In his many writings and articles, he makes occasional reference to Beethoven, including the following:

> 'Fate seems to have shaped [Beethoven] with the conscious and deliberate hand of an artist bending a mass of inchoate material to the realization of his own. It pruned him as an horticulturist prunes a tree, destroying a dozen shoots that one may bear richer fruit. [A reference to Beethoven's tireless rejection of one musical idea in search of a superior one.] We can only dimly speculate on what would have become of him had not disease laid her ugly and terrible hand on him.'

Newman continues:

> 'I fancy we have, by a sort of paradox, another evidence of the clairvoyant nature of Beethoven's genius — genius that was simply the medium through which a power beyond himself delivered oracles — in the very slowness of some of his conceptions. His sketch books show us that his themes were, as a rule, arrived at by a series of experiments: as first set down they are often incredibly commonplace: then they are altered by a touch here and a touch there, until, after a score of hackings and hewing, they take the shape in which we know them.'

Ernest Newman, *Testament of Music: Essays and Papers*, London, Putnam, 1962, p. 279. Originally published as *Beethoven* in 1917.

Writing in the *Sunday Times* (17 Feb. 1929), Newman discussed Beethoven in the context of prevailing music criticism:

> 'The only composer who has been at all adequately studied is Beethoven, the reason being that only in his case have we sufficient documents (his sketch books are particularly valuable) that throw light on the structure of his musical faculty. But even the mind of Beethoven still holds mysteries for us. Personally, I have no further use for the kind of Beethoven criticism that ranges in merely literary fashion over his music, telling us, with more-or-less eloquence, how that music affected the writer, which philosophy, of course he innocently proceeds to attribute to Beethoven himself. My contention is that three-fourths of what is written about Beethoven is "literature", not music. Misled by this or that story from his life, our writers read something into the music that is not really there. They would never have discovered, or thought they had discovered, these things had all the records of Beethoven's life perished the day he had died. They form a certain conception of him from the story of his life, and then innocently proceed to foist that conception upon his music.'

Ernest Newman, *From the World of Music: Essays from "The Sunday Times"*, London, J. Calder, 1956, pp. 24–5.

Later in his career (1950) Newman contributed to *The Atlantic Monthly*. His articles belonged to a series, the object of which formed part of the study of a great thinker or man of action in a period of crisis in his life. Newman's subject was Beethoven. Of the composer's later works he writes:

> 'On one point ... everyone is agreed — that in the works unmistakably of his third period, of which the last two piano sonatas and the last five quartets (with the Great Fugue) constitute a definite unity, a territory with a spiritual climate and a flora and fauna entirely its own, we are confronted with what seems to be virtually new Beethoven: such music had never been heard in the world before, and we may doubt whether its like will ever be heard again. All who have fallen under its spell agree that here music explores the profoundest depths of the spirits and soars to the loftiest mystical heights.'

At the close of his article, Newman reflects:

> 'Of all the mystics of art, the Beethoven of the last few years is the greatest: one has to go back to the thirteenth-century Persian poet Rumi to find his parallel, and we can only be grateful for the tremendous inner change, whatever its hidden origins may have been, that took place in him in his final years. But he was hardly more than fifty-six when he died; and inevitably we ask ourselves what his next phase might have been. Is a "next phase" conceivable? He could hardly have travelled further along the mystical road than he had done already; and we may ask ourselves whether, on the other hand, it was within the bounds of human possibility for him to have gone back once more to the outer world. Has any born

mystic ever made that backward journey after ... "he on honey dew hath fed" [*Kubla Khan*, Samuel Taylor Coleridge]?'

Ernest Newman, *Testament of Music: Essays and Papers*, London, Putnam, 1962, p. 242, and p, 251.

RICHARD OSBORNE

In the introduction to his study of Beethoven, the British author Richard Osborne makes reference to the writings of others in support of his own convictions:

'Writing about the Beethoven symphonies in a letter to Elgar in January 1919, the critic Ernest Newman remarked: "The music unfolds itself with perfect freedom; but it is so heart-searching because we *know* all the time it runs along the quickest nerves of our life, our struggles & aspirations & sufferings & exaltations." Years later, in a series of background notes prepared for the BBCs Third Programme, Hans Keller suggested that "in the entire history of the symphony, no composer traversed so much *spiritual space* [Osborne's italics] as did Beethoven between his First and Ninth Symphonies". Such judgements are, I think, worth quoting at the outset of any latter-day survey of the Beethoven symphonies because they reassert — in a sceptical and at times needlessly analytical age — the source of the music's wide and long-standing appeal. There will always be those, of course, who will be happy to echo the turn-of-the-century critic who claimed that "the Fifth Symphony is not what it was"; and after Belsen and Buchenwald we might have even greater cause to question Beethoven's transcendent optimism at the end of that particular work. And yet it endures, not because of the originality, the craggy individuality, of Beethoven's finale during which the scherzo's eerie theme reappears, very much the spectre at the feast. E. M. Forster put it well in a famous description of the Fifth Symphony in his *Howard's End*: "But the goblins were there. They could return. He had said so bravely, and that is why one can trust Beethoven when he says other things".'

Osborne continues in a more personal vein:

'By the 1820s, there is evidence of expanding numbers of orchestral players and of strategic reinforcements of the sound in some tutti passages, but throughout his career as a symphonist Beethoven is a man for whom force of argument is always preferable to force of numbers. The sense of huge and unalloyed power we often take from his music is a result, not of brute force, but of Beethoven's astonishing command of time and symphonic space. The harmonic reach of his music is phenomenal yet it is never won at the expense of a symphony's essential rootedness; it is simply that Beethoven roams on a longer and stronger lead than other men.'

Richard Osborne, *Beethoven* in: Robert Layton editor, *A Guide to the Symphony*, Oxford, Oxford University Press, 1995, pp. 80—82.

HUBERT PARRY

Sir Charles Hubert Hastings Parry was a former pillar of the English musical establishment, occupying the professorship in music at the University of Oxford and later the headship of the Royal College of Music where his pupils included Vaughn Williams, Gustav Holst, Frank Bridge and John Ireland. From his substantial musical output, Parry is perhaps best remembered today for his choral song *Jerusalem* and his setting for the coronation anthem 'I was glad when they said unto me'. In his undergraduate days at the University of Oxford, Parry was co-founder of *The Music Club* and it was at this period when Beethoven's pianos sonatas 'cast a powerful spell' upon him. His diary for 27 December 1866 records: 'Practised all morning — Beethoven mostly.'

The work he studied intently was the Piano Sonata in F, Op. 10, No. 2. When Parry succeeded Sir Charles Grove as Director of the Royal College of Music, of necessity he devoted much of his time to college administration but not to the neglect of composition and musicology. In the latter capacity he published a study of Beethoven (1886) that includes an evaluation of his works, including the piano sonatas. In this he writes: 'The imagination and the reason must both be satisfied, but above all things the imagination.'

C. Hubert H. Parry, *Beethoven* in: David Ewen, *From Bach to Stravinsky: The History of Music by its foremost Critics*, New York, Greenwood Press, 1968, pp. 105–131.

Aware that his technique in piano had many shortcomings, Parry took lessons from his music teacher Professor James Taylor — remembered today for establishing Oxford's chamber music recitals. According to Parry's diary (27 December 1866), 'Taylor soon had him tackling the Op, 57

Piano Sonata — The *Appassionata*.' Writing of Parry's student days, Anthony Boden recalls:

> 'He had discovered the music of Beethoven and begun to explore the sonatas, and with Taylor's guidance was soon scaling the peaks of the *Appassionata*, but only after the ending of the Trinity term would the full impact of Beethoven's genius take him like a flood.'

It was then that Parry heard Beethoven's Fifth Symphony for the first time, prompting him to enthuse: 'Words cannot express the hopeless gloriousness of this old ruffian! Such a whacker! So tremendously massive!'

Jeremy C. Dibble, *Hubert H. Parry: His Life and Music*, Oxford, Clarendon Press, 1992, pp. 50—1 and Anthony Boden, *The Parrys of the Golden Vale: Background to Genius*, London, Thames Publishing, 1998, 120—1.

THE PHILHARMONIC SOCIETY

The Philharmonic Society of London was founded in 1813. Its stated aims were 'to promote the performance, in the most perfect manner possible, of the best and most approved instrumental music', and 'to encourage an appreciation by the public in the art of music'. The founding Directors were enterprising insofar as they resolved to promote 'that species of music which called forth the efforts and displayed the genius of the greatest masters'. These included contemporary composers such as Beethoven, Cherubini, and Carl Maria von Weber. Beethoven's pupil Ferdinand Ries was elected a Director of the Society and was active in the promotion of his teacher's symphonies.

Perhaps Ries's most significant contribution, in this context, was the role he played in 1822 in the Philharmonic Society's commissioning of Beethoven's *Choral* Symphony.

The following is a record of the number of occasions the Philharmonic Society performed Beethoven's symphonies from the period of its inception to the close of the nineteenth century: Symphony No. 1, (19); Symphony No. 2, (39); Symphony No. 3, (52); Symphony No. 4, (54); Symphony No. 5; (77); Symphony No. 6; (69); Symphony No. 7, (65); Symphony No. 8, (47); and Symphony No. 9, (73).

The Society gave its first concert in the Argyll Rooms, Regent Street, London on Monday 8 March 1813. The impresario Johann Salomon was the Leader and Muzio Clementi directed at the piano. A Beethoven symphony was performed but was not identified in the records. At the second concert on Monday 15 March another Beethoven symphony was performed, also not identified. At the fourth concert on 3 May, the British-African violinist George Polgreen Bridgetower took part in a performance of a Beethoven string quartet; Bridgetower is remembered today as the intended dedicatee of the *Kreutzer* Violin Sonata. In this opening season of concerts, J. B. Cramer and Charles Neate — an associate of Beethoven and a founder member of the Society — performed at the pianoforte. On 21 June, another Beethoven symphony was performed. Authorities consider these unidentified entries in the Society's records refer to one or other of the composer's Symphonies 1–4.

The *Eroica* Symphony made its first appearance at a concert of the Philharmonic Society on Monday 28 February 1814. However, this was not the first English performance. The Symphony had been premiered on 26 March 1807 at the Covent Garden Theatre — and, remarkably, overseas in Boston on 17 April 1810 by the newly founded Boston Philharmonic Society. The 1815 London Philharmonic music season was significant insofar as the Society purchased from Beethoven, for the considerable sum of £200, the performing rights for three Overtures. These were, incorporating Beethoven's sub-titles: *King Stephen* – 'To Hungary's first benefactor'; *The Ruins of Athens*, and *Overture in C – The Consecration of the House* – 'Written for the opening of the Josephstädter Theater'.

The Society performed the Fifth Symphony for the first time in England on Monday 29 April 1816. The notes accompanying the programme enthused: 'It is scarcely necessary to enlarge upon this important production, for it is so well known, and likely to become even more so as the Symphony in which Beethoven revealed himself and his own rugged strength, having discarded the formalism which restricted his earlier works.' Regarding its construction, the Society's music correspondent noted: 'It is orchestrally interesting as first employing trombones and double-bassoon in a symphony.' The pianist-composer Cipriani Potter received a mention in the Society's notices for 1816. He was acquainted with Beethoven who once remarked to Ries: 'Potter visited me several times; he seems to be a good man and has a talent for composition.'

The 1817 music season was noteworthy for the Society's first performance of the Seventh Symphony on 26 May, with the *Pastoral* Symphony having been presented earlier at a concert on 24 March. Of related interest is that the Directors of the Society, through the offices of Ferdinand Ries, invited Beethoven to compose and direct two symphonies for the sum of three-hundred guineas. His response was to request four-hundred and fifty guineas that the Directors declined; the outcome was Beethoven never visited England – as he had intended. The 1821 season was noteworthy for the performance of no fewer than six Beethoven symphonies, namely, Nos. 1, 2, 4, 5, 6, and 7.

In the second decade of the Society's programmes, it became usual for six or seven Beethoven symphonies to be performed each year. 1825 was memorable in the history of the Society for realizing, on 21 March, the first performance in England of the *Choral* Symphony. It was described as a 'New Grand Characteristic Sinfonia with Vocal Finale ... (composed expressly for the Society).' On the Title Page of the MS copy of the score, that Beethoven sent to the Society, he inscribed the words 'Geschrieben für die Philharmonische Gesellschaft, London'.

In 1827, the Directors were informed by Ignaz Moscheles that Beethoven was ill and was in need of financial assistance. The Society undertook to give a concert for his benefit and to send him the sum of one hundred pounds. On receiving the gift Beethoven later expressed his thanks: 'May Heaven soon restore me to health, and I will then prove to the generous English how much I appreciate the sympathy which they have shown for my condition.' He undertook to write a new symphony for the Society — that he described as 'already sketched in outline'; his death on 26 March precluded its completion.

1929 was a significant year in the annals of the Society since it heralded the appearance of Felix Mendelsohn in its concert programmes for the first time. He would in due course exert a considerable influence on English musical taste and become a favourite of Queen Victoria and Prince Albert. On 6 February 1830, the Society's premises in the Argyll Rooms were destroyed by fire but the contents of the Library were saved — including precious Beethoven memorabilia. The Society relocated to the King's Theatre but the accommodation proved unsatisfactory. A later move in 1833, to premises in Hanover Square, offered better facilities and was the home of the Society until 1869.

The 1844 season was memorable insofar as the *thirteen-*

year old boy-violinist Joseph Joachim performed Beethoven's Violin Concerto from memory — then something of an innovation — also supplying his own cadenzas. Beethoven's Overture *Leonora* No.1 was performed for the first time disposing the Society's music correspondent to enthuse 'its large proportions and grand style almost gave it the importance of a symphony'.

During his stay in London, in 1856, Richard Wagner conducted the Philharmonic Society Orchestra and complimented it for being a '*strong esprit de corps*' possessed of 'superb tone' and 'the finest instruments'. He complained though of the length of the Society's programmes that typically did not finish until after 11.00 p.m.! In 1873 the eminent interpreter of Beethoven, Hans von Bülow made his debut on 28 April with a performance of Beethoven's *Emperor* Piano Concerto and would earn fame later in his capacity as an orchestral conductor — for both of which endeavours he received the Philharmonic Society's coveted Beethoven Gold Medal.

In 1885, the Society appointed Sir Arthur Sullivan as its resident conductor, a position he held for the next three years; his failing health deprived him of remaining in office for longer than he wished. The Philharmonic Society's Centenary Year of 1912–13 provided the opportunity for a reflection of its achievements. The contributor to the records enthused:

> 'If the reader has the patience to wade through the pages of this long history, a history unique in the annals of musical institutions of this kind ... he will see what efforts were made to keep pace with all the changes in musical progress; what numbers of works, since acknowledged everywhere as masterpieces, first made their appeal to

English audiences at the Philharmonic Concerts, and what crowds of singers and players, since acclaimed great, first sang and played there.'

Beethoven's connection with the Society was honoured with a performance of the *Choral* Symphony.

Cyril Ehrlich, *First Philharmonic: A History of the Royal Philharmonic Society*, Oxford, Clarendon Press, 1995.

SERGEI RACHMANINOFF

During his years of study at the Moscow Conservatory, the youthful Rachmaninoff enjoyed displaying his formidable pianistic gifts by performing piano reductions of the Beethoven symphonies. One of his teachers at this period was Nicolay Zverev. His pedagogical regimen included exploring the musical symphonic literature at four-and eight-hands piano, combined with lessons on theoretical subjects — a combination conceived to assist his students mount the *Gradus ad Parnassum*. Such piano playing appears to have extended to social occasions, as we learn from an account of this period in the young pianist-composer's life:

> 'At Zverev's request a competent pianist, Madame Belopolskaya, came once a week to the house to play with them [Rachmaninoff and fellow students] all the classical and new symphonic works in two-piano arrangements for eight hands — an experience that the boys enjoyed. They played through many Haydn, Mozart, and Beethoven symphonies as well as the overtures of Mozart, Beethoven and Mendelssohn. Their favourites were the Beethoven symphonies, and in these they achieved such virtuosity that Zverev

> suggested to the Conservatory's Examining Committee that it should hear them play eight hands.'

Rachmaninoff's grandfather Arkadi Alexandrovich was himself an accomplished pianist and enjoyed playing symphonic duet arrangements with his grandson. From one such occasion we learn:

> 'That same evening the grandfather and grandson once again took their place side by side at the piano and astounded the crowd of guests who had arrived with the majestic sounds of the *andante* from Beethoven's Fifth Symphony.'

Grandfather Alexandrovich was so pleased with his grandson's prowess at the keyboard that he prophesised 'the laurels of a future Steibelt' for him. Daniel Steibelt, who settled in Saint Petersburg, was a contemporary of Beethoven's and had once taken part in a pianistic contest with him – to his disadvantage. Alexandrovich's prediction proved well-founded as Rachmaninoff fulfilled himself as composer, virtuoso pianist, and conductor of the late Romantic period.

Victor I. Seroff, *Rachmaninoff*, London, Cassell & Company, 1951, p. 10 and pp. 20–21.

SIMON RATTLE

When Helena Matheopoulos interviewed Sir Simon Rattle in the 1980s, he shared his thoughts with her about the challenges of conducting Beethoven's symphonies:

> 'Technique is easy, although it obviously takes time to learn. But once you are faced with the real musical problems, it becomes harder and harder.

For instance, I find myself less and less capable of conducting the Beethoven symphonies as I grow older, and they weren't so hot to begin with! But now, as I grow more and more aware of all the different layers, of their unfathomable depth, I am left gasping at the sheer amount that I have to take in.

'It's in those works, the real works, the works of the Classical tradition — Bach, Mozart, Beethoven, Brahms — that the mirror is at its clearest. These works are almost conductor-proof and mirror your weaknesses very strongly. There is always an enormous choice of possibilities in Beethoven and Brahms. In Beethoven, the most difficult thing is those rhythms — you ask any string player and he will tell you that the hardest task in Beethoven is to make the rhythm work, because there is a little life-pulse underneath it, and you have to be *in* it. You can't get it right just like that, by skimming the surface, from outside.

'Doing things for the first time, when you are virgin to them, can never be satisfactory *ever*, but especially not when it comes to the great Classical and Romantic literature. Because everything important only happens in maturing performances. Who wants to listen to a twenty-five-year-old's Beethoven?'

Helena Matheopoulos, *Maestro: Encounters with Conductors of Today*, London, Hutchinson, 1982, p. 525 and p. 512.

MAURICE RAVEL

As a student at the Paris Conservatoire, Maurice Ravel showed great promise as a pianist, winning the Conservatoire's first prize in piano. He soon realised, however, that his true vocation was in composition and that his idol was Mozart. His writings bear testimony to this, generally, though, to the detriment of Beethoven:

> 'For me it is Mozart. Mozart is perfection: he is Grecian, whereas Beethoven is Roman. The Greek is great, the Roman is colossal. I prefer the great. There is nothing as sublime as the third act of Mozart's *Idomeneo.*'

Ravel was given to proclaiming:

> 'My music is unequivocally French. Anything except Wagnerian. And just as little like that of Richard Strauss or the modern Viennese. That's why I hope it may please the Viennese, since it's so different from their own! Frenchmen, in turn, enjoy Viennese music. I personally feel particularly close to *Mozart.* My admirers exaggerate when they compare me with him. Beethoven strikes me as a classical Roman, Mozart as a classical Hellene. I myself feel closer to the open, sunny Hellenes.'

Ravel's biographer Arbie Orenstein reminds us that the music of Beethoven and Wagner was performed regularly in France during the composer's lifetime. He suggests that Ravel's response to this was complex and somewhat contradictory. Ravel considered Wagner and Beethoven to be "philosophical" composers and his response to them 'combined elements of respect, awe, and jealousy, coupled with a marked rejection of their influence on French composers'.

In March 1911, Ravel gave an interview in which he expressed his opinions on contemporary French music; Ravel was by then considered to be one of France's leading composers. His views were subsequently published under an anonymous hand. Passages of his text more-or-less reiterate the thoughts quoted above:

> 'Beethoven can be considered a decadent Mozart from the point of view that he brought to its height and to its close the life which Mozart's music expresses, just as the Byzantine Art can be called a decadent Greek art because it brought to a close the Greek Art. Mozart, in music, like Raphael in painting, possessed a certain perfection which was marked, nevertheless, by a certain dryness. Beethoven, who was less perfect, was also less dry.'

Twenty years later, Ravel gave a further interview a synopsis of which was subsequently published. By then Ravel was at the height of his fame and had just completed work on his piano concerto for the left hand — written for the pianist Paul Wittgenstein who had been seriously injured in the Great War. Time had clearly not weakened its hold on Ravel's musical opinions. With his own piano concerto in mind, he remarked:

> 'One should not make pretentious assumptions about this concerto which it cannot satisfy. What Mozart created for the enjoyment of the ear is perfect, in my opinion, and even Saint-Saëns

achieved this goal, although on a much lower level. Beethoven, however, overacts, dramatizes, and glorifies himself, thereby failing to achieve his goal.'

Arbie Orenstein editor, *A Ravel Reader: Correspondence, Articles, Interviews*, New York: Columbia University Press, 1990, p. 378, p. 409, p. 433, p. 473, and p. 488.

A further anecdote bears testimony to Ravel's antipathy towards Beethoven. The fashionable portrait painter Jacques-Emile Blanche was a good amateur pianist who enjoyed playing piano duets. He initially persuaded Ravel to be his duet partner, but the planned enterprise foundered as Blanch explains:

> 'We agreed ... that [Ravel] would come twice a week to my studio to play duets. These meetings were planned, postponed and finally abandoned, for the curious reason that Ravel asked me to exclude Beethoven, Wagner, Schumann and any other "romantics" from our repertoire and indicated we should stick to the numerous works of Mozart. I was not very happy with the idea and roused in him a mixture of disdain and pity.'

Roger Nichols, *Ravel Remembered*, London: Faber and Faber, 1987, pp. 15–16.

JOHANN FRIEDRICH REICHARDT

In 1809 the composer, writer, and music critic Johann Friedrich Reichardt arrived in Vienna and has left a description of Europe's capital of music with which Beethoven would have been familiar:

> 'For everyone, surely, who can enjoy the good things of life, especially for the artist, perhaps quite especially for the musical artist, Vienna is the richest, happiest, and most agreeable residence in Europe. Vienna has everything that marks a great capital in a quite unusually high degree. It has a great, wealthy, cultivated, art-loving, hospitable, well-mannered, elegant nobility; it has a wealthy sociable, hospitable middle-class and bourgeoisie ... All classes love amusement and good living, and things are so arranged that all classes may find well-provided, and may enjoy in, all convenience and security every amusement that modern society knows and loves.'

Reichardt makes reference to Vienna's theatres:

> 'In the city and in the suburbs, five theatres of the most varied sort give performances all the year round. At two court theatres in the city itself, one sees everything outstanding in the way of grand and comic opera, comedy, and tragedy that Germany produces – and, in some measure, Italy and France as well; the same is true of the great suburban Theater an der Wien, where, in addition, the great romantic operas are given with unusual magnificence. At all three theatres, great pantomimic ballets, heroic and comic, are often given also. The two smaller theatres in the Leopoldstadt and Josphstadt play popular dramas of the jolliest kind. On days when no play is scheduled,

> all these theatres give great concert performances of the most ancient and modern music for church and concert hall. Aside from this, all winter long there are frequent public concerts, by local and visiting musicians, and excellent quartet and amateur concerts by subscription.'

As a consequence of his deafness, Beethoven had withdrawn from the Vienna Reichardt describes, as is evident from a later part of his account:

> 'I have called on the excellent Beethoven, having found him out at last. People here take so little interest in him that no one was able to tell me his address and it really cost me considerable trouble to locate him. I found him finally in a great deserted and lonely house. At first, he looked almost as gloomy as his surroundings, but presently he grew more cheerful ... His is a powerful nature, outwardly Cyclops-like, but in reality, sincere, friendly, and kind.'

On 25 December 1808, Reichardt attended the concert of Beethoven's music that has passed into musical history. The venue was the Theater an der Wien, it was winter and the theatre's heating system was out of order. The first part of the concert included: the *Pastoral* Symphony, Op. 68; the concert aria *Ah! perfido*, Op. 65; the *Gloria* from the Mass in C, Op. 86; and the Piano Concerto No. 4, Op, 58. The second part included: the C minor Symphony No. 5, Op. 67; the *Sanctus* from the Mass in C, Op. 86; a Beethoven pianoforte extemporisation — later written out as the Fantasia in G, Op. 77; and to close the Choral *Fantasy*, Op. 80. Of this musical feast Reichardt wrote:

'There was sat, in the most bitter cold, from half past six until half past ten, and confirmed for ourselves the maxim that one may easily have too much of a good thing, still more of a powerful one ... The singers and orchestra were made up of very heterogeneous elements, and it had not even been possible to arrange one full rehearsal of all the pieces on the programme, every one of which was filled with the greatest difficulties.'

Reichardt gave his impressions of the two symphonies:

'To begin, a pastoral symphony, or recollections of country life. First movement: "Agreeable impressions awakening in man on arrival in the country". Second movement: "Joyous amusements of the country folk". Fourth movement: "Thunder and storm". Fifth movement: "Benevolent feelings after the storm, joined with thanks to the Divinity". Each number was a very long and fully worked-out movement, filled with the liveliest images and the most brilliant ideas and figures; as a result, this one pastoral symphony alone lasted longer than an entire concert is allowed to last with us. Ninth piece [C-minor Symphony]: A great symphony, very elaborate and too long.'

Oliver Strunk, *Source Readings in Music History, 4: The Classic Era*, London, Faber and Faber 1981, pp. 154–55 and pp. 163–64.

HANS RICHTER

As with Maurice Ravel (see above) the Austro-Hungarian conductor Hans Richter clearly preferred the music of Mozart to that of Beethoven. He revealed this, albeit in a somewhat backhanded and amusing manner, when he was once asked to name the composer who, in his opinion 'was the greatest of them all'. Without hesitation he responded, 'Beethoven, undoubtedly'. The questioner expressed surprise at a reply so positive: 'Undoubtedly, Herr Doktor? But I thought you might have considered Mozart.' 'Oh', replied Richter, 'I didn't understand that you were bringing Mozart into the argument; I thought you were referring to the rest!'

As told in: Neville Cardus, *Talking of Music* (brief description), London: Collins, 1957, p. 69.

The American music critic Louis Engel heard Richter conduct a concert in Birmingham, UK on 19 May 1884. This disposed him to describe his command of the orchestra, and respect for Beethoven, in the following terms:

> 'A more magnificent orchestral performance than that of Wagner's *Siegfried's Journey* ... at the fifth Richter concert I never heard, and it once more shows what Napoleon said to be perfectly correct: "A general can make the best army out of any soldiers." What was the orchestra when Richter took it in hand? What is it today? Equal to any demand, but mind you well, under him only. Hans Richter's conducting is so perpetual, he does not merely superintend the time, he plays the piece with his head, with his left hand, the way he bends forward more-or-less, the immense, the perplexing knowledge of each entry which his

memory never misses; the great respect and unbounded confidence of all the performers, who, with the music before them, trust to him without the music, render him a phenomenon at the conductor's desk ... Beethoven's symphonies many people know by heart. But then see the perpetual *rapport* of Richter with his orchestra; his eye is everywhere and it could not be everywhere on paper too. He can carry or steady his hand just as he pleases and what a force of will that requires, only those who understand the affair thoroughly are able to say.'

Christopher Fifield, *True Artist and True Friend: A Biography of Hans Richter*, Oxford, Clarendon Press, 1993, pp. 211–12.

FERDINAND RIES

The German composer and pianist Ferdinand Ries was a pupil of Beethoven from 1801 to 1804, the period when he made his public debut as a concert pianist playing the composer's C minor Piano Concerto, Op. 37 — with his own cadenza. In 1838, Ries published a collection of reminiscences of Beethoven, co-written with the composer's life-long friend, the distinguished physician Franz Wegeler. These appeared under the original title *Biographische Notizen über Ludwig van Beethoven* and are considered to be an important and reliable source of information. They are available in English as: Franz Wegeler and Ferdinand Ries, *Remembering Beethoven: The Biographical Notes of Franz Wegeler and Ferdinand Ries*, London: Andre Deutsch, 1988. Perhaps the most repeated anecdote told about Ries relates to the occasion of the first rehearsal of the *Eroica*

Symphony. During this, Ries mistakenly believed the horn player had come in too early and said so to Beethoven — incurring his displeasure. It is also from Ferdinand Ries that we learn of the deterioration of Beethoven's hearing. When out walking in the countryside one day, Ries heard a shepherd playing his pipe — possibly a shawm. It was apparent to him that Beethoven was quite unaware of its sound and so he discreetly made out that he too could not hear anything. Recalling his days in Vienna, when he received piano instruction from Beethoven, Ries states:

> 'If I missed something in a passage, or played wrongly the notes and leaps he often wanted me to bring out strongly, he rarely said anything; but when I fell short as regards expression, crescendos, etc., or the character of the piece, he got exasperated because he said, the first was an accident, but the other was a lack of judgement, feeling or attentiveness. The former happened to him quite often too, even when he played in public.'

Wegeler-Ries, 1988, p. 94 et seq. See also: Ferdinand Ries cited in Alfred Brendel, *Alfred Brendel on Music: Collected essays*, Chicago, Illinois, A Cappella Books, 2001, p. 48.

Sometime late in 1806, Ries felt an obligation to acknowledge the debt he felt he owed to his teacher and duly wrote to Beethoven informing him of his intention to dedicate to him his own two Piano Sonatas Op. 1:

> 'I shall take this occasion to express my gratitude to you publicly; the sincere and the more ardent for the intimacy that you have allowed me, and for the friendship with which you have honoured

me. The memory of pleasant hours spent near you will never fade from my heart, and if my efforts are rewarded by any success, it is to your counsel that I shall be indebted.'

Derived from Theodore Albrecht, editor and translator, *Letters to Beethoven and other Correspondence*, Lincoln, New England, University of Nebraska Press, 1996, Vol. 1, Letter No. 121, pp. 189–90.

Ries played an important role in establishing Beethoven's orchestral works in England, particularly in connection with the Philharmonic Society of London — later the Royal Philharmonic Society. He took up residence in London in April 1813 and was elected a Director of the Society two years later. He was active in the promotion of his own compositions that included eight piano concertos, eight symphonies and 26 string quartets. These works reveal a style, not unsurprisingly, owning a debt to his teacher. Beethoven was once disposed to remark: 'Ries is the crow who follows my plough!' Ries maintained contact with Beethoven to the end and was instrumental (no pun intended) in bringing before the English public several of Beethoven's piano sonatas and other compositions. Perhaps Ries's most significant contribution in this context was the role he played, in 1822, in the Philharmonic Society's commissioning of Beethoven's *Choral* Symphony. Ries once said of his master:

'Without wanting to hurt the feeling of any composers living or dead, I must reaffirm my belief that no one else showed such a wealth and variety of ideas, nor such originality, as Beethoven did in his works.'

Franz Wegeler and Ferdinand Ries, *Remembering Beethoven: The Biographical Notes of Franz Wegeler and Ferdinand Ries*, London, Andre Deutsch, 1988, p. 113.

NIKOLAY RIMSKY-KORSAKOV

Nikolay Rimsky-Korsakov recalls his early studies and encounters with Beethoven. Writing of the summer of 1859—60, when he was age sixteen, he attended the Imperial Theatre and Grand Theatre at St. Petersburg where he heard Beethoven's *Pastoral* Symphony and Second Symphony, prompting him to play four-hand arrangements with his friend P. N. Novikova. 'In this way', he recalls, 'I developed a passion for symphonic music'. He enthuses:

> 'I took delight in Beethoven's Second Symphony, especially the end of its *Larghetto* (with flute), when I heard it at the University; the *Pastoral* Symphony enraptured me.'

Carl van Vechten, editor, Nikolay, Rimsky-Korsakov: *My Musical Life*, London, Martin Secker & Warburg Ltd., 1942, pp. 13—14.

ROMAIN ROLLAND

Notwithstanding his celebrity as a philosopher, dramatist, novelist, essayist, art historian and Nobel Laureate (prize for literature in 1915) Romain Rolland wrote extensively on music and was appointed to the first chair of music history at the Sorbonne in 1903. His passion for music — he was an accomplished pianist — found expression in several studies of Beethoven who for Rolland was 'the universal musician above all the others'. His writings about the composer and his works include: *Beethoven and Handel* (1917); *Goethe and Beethoven* (1930); and *Beethoven the Creator* (1937). His *Essays on Music* (1915) also includes a study of Beethoven in his thirtieth year. Typical of Rolland's word-imagery is:

> 'The music of Beethoven is the daughter of the same forces of imperious Nature that had just sought an outlet in the man of Rousseau's *Confessions*. Each of them is the flowering of a new season.'

Rolland is here making reference to the autobiographical work, *The Confessions of his fellow countryman Jean-Jacques Rousseau — published in 1782*. Cited in: David Ewen, *Romain Rolland's Essays on Music*. New York: Dover, Publications, 1959, p. 262.

In Rolland's study of the composer *Beethoven the Creator*, written shortly after the horrors of the Great War, Rolland had to confront not only its divisions and the new musical horizons that were dawning but also the challenge to the supremacy Beethoven and his music had held through the nineteenth century. We recall, for example, the stir that Igor Stravinsky's *The Rite of Spring* (*Le Sacre du printemps*) had created at its first performance in 1913; the police had to be summoned to quell the ensuing riot amongst the audience. Unshaken in his admiration for Beethoven, Rolland wrote:

> 'After a life of combat, Beethoven, from his tomb, continued the fight for half a century in the kingdom of the spirit, where, high above our heads, our gods wage their eternal warfare ... We know that everything must pass — we and you, all that we believe in, all that we deny. The suns themselves are mortal. Yet the beams they gave

out thousands of years ago still bear their message through the night; and thousands of years later we see by the light of these extinct suns.'

Rolland continues:

'I will refresh my eyes, a last time, at the sun of Beethoven. I will say what he was for us — for the peoples of a century. What that is I know now better today than I did when, as a young man, I poured out my song to him. For at that time his light, unique as it was, penetrated us, Today, the shock of the meeting of two epochs of humanity — of which the war [the Great War] has been not so much as the separation as the landmark at the crossroads, where so many runners have come to grief — has had the advantage, that it has forced us to come to full conscience of ourselves, of what we are, of what we love ... I love, therefore I am. And I am which I love.'

Rolland movingly concludes:

'We had become so accustomed to living in our Beethoven, to sharing with him from our infancy the bed of his dreams, that we had failed to perceive to what degree the tissue of his dreams was exceptional. Today, when we see a new generation detaching itself from this music that was the voice of our inner world, we perceive that the world was only one of the continents of the spirit. It is nonetheless beautiful for that, nonetheless dear to us; nay, it is dearer still. For only now do our eyes clearly perceive its delimiting lines, the definite contours of the imperial figure that was our *Ecce homo*. Each great epoch of humanity has its own, its Son of God, its human archetype, whose glance, whose gestures, and whose word are the common possession of millions of the living. The whole being of a Beethoven — his sensibility, his conception of the world, the form of his intelligence and of his will, the laws of his construction, his ideology, as well as the substance of his body and his temperament — everything is representative of a certain European epoch. Not that that epoch modelled itself on him! If we resemble him, it is because he and we are made of the same flesh. He is not the shepherd driving his flock before him; he is the bull marching at the head of the herd.'

Romain Rolland, *Beethoven the Creator*, Garden City, New York, Garden City, 1937, derived from the Introduction pp.19–21.

STEPHEN RUMPH

The American musicologist and academic Stephan Rumph identifies Beethoven in the context of politics:

'Beethoven was a political composer. Like few other musicians in the Western canon, he stubbornly dedicated his art to the problems of human freedom, justice, progress, and community. Beethoven found his voice with a cantata memorializing the enlightened reforms of Joseph II, and he crowned his public career in Vienna with the Ninth Symphony's hymn to universal brotherhood. No intervening work drew more labour or revisions from him than *Fidelio* (née *Leonora*), the first political opera to remain in the permanent repertory ... The political note in Beethoven's music echoes the cataclysmic times in which he lived ... While Napoleon was gathering laurels in Italy and Egypt, Beethoven was conquering the salons and halls of Vienna, undertaking a deliberate campaign to annex all current musical genres.'

Rumph reflects on the origins of the estimations of Beethoven the romantic:

'For two centuries the evolving image of Beethoven has taken shape in the passionate echolalia of critical prose, no less than in the concert hall, the classroom, or the sculptor's studio. E. T. A. Hoffmann stands at the head of this line as its first great genius. His reviews, literary rhapsodies, translated the heroic style into Romantic terms, bequeathing the nineteenth century a compelling portrait of Beethoven as mystic visionary and conquistador of the spirit of the world. Hoffmann's was, of course, a distorted image; like any interesting critic, he brought strong prejudices to his material. In particular, his allegiance to the transcendent metaphysical realm blinded him to the enlightened aspects of the heroic style. Yet even this distortion proves illuminating. As we watch Hoffmann tailoring the Fifth Symphony to his specifications, we see a fascinating preview of the way Beethoven himself would rework his style as he fell under the Romantic spell.'

Rumph provides the reader with detailed commentaries on the writings of the following Beethoven authorities: Walter Riezler, Heinrich Schenker, Joseph Kerman, Charles Rosen, Maynard Solomon, and Theodor Adorno. He concludes by turning to the works of Beethoven's final period:

> 'Studying late Beethoven ... means coming to terms with the modern legacy. Our understanding of this repertory is twisted up at the roots with the axioms of a bygone age. It seems telling that the most vital new studies of Beethoven have turned to the *Eroica* and the heroic works, resuscitating modes of interpretations the earlier critics disdained. The late works await the same kind of research by critics who will not shy away from paradoxical and contingent aspects of this music. Mythology will have to give way to history, the cultic Beethoven to a more human figure. Then perhaps these fascinating works can tumble from their pedestal of absolute music into the melee of real human discourse.'

Stephen C. Rumph, *Beethoven after Napoleon: Political Romanticism in the Late Works*, Berkeley; London, University of California Press, 2004, pp. 1–2 and p. 222.

CAMILLE SAINT-SAËNS

The French composer, organist, conductor and pianist Camille Saint-Saëns was one of the most remarkable musical child prodigies in history. At the age of five he performed to private audiences and when age ten made his public debut in Paris at the Salle Pleyel. His programme included Mozart's Piano Concerto in B flat, K450 and Beethoven's Third Piano Concerto. Most remarkably, Saint-Saëns played from memory. At the close of the concert he offered to give as an encore any of the Beethoven Piano sonatas! At over the age of sixty he repeated the offer at a concert to the musical elect of Madrid. Towards the end of his long life (86), Saint-Saëns maintained diligent morning practice by performing scales and arpeggios — relieving what he considered to be the tedium by simultaneously reading the morning newspaper that he placed on the piano's music rack!

Adapted, in part, from James Harding, *Saint-Saëns and his Circle*, London, Chapman & Hall, 1965, p. 18.

The Polish-American virtuoso pianist, composer, and teacher Leopold Godowsky was one of the most highly regarded virtuosi of his time. Something of his performance-style can still be appreciated today since he was a pioneer in the art of the piano-roll recording. Godowsky was on close terms with Saint-Saëns and played for him regularly. In turn, Saint-Saëns also performed — almost anything from his prodigious repertoire that included not only piano music but keyboard reductions of Beethoven symphonies, overtures, and chamber music. Even Liszt held Saint-Saëns in high regard, as a recollection from Godowsky's memoirs confirms:

> 'Saint-Saëns could talk most delightfully about music, and many an interesting séance have I had with him in his Paris apartment, climbing four flights of stairs to reach it. Liszt gave him a photo

of himself inscribed "Au Beethoven français", which seems not altogether appropriate; but then Liszt had a tendency to exaggerate when he praised.'

Jeremy Nicholas, *Godowsky: The Pianists' Pianist; A Biography of Leopold Godowsky*, Hexham, Appian Publications & Recordings, 1989, p. 23.

MALCOLM SARGENT

The English conductor Sir Malcolm Sargent was known to many through his association with the internationally famous London music festival known as the Henry Wood Promenade Concerts. Being such an 'establishment' figure somewhat eclipsed his astonishing youthful musical attainments: A.R.C.O (age 16), B, Mus. (age 18), and D. Mus. (age 24). On the concert platform, his debonair appearance earned for him the nickname Flash Harry! *The Times* obituary said of Sargent: '[He] was of all British conductors in his day the most widely esteemed by the lay public ... a fluent, attractive pianist, a brilliant score-reader, a skilful and effective arranger and orchestrator ... as a conductor his stick technique was regarded by many as the most accomplished and reliable in the world.'

A musicologist friend once asked: 'Sargent, do you think that probably we can do better justice to Beethoven today than could have been done in his lifetime?' Sargent replied:

> 'Well, I'm sure the playing of even amateur orchestras today is much better than orchestral playing was in his day. The wind instruments must be much more in tune now ... I should imagine woodwind

intonation was extremely faulty. Our ears being more trained, we should find it disturbing today. Two extraordinary things ... Trumpets were able to play only certain notes. Same with the horns. In Beethoven you will come across successions of four chords. Three of these chords will include trumpet and horn notes because those notes could be played on those instruments. But the fourth chord notes were missing because those instruments couldn't play them; they weren't available. From Wagner's and Weingartner's onwards, everybody has added notes we feel sure Beethoven would have put in had they been available then.'

Charles Reid, *Malcolm Sargent: A Biography*, London, Hamilton, 1968, pp. 320–21. (See also: Robert Simpson)

ANTON FELIX SCHINDLER

Anton Felix Schindler was an associate of Beethoven and acted as his secretary, assistant and spokesman in the latter period of the composer's life. He was by training a lawyer, although his vocation was in music; he was appointed leader of the violins in the Josephstadt-theatre. Schindler's claim to Beethoven fame rest in his early study *Biographie von Ludwig van Beethoven* that was published in Münster in 1840 and again in 1860 in two volumes with extensive revisions and additions. English-speaking readers know this work as *Beethoven as I Knew Him*, edited with commentaries and emendations by Donald W. MacArdle in a translation by Constance S. Jolly, London, Faber and Faber, 1966.

Throughout the nineteenth century, and well into the twentieth, Schindler's *Life* had a considerable influence on the perception of Beethoven and Beethoven biography. Unfortunately for posterity, it is believed Schindler destroyed some of the composer's Conversation Books — although not as many as the 400 that has been previously suggested. In addition, his reliability as a credible chronicler of Beethoven has been called into question. It is now considered he may have inserted spurious entries into a number of the composer's surviving Conversation Books and that his accounts of alleged conversations with the composer, notably about the nature of his music, may have been exaggerated or even invented. See: Peter Stadlen, *Schindler's Beethoven Forgeries, The Musical Times*, Vol. 118, No. 1613, July 1977, pp. 549–552.

The Beethoven scholar Barry Cooper discusses the problem of Schindler's alleged falsifications in his *The Beethoven Compendium: A guide to Beethoven's Life and Music,* London: Thames and Hudson, 1991. Others have attempted to exonerate Schindler, at least in part, from some of the more extreme accusations charged against him. See, for example, Theodore Albrecht, translator and editor, *Letters to Beethoven and other Correspondence*, Lincoln, New England: University of Nebraska Press, 3 vols., 1996. Notwithstanding Schindler's indiscretions, as Donald W. MacArdle, the editor to the 1960 edition of Schindler's text remarks: 'The Beethoven who steps forth from these pages is indeed the Beethoven of the *Eroica* and last Quartets ... [and] will give much that cannot be found elsewhere.' (Anton Schindler, 1966, p. 19.

To the foregoing remarks may be added the further observation that Schindler makes reference to all Beethoven's symphonies, including details of their first performance and their critical reception.

JOHANN ALOYS SCHLOSSER

Johann Aloys Schlosser is significant to Beethoven musicology for being the composer's first biographer. His *Biographie* was written in the year of Beethoven's death (1827) when it may also have been published — although the Title Page gives 1828. The work's full title reads, in translation: *Ludwig van Beethoven, A Biography, together with Assessments of his Works; published with the aim of erecting a monument to his teacher, Joseph Haydn.* Of interest here is the regard in which Beethoven's teacher Haydn was held, and the value already being attached to Beethoven's correspondence as a source of information about him.

In his introduction to Richard G. Pauly's modern-day translation of Schlosser's text (1996), Beethoven authority Barry Cooper remarks how little of Schlosser himself is known. He was a partner in a publishing firm in Prague and may have become aware of the young Beethoven when he performed there in 1796 and 1798. Cooper remarks how Schlosser's brief *Biography* 'satisfied an immediate need' about a composer whose funeral cortege was witnessed by several thousand spectators — an honour normally reserved for emperors. Although subsequent research has corrected errors and flaws in Schlosser's text, it is still held in high regard for providing a contemporary view of Beethoven and what was believed about him in Vienna and Prague in 1827. For example, Schlosser opens his account:

> 'Beethoven's death has been noted with more grief, in Germany and throughout Europe, than anyone else's for a long time. His art reached a level far above what others will attain. We therefore grieve not only because of our loss but also

because there is no one able to take his place. Beethoven was not only a great artist but also a great human being.'

Later Schlosser pays tribute to Beethoven the virtuoso:

'People marvelled at the facility with which he executed difficult passages. His playing may not always have been delicate, and at times may have lacked clarity, but it was extremely brilliant. He excelled particularly at free improvisation. Here it was really quite extraordinary with what ease, and yet soundness in the succession of ideas, he would improvise on any theme given to him.'

Of the composer's working method, Schlosser observes:

'Beethoven liked to compose outdoors: there he could best find ideas. When they came he treasured them as the inspirations of the moment but did not concern himself with developing them immediately. While still outdoors, however, he would commit them to paper and would continue them on his way home ... Only the working out of these ideas in score was carried out in his room ...'.

Schlosser remarks on the public acclaim Beethoven received at the period of the Congress of Vienna, when his so-called *Battle Symphony* was performed — *Wellington's Victory, or, The Battle of Vitoria* (*Wellingtons Sieg oder die Schlacht bei Vittoria*):

'This work, now faded from the concert repertoire, together with the Seventh Symphony, elevated Beethoven's public reputation to a greater extent than he had ever previously enjoyed — or would ever again experience.'

Writing about Beethoven's Op. 1, the set of three piano trios that were first performed in 1795, Schlosser remarks:

'They display extraordinary deep sentiments, which have not yet found their true outlet. This has caused some to complain of disorder in these and some subsequent compositions, and not without reason. In these and some later works Beethoven reveals his heart, in a great surge of feeling. With this music we enter a new world, which he was to conquer triumphantly.'

Of Beethoven's first venture into writing for the medium of the string quartet, namely the six quartets Op. 18, Schlosser comments prophetically: '[These] are works of a maturing artist, so that not surprisingly they contain many hints of the later period.'

Remarking on Beethoven's later compositions he adds:

'The works of the last period are shaped by inner necessity. Everything follows organically from what preceded, so that everything accidental, uncertain, or extraneous is excluded. Thus, each composition is meaningful, coherent, and a unified whole. In the same way, the fruit emerges from the blossom, which itself owes its life to the living tree: that is the mysterious law of life, in nature and in art.'

Of Beethoven himself, Schlosser concluded: 'He was an artist, but also a man — a human being in the word's most perfect sense.'

Johann Schlosser, *Beethoven: The First Biography, 1827*; translated by Richard G. Pauly and edited by Barry Cooper, Portland, Oregon, Amadeus Press, 1996, pp. 9–34, pp. 70–80, p. 116, p. 138 and p. 141.

PERCY ALFRED SCHOLES

The English musician and writer Percy Alfred Scholes is widely known for being editor of *The Oxford Companion to Music*. In another of his many writings about music, he expressed his disapproval of the editing (truncating) of Beethoven's symphonies:

> 'I am always pleased to see in *The Musical Times* the often-repeated suggestion of its editor that the best movements of Beethoven's symphonies should sometimes receive separate performance as independent concert items. I would not have the symphonies as wholes drop out of the repertory, any more than I would have the official shortened versions of Wagner's music dramas, which I have recently proposed, entirely supersede the full-length performances. But of the thirty-six symphony movements, some have much greater value than others, and I see little sense (in the cyclic works of this period, where the movements have no organic connection) in the equal frequency of the performance of the inferior and superior movements. This, of course, applies equally to the string quartets.'

Percy Alfred Scholes, *Crotchets: A few short Musical Notes*, London, John Lane, 1924, p. 181.

HAROLD C. SCHONBERG

The American music critic Harold C. Schonberg draws on contemporary accounts of
Beethoven's mannerism and gesticulations when conducting the orchestra:

> 'There is considerable evidence that Beethoven ... cut the air with both hands. But from all accounts, Beethoven seems to have been one of the worst conductors in history. Stubborn, defiant, he refused to bow to his deafness and often insisted on conducting first performances of his works. The result was invariably a tragi-comedy, though with much more tragedy than comedy: a handicapped giant in awesome throes, fighting to do that which could not be done. On top of that, he never could get along with people even before his deafness, and was constantly antagonising every orchestra with which he was associated. Yet he stubbornly kept on. Even when the orchestra refused to play under his direction, as happened in 1808 at the premiere of his Fifth and Sixth Symphonies.' (See Friedrich Reichardt)
>
> 'Nevertheless, Beethoven as a conductor is a fascinating figure: a solid, even prophetic, link between divided leadership and the tyrannical, choreographic, virtuoso conductors who were to follow not much later. During his lifetime, the baton came into use but there is no real evidence Beethoven ever used one. And as late as the

premiere of the Ninth Symphony, in 1824, several conductors shared the performance. But Beethoven insisted on making his presence felt, as he always had done.

'Every musician spoke of Beethoven's conducting motions with amazement and disbelief. Ludwig [Louis] Spohr, the important violinist-composer-conductor [see below], played in the orchestra when Beethoven conducted the premiere of his *Wellington's Victory* and Seventh Symphony in 1814. Spohr discussed the composer's "extraordinary" motions. "Whenever a sforzando occurred he tore apart his arms, which he had previously crossed on his breast, with great vehemence. At a soft passage he bent himself down, and the softer he wished to have it, the lower he bent." The reverse happened, says Spohr, as the music grew louder; and "to increase the forte yet more he would sometimes, also, join in with a shout to the orchestra without being aware of it".'

Harold C. Schonberg, *The Great Conductors*, Simon & Schuster, 1967, pp. 57–60. See also the entry under Ignaz von Seyfried.

ROBERT SCHUMANN

The Romantic composer Robert Schumann was recognised in his lifetime for being an authoritative and influential music critic. In an essay from 1829 – just two years after Beethoven's death – he published a survey of the state of symphonic writing in Germany. He opens his account:

'When the German speaks of symphonies, he

means Beethoven; the two names are for him one and indivisible — his joy, his pride. As Italy has its Naples, France its Revolution, England its Navy, etc., so the Germans have their Beethoven symphonies. The German forgets in his Beethoven that he has no school of painting; with Beethoven he imagines that he has reversed the fortunes of the battles he lost to Napoleon; he even dares to place him on the same level with Shakespeare.'

Schumann reflected on Beethoven's symphonic legacy and the challenge his writing posed to those composers following after him — he did not start work on his own *Spring* Symphony until 1832–33:

'Since the compositions of this master have become an integral part of us, since some of his symphonic works have become popular, one could suppose that they had left deep traces behind them and begotten works of the same nature during the period following that of Beethoven. But this is not so. We find imitations — and, oddly enough, principally of his earlier symphonies, as if each one needed a certain time to be understood and copied; we find many too-close imitations, but very, very seldom, with few exceptions, any true maintenance or mastery of this sublime form in which, bound in a spiritual union, continually changing ideas succeed one another. The great number of recent symphonies drop into the overture style, especially in their first movements; the slow movements are there because slow movements are required; the scherzos have nothing about them save the name; the last movements completely forget what the former ones contained.'

That Schumann was alert to musical developments is evident in his early recognition of the pioneering innovations of Hector Berlioz, as exemplified in his *Symphonie Fantastique*:

'Berlioz was announced to us as a phenomenon. Little more than nothing is known about him in Germany; what is known of him by hearsay seems to have so alarmed the Germans that considerable time must pass before he will be accepted here. Assuredly, he has not laboured in vain; no phenomenon comes singly. This will be shown in the near future.'

In 1838, ten years after Franz Schubert's death, Schuman visited Vienna where he was shown the manuscript of Schubert's so-called *Great* C major Symphony, No.9. He returned to Leipzig with a copy that was used by Felix Mendelssohn in the work's first public performance, in March 1839. Schumann's admiration for the spacious grandeur the C major Symphony prompted him to coin the expression *heavenly length* — used also in descriptions of the composer's last piano sonatas. Schumann recognised that Schubert was a worthy successor of Beethoven, describing him as 'the imaginative painter, whose pencil was steeped now in moonbeams, now in the full glow of the sun'.

Robert Schumann, *Music and Musicians: Essays and Criticisms*, London, William Reeves, 1877, p. 61 and p. 165.

ROGER SESSIONS

The American composer, educator and writer on music Roger Sessions was blessed with a long life. He died just short of his 100th birthday and during his lifetime became an icon of American contemporary music. His writings also reveal the scholarly musicological erudition that he formed in his formative years at both Harvard and Yale Universities. In 1937 he wrote an essay titled *The New Musical Horizon* in which he commented on the musical ideals of the current generation.

He first reflected on the pioneering transformations of the musical horizon as shaped, initially, by such composers as Strauss, Debussy, Ravel, Mahler and Scriabin and, nearer to his own time, those of Schoenberg, Stravinsky, Hindemith, Berg and Bartok. Sessions, the modernist, took issue with the manner in which music critics wrote about music. By way of illustration, he chastises them for sentimentally alluding to 'the tears that fall on the hero's grave' at the close of the Funeral March in the *Eroica* Symphony and to the evocation of 'frosty northern landscapes' in the music of Sibelius. Such writings he dismissed as 'a mess of verbiage'. Some of Sessions' vexation is apparent in the following passage that he devotes to Beethoven:

> 'Beethoven's ideas for or against the Revolution were precisely what he shared with millions of his contemporaries. What is great in his work is what he alone was capable of achieving — his music, the sounds, the musical shapes which he conjured up, of which the profoundly human significance transcends his specific preoccupations only somewhat less completely than it does the fundamentally meaningless pomposities of M. Rolland [French writer on music — see above] or Mr. Ernest Newman [English music critic — see above]. The

content lies — as Beethoven himself pointed out — in the tones, the lines, accents and contrast, and not in the thousand experiences which, fused together in a single gesture, take composite shape as a musical impulse or idea. It can never be too clearly stated that if musical expression is something unique and untranslatable it does not therefore follow that it is without human significance.'

Sessions maintained: 'Every Beethoven symphony is unique; every Beethoven sonata is unique.' He took issue with a commonly expressed generalisation: 'Do we not all sometimes hear the statement that Beethoven's odd-numbered symphonies are superior to his even ones (as if the *Eroica* and the *Pastoral* were in any real sense comparable except on the most primitive quantitative level)?' Sessions made a passing reference to Schubert:

'[Schubert] died when he was thirty-one years old, which is quite young after all. He'd have been Beethoven's equal, if he'd lived. In a certain way he was, almost.'

Sessions conceded tempo markings in Beethoven's symphonies 'are always a big problem'. He elaborated:

'I think there's a very easy explanation for that. The metronome was invented when Beethoven was in mid-career. It was something quite new and he used it. I think his tempi are too fast. That's the problem.'

He offered the following explanation:

> 'You read music very fast, in about a third of the time it takes to play it or hear it. You read it and you aren't expending a tenth of the energy you're expending when you're listening. The physical impacts of the sounds — they've got to begin and end. When you look at the music, that's not there.'

Andrea Olmstead, *Conversations with Roger Sessions*, Boston, Northeastern University Press, 1987, p. 68, pp. 72–73, and pp. 196–97.

Sessions held the Charles Eliot Norton Professorship for 1968–69 at the University of Harvard. In one of his lectures he discussed the hard-one freedom of the artist, remarking:

> '[In] the case of artists, everyone who has mastered his art feels fully free, simply by virtue of his mastery of his materials, and in strict proportion to his mastery of them. He can do with them anything he chooses.'

Sessions then called to mind his reading about Beethoven:

> 'I remember a book that appeared many years ago, entitled *Beethoven, the Man who Freed Music* [Robert Haven Schauffler, 1929]. The question arose in my mind: "What did he free it from?" From Mozart, perhaps, or Haydn? I do not mean to labour the point; simply to draw attention to the fact that the artist — barring forces quite external to his art — *is* free, in proportion to his mastery of his materials, in every way that has any importance to him. He is free, that is, to make the music which is his own, that which he wants to make. Once he

has clearly envisaged what this is, he must follow its demands. In so doing, he is enjoying the most intense musical experience that is open to him, and presumably he finds fulfilment in it.'

Roger Sessions, *Questions about Music*, Cambridge, Massachusetts: Harvard University Press, 1970, pp. 92–3.

IGNAZ VON SEYFRIED

Ignaz von Seyfried studied piano with Mozart and had lessons in counterpoint with Johann Albrechtsberger — one of Beethoven's teachers. As a conductor, he was familiar with Beethoven's orchestral scores and directed performances of his Second, Fifth, and Sixth Symphonies, the Third and Fourth Piano Concertos, and a rehearsal performance of *Fidelio*. Of Beethoven's style and manner of conducting he writes:

'As a conductor Beethoven could by no means be considered as a model. Woe to the orchestra which did not exert all attention to prevent being led astray by his baton, for he had no feeling but for the poetry of his composition, and was incessantly in motion, through the numerous gesticulations by which he was accustomed to betray its effect upon him. [Von Seyfried's reference here to Beethoven's baton is somewhat perplexing since other of his contemporaries remark how he conducted by 'cutting the air with his hands'] Thus, he frequently gave the down beat in any forcible passage, although it occurred on the false accent of the bar. He was accustomed to mark the whole progress of a diminuendo passage, indicating the most gradual decrease possible, and literally almost slipping down under his desk when the *pianissimo* was reached. So, when the sound was required to increase, he himself rose up as from below, and with the commencement of the *tutti*, he raised himself on tiptoe almost to a giant height, and with both his arms spread out he appeared as if about to take his flight into the clouds; every nerve and muscle seamed in action.'

Von Seyfried remarks on the worsening of Beethoven's hearing and his increased difficulty in being able to direct an orchestra:

'As his deafness increased, however, most woeful discords frequently occurred, the conductor beating in one time and the band accompanying in another. *Piano* passages were most easily conveyed to him, of the *fortes* he heard absolutely nothing; all was confusion. In such cases, he would only be guided by his eye; he watched the bowing of the stringed instruments, guessed at the musical phrase which was being executed and soon set himself right. But he did not possess the mechanical gift of conducting, which indeed is seldom to be met with in any composer of real genius and fiery imagination.'

According to von Seyfried's account, Beethoven could be quite tolerant — at least on occasions — with wayward orchestral players:

'Our composer by no means belonged to that class of musicians who think no orchestra in the world can be deserving of thanks. Sometimes, indeed, he was too indulgent in not requiring faulty passages at rehearsal to be repeated, "It will go right next time" he would say. With regard to expression, he was strict in enforcing the most delicate nuances, the most nicely-proportioned distribution of light and shade, as well as an effective *tempo rubato*, and discussed these points without restraint or want of temper with anybody. When, however, he perceived the musicians entered into his ideas, and went together with increasing unanimity, wrought upon by the magic of his artistic creations, his countenance lighted up in a moment, every feature was animated by satisfaction, a happy smile played about his mouth, and a thundering *bravi tutti* rewarded the excited artists; it was the finest moment of triumphant self-consciousness, before which the shout of applause from a large and eager audience faded into insignificance.'

Ignaz von Seyfried, *Louis van Beethoven's Studies in Thorough-Bass, Counterpoint and the Art of Scientific Composition*, Leipzig, New-York, Schuberth and Company, 1853, pp. 12—14.

GEORGE BERNARD SHAW

George Bernard Shaw's fame as a playwright and polemicist has eclipsed his reputation for being a discerning music critic. Eugene Gates, of the Faculty of the Royal Conservatory of Music, Toronto, writes:

'[Shaw] was ... the most brilliant British music

critic to emerge in the late-nineteenth century. His vision of the ideal critic was not a passive reporter of musical events, but rather a vital and initiating force within the music community.'

(*Journal of Aesthetic Education*, Vol. 35, No. 3, 2001)

Shaw was committed to the principle of making music criticism both intelligible and entertaining. To this end he invented the persona of *Corno di Bassetto* (in music, the basset horn) to serve as his spokesperson. Shaw's collected writings on music by Dan Laurence fill no fewer than three sturdy volumes.

In Beethoven's Centenary Year, Shaw contributed an article in the *Radio Times* of 18 March 1927. In this he states:

> 'Now what Beethoven did, and what made some of his greatest contemporaries give him up as a madman with lucid intervals of clowning and bad taste, was that he used music altogether as a means of expressing moods, and completely threw over pattern-designing as an end in itself. It is true that he used the old patterns all his life with dogged conservatism ... but he imposed on them such an overwhelming charge of human energy and passion, including that highest passion which accompanies thought, and reduces the passion of the physical appetites to mere animalism, that he not only played Old Harry with their symmetry but often made it impossible to notice that there was any pattern at all beneath the storm of emotion.'

In another article, Shaw cites Beethoven, alongside Mozart, as pioneering a new epoch in music — taking the time of

Wagner's birth as a benchmark:

> 'When Wagner was born in 1813, music had newly become the most astonishing, the most fascinating, the most miraculous art in the world. Mozart's *Don Giovanni* had made all musical Europe conscious of the enchantments of the modern orchestra and of the perfect adaptability of music to the subtlest needs of the dramatist. Beethoven had shown how those inarticulate mood-poems, which surge through men who have, like himself, no exceptional command of words, can be written down in music as symphonies. Not that Mozart and Beethoven invented these applications of their art; but they were the first whose works made it clear that the dramatic and subjective powers of sound were enthralling enough to stand by themselves quite apart from the decorative musical structures of which they had hitherto been a mere feature'.

Dan H. Laurence, editor, *Shaw's Music: The Complete Musical Criticism in Three Volumes*, London, Max Reinhardt, the Bodley Head, 1981, Vol. 3, p. 528 and pp. 746–7.

In the *Saturday Review* of 14 November 1896, Shaw wrote an article concerning the recently published *Beethoven and his Nine Symphonies* by George Grove (London and New York, Novello, Ewer & Co.). Of Beethoven, Shaw remarks:

> 'Beethoven was the first man who used music with absolute integrity as the expression of his own emotional life. Others had shown how it could be done – had done it themselves as a curiosity of their art in rare, self-indulgent, *unprofessional* moments

— but Beethoven made this, and nothing else, his business. Stupendous as the resultant difference was between his music and any other ever heard in the world before his time, the distinction is not clearly apprehended to this day, because there was nothing new in the musical expression of emotion: every progression in Bach is sanctified by emotion; and Mozart's subtlety, delicacy, and exquisite tender touch and noble feeling were the despair of all the musical world. But Bach's theme was not himself, but his religion; and Mozart was always the dramatist and story-teller, making the men and women of his imagination speak, and dramatizing even the instruments in his orchestra, so that you know their very sex the moment their voices reach you. Haydn really came nearer to Beethoven, for he is neither the praiser of God nor the dramatist, but, always within the limits of good manners and of his primary function as a purveyor of formal decorative music, a man of moods. This is how he created the symphony and put it ready-made into Beethoven's hand. The revolutionary giant at once seized it, and, throwing supernatural religion, conventional good manners, dramatic fiction, and all external standards and objects into the lumber room, took his own humanity as the material of his music, and expressed it all without compromise, from his roughest jocularity to his holiest aspiration after that purely human reign of intense life.'

George Bernard Shaw, cited in: Percy M. Young, *George Grove, 1820–1900: A Biography*, London, Macmillan, 1980, Appendix B.

Towards the end of his long life, Shaw reflected on the social changes bearing on the accessibility of Beethoven's music and of his own discovery of the composer's symphonies:

> 'Radio music has changed the world in England. When I made my living as a critic of concerts in London, fifty years ago, I heard a Beethoven symphony once in a blue moon in the old St. James's Hall or the Crystal Palace as part of a musical set of perhaps a thousand people who could afford to pay and were quite accidentally musical in their tastes. My own familiarity with the orchestral classics was gained by playing arrangements of them as piano duets with my sister. As to the Ninth Symphony, performances of it were extraordinary events separated by years.
>
> 'Today, with radio sets as common as kitchen clocks, the *Eroica*, the Seventh, the Ninth, are as familiar to Tom, Dick, and Harriet as Nancy Lee used to be when it was played incessantly on every street piano.'

Originally published in *The Musical Times*, January 1947 and reproduced in: Bernard Shaw, *How to Become a Musical Critic*, London, R. Hart Davis, 1960, p. 321.

JEAN SIBELIUS

Santeri Levas was the personal secretary to Jean Sibelius for twenty years and had many opportunities to observe him at work and to record his personal beliefs. He relates the occasion when Sibelius visited Berlin's State Library, then known as the Royal Library, where he consulted the original score of the Ninth Symphony. Lavas recalls Sibelius remarking:

'It was full of cancellations and alterations' prompting him to add: 'At first glance one could see that it was a matter of life and death, a contest with God!' Levas adds:

> 'His eyes shone as he spoke of Beethoven's gigantic struggle. He was obviously thinking of his own life's work and found satisfaction in the knowledge that he alone did not have to bear the labour-pains of a great musician.'

One day Sibelius gave Levas a copy of F. S. Noli's *Beethoven and the French Revolution* [New York, 1947]. This had apparently given the Finnish composer great pleasure and a sense of personal identification with Beethoven. Levas writes:

> 'I had the impression that it gave him some satisfaction to compare himself with that musical giant, the account of whose personal characteristics afforded Sibelius a greater understanding.'

Sibelius, the great tone poet, clearly felt a sense of identification with Beethoven when he remarked: 'One could have said of Beethoven — if one absolutely insists — that he wrote programmatic music. For his point of departure was always a specific idea.'

Reflecting on this remark, Levas comments:

> 'In relation to musical history one could perhaps say that Beethoven was the first Romantic and Sibelius the last. But neither was solely a Romantic; both stood on the watershed between two great musical epochs.'

According to Levas, Sibelius most admired in Beethoven

'the inflexible determination to create, and the moral depth of his works'. He recalls Sibelius once expostulated:

> 'It is inconceivable that they don't appreciate Beethoven's greatness ... Beethoven's works have many failings, especially from the period of his deafness. But they live.'

Levas closed his writing about Sibelius with an *epilogue* that he titles *The Place of Sibelius in the History of Music*. In this he philosophises:

> 'When a small nation of four million people produces an artist whose acclaim is truly universal, it is easy to understand that in his own country his importance is unreasonably exaggerated. This is particularly the case when admirers have only a slender idea of musical history.
>
> 'It is, then, much more significant that foreign critics and scholars, important ones among them, have often compared Sibelius with Beethoven. Cecil Grey [English composer and music critic] has gone so far as to say that Sibelius is the only true symphonic composer since Beethoven, and not only the greatest figure of his own generation but one of the greatest in the history of music. One finds similar enthusiastic assertions in what other English and Americans have written.'

Santeri Levas, *Sibelius: A Personal Portrait*, London, J. M. Dent, 1972, pp. 60–63, and p. 131. In support of Levas's closing remarks, see Wilhelm Furtwängler and Constant Lambert.

ROBERT SIMPSON

Robert Simpson was an English composer and was well known as a long-serving BBC producer and broadcaster. His primary interests were the orchestral music of Beethoven, Bruckner, Nielsen, and Sibelius. For the present writer's generation, he will be remembered for introducing a series of broadcasts on the BBC's Third Programme titled *The Innocent Ear*. As he remarked on the evening of 2 November 1959, when the series commenced:

> 'The names of the composers in this programme will be announced only *after* [italics added] the performance of their works. The listener is invited to preserve his "innocence" by not trying to guess the composer, and by approaching the music with fresh judgement freed from prejudice.'

In some measure it may be argued the youthful Franz Liszt anticipated Simpson's ploy by almost 150 years. By his own account, when a young man, he would on occasions play one of his own compositions, or one by his teacher Carl Czerny, only to have the audience respond indifferently with polite applause. At a later performance he would play the same piece and declare it to be by Beethoven — at which the audience responded with fulsome applause and bravos!

Simpson introduced his study of the Beethoven symphonies with the following words:

> 'Some years ago Sir Malcolm Sargent set me thinking by casually remarking that if Beethoven's symphonies had been unnumbered and undated it might have been difficult to find out their correct order; the first two, he thought, would fall obviously into place and most people would

guess that the Ninth was the last. The others, he said, might be in almost any order. I agreed with him, up to a point, when he confirmed that he really meant that with Beethoven what is usually called "style" is not chronologically easily traceable by the usual methods, that it is in fact nothing but a function of his purpose, changing radically and rapidly as his purpose changes. In other words, the development of Beethoven's deeper purpose, artistic and human (the same thing with him), is itself organic throughout his life. Superficial talk about "style" gets us nowhere. Beethoven's identity is shown by the supreme authority with which he directs and redirects his powers, rather than by personal fingerprints which, though they markedly exist, fade before the force of his humanity. In no other composer is this so strikingly evident. Most great composers, having once settled an individual way of expression, maintain it more materially than Beethoven, either within the scope of a definable period manner, like Bach, Handel, Haydn, or Mozart, or as a set of notably personal devices that remain fixed for life — Berlioz, Schumann, Chopin, Wagner, Liszt, Brahms, Bruckner, and many others. It is no doubt significant that Beethoven's historical position lies between these two opposite groups, but his achievement would not have been possible without unprecedented human power.'

In support of Simpson's contention, bearing on Beethoven's individuality of expression, we may cite here Beethoven's own self-imposed injunction 'I never repeat myself'.

*

Simpson considered Beethoven's first three symphonies:

'The first three symphonies show a continuous process of physical expansion that could go no further without threatening a looser kind of romantic expression alien to Beethoven's nature. Having used the full power of his muscles in the *Eroica*, his instinct was to concentrate his new strength in denser discharges. The C minor Symphony would be the obvious vehicle; he would demonstrate that he was now able not only to span vast territories but also to pack confined spaces with unheard-of concentration.'

Robert Simpson, *Beethoven Symphonies*, London, British Broadcasting Corporation, 1970, pp. 7–8. See also: Karl Heinrich Stockhausen.

NICOLAS SLONIMSKY

For many of his 101 years, the Russian-born American Nicolas Slonimsky enjoyed a career as a composer, pianist, and author. He was also a conductor — for example he directed the 1933 summer concert season at the Hollywood Bowl. Notwithstanding the personal pleasure he derived from conducting — he once described it as 'the nearest approximation to music in motion' — he had some challenging things to say about conducting and conductors:

'To the average musical critic every orchestra conductor is a sceptred personification of the heterogeneous body of string-bowers, reed-blowers, and drum-beaters. To the average orchestra musician every conductor is a fake and a nuisance.'

Turning to the conductor in history, Slonimsky avows:

'The evolution of the conductor as a separate species is edifying to follow. Some two hundred years ago his presence was really an insinuation against the musicians' competence ... Early conductors were pathetically unaware of their latent possibilities, and knew nothing about the psychology of hero worship. They beat time with a scroll of paper, or else, sitting at the cembalo, contributed to the musicians' efforts. There was much nodding, rhythmical wheezing, much swaying of the body and foot stamping. The maintenance of the proper tempo seemed to be all their concern. The conductor was then held in no greater esteem than a competent coach is now. He was often the composer of the music, and his office as conductor was not yet clearly differentiated. He was also a drillmaster and a disciplinarian.'

Slonimsky directs his narrative to the age of Beethoven and the vexed problem of the interpretation of his suggested orchestral tempi:

'[The] nineteenth century of music was still young. Beethoven, with his sombre moods, sudden digressions and programmatic designs afforded a great field for experiments. For a hundred years the Big Controversy has raged, producing schools, creating schisms, establishing reputation.'

Originally published in *The Overture*, September 1931 and reproduced in: Electra Slonimsky Yourke editor, *Nicolas Slonimsky: Writings on Music*, New York, N.Y., London, Routledge, 2003–05, pp. 282–83.

ALEXANDER BRENT SMITH

To celebrate Beethoven's Death Centenary, *The Musical Times* issued a *Special Issue* in April 1927 devoted entirely to Beethoven and his music. Alexander Brent Smith was an organist, Director of Music at Lancing College — where Peter Pears was one of his pupils — and, in the role of musicologist, was an occasional contributor to *The Musical Times*. In his essay, 'His Infinite Variety' he has the following to say of Beethoven's powers of invention:

'For those who are influenced and impressed by statistics, it may be interesting to remember a few hard facts about the extent and variety of Beethoven's invention, such as, that each of his many piano sonatas, violin sonatas, cello sonatas, trios, quartets, concertos, and symphonies have, on average, four movements, and that each of the four movements has at least two subjects, that is, he wrote at least seven-hundred tunes each so full of character, and so independent of each other, that many musicians could easily locate each separate tune. And not only had Beethoven the power of creating individual melodies, but he had the additional power of creating subjects in pairs, or of providing each first subject with a suitable yet well-contrasted second subject. In this power of creating themes (subjects distinguished by heroic and manly qualities) and melodies (subjects distinguished by beauty grace and tenderness) other composers have not been so wholly successful as Beethoven.'

Smith placed Beethoven alongside Shakespeare:

'It is this infinite variety ... of invention and expression which has brought Beethoven such a widespread popularity, a popularity which he did not seek but which has been thrust upon him. From his early manhood, in the year 1796, men began to discover that his music was not written for the few but that it had that Shakespearian quality which transmutes the simplest emotions of common man into something splendid and serene.'

Smith concluded his estimation of Beethoven with a paean of praise:

'The great popularity of Beethoven and the reverence felt by the multitude for his personality and music are due, in a great measure, to his capacity for expressing with the utmost intensity and vividness the common emotional experiences of mankind. And because he addresses himself to the common experience of men, there seems to be no reason why the infinite variety of his appeal should not secure for him a greater popularity during the next hundred, two hundred, or even two thousand years.'

Alexander Brent Smith, *His Infinite Variety* in: *The Musical Times*, Vol. VIII, No. 2, April, 1927, pp. 202–5.

MAYNARD SOLOMON

The American musicologist Maynard Solomon has an established reputation for being an authority on Beethoven. His work is characterised by a scholarly presentation of the available evidence and the construction of plausible hypotheses. In his Introduction to *Beethoven*, he writes:

> 'The proper study of Beethoven is based on contemporary documents — on letters, diaries, conversation books, court and parish records, autograph manuscripts and sketches, music publications reviews, concert programmes, and similar materials. These may be utilized by a biographer with relative confidence as to their authenticity, although even they ... must be approached with some caution. A second major source of material bearing significantly on Beethoven's life and personality consists of the reminiscences of his contemporaries. Here, more serious questions arise as to the validity of anecdotes, reports, and memoirs that were written down long after the fact by a wide variety of individuals.'

Commenting on Beethoven's first ventures into the realm of symphonic composition, Solomon elucidates:

> 'Sketches from around the mid-1790s, for an unwritten Symphony in C major survive, but it was not until 1800 that Beethoven ventured to complete his First Symphony, Op. 21. It was then five years after Haydn's final effort in the form, and twelve years after Mozart's *Jupiter* Symphony. In the interim, numerous symphonies by such composers as [Paul] Wransky, [Joseph] Eybler, and

[Antonio] Cartellieri — none of which made any lasting impression — had found their way into concert programmes in Vienna. In light of the risks involved as well as the newness of the task, it was natural that Beethoven's First Symphony, scored for the standard orchestra of Haydn and Mozart, with clarinets added, should lean heavily on the traditional inheritance. Perhaps this is why it became one of the most popular of Beethoven's symphonies during his lifetime. Tovey, who calls it Beethoven's "fitting farewell to the eighteenth century", stresses that it "shows a characteristic caution in handling sonata form for the first time with full orchestra". However, contemporary critics did not by any means regard it as a timid or imitative work. The reviewer in the *Allgemeine musikalische Zeitung* spoke of its "considerable art, novelty, and ... wealth of ideas", thinking, no doubt, of the audacious "off-key" opening; the striking use of the timpani in the *Andante*, which foreshadows similar solos in Beethoven's later works; and the teasing scale-passages which initiates the closing *Allegro*.'

Maynard Solomon, *Beethoven*, New York, Schirmer, 1977, pp. xi–xii and p. 103.

Elsewhere, Solomon writes:

'It is common knowledge that Beethoven was a founder of the Romantic movement in music and that his works influenced most of the romantic composers and were models against which nineteenth-century romanticism measures its achievements and failures ... [During] his own lifetime,

> Beethoven was widely regarded as a radical modernist, whose modernism was seen sharply to distinguished him from the classical standards established, in the main, by Mozart and Haydn. Of course, they too had their share of hostile notices before they were elevated to canonical status; but the classicizing critiques of Beethoven were too intense and pervasive to be regarded as merely the usual, provisional resistance to modifications of cultural traditions. His contemporaries — including many of his advocates — saw him as subverting classical principles and procedures, as radical iconoclastic, and eccentric. They did not regard him as an eighteenth-century composer.'

Maynard Solomon, *Beethoven: Beyond Classicism*, in: Robert Winter, and Robert Martin, editors *The Beethoven Quartet Companion*, Berkeley, University of California Press, 1994, p. 59 and pp. 70–1.

OSCAR GEORGE SONNECK

Oscar George Sonneck was an American musicologist who received his higher education in Germany at the universities of Heidelberg and Munich. A few years before his death, in 1928, he conceived the idea of compiling a series of recollections from the writings of those who knew Beethoven or who had visited him at some time or other in his lifetime. The impending Beethoven Death Centenary of 1927 also provided Sonneck with the added incentive to create such a biographical survey. This was duly published in 1926 by G. Schirmer, Inc. under the title *Beethoven: Impressions by his Contemporaries*. In his Preface, Sonneck pays tribute to the pioneering efforts of Anton Schindler

(*Beethoven Biography*, 1845), Ludwig Nohl (*Beethoven as Depicted by his Contemporaries*, 1877) and Alexander Wheelock Thayer (*Life of Beethoven,* 1921).

Initially, Sonneck studied the works of the hundred and fifty or so recorded reminiscences of contemporaries who visited Beethoven and from these he selected thirty-six for final inclusion in his *Impressions.* Sonneck did not attempt to significantly edit or adapt his chosen writings, but he does provide each of his selected texts with prefatory contextual words that include occasional corrections of fact relating to such matters as the chronology of particular events. Introducing Sonneck's work, the publishers wrote:

> 'Beethoven, being what he was could not very well appear in a different light to every visitor — and yet, how amazingly at times the impressions of him contradict one another.'

One of the virtues of Sonneck's study is that he presents his selected recollections in a chronological sequence. Thereby, the reader is offered an unfolding picture of Beethoven from his earliest years to his death. The following is a list of those from whom, or to whom, Sonneck makes reference together with the date to which the text in question relates:

Gottfried Fischer (1770 onwards), Christian Gottlob Neefe (1783), Mozart (1787), Carl Ludwig Junker (1791), Johann Schenk (1792), Franz Gerhard Wegeler (1794–96), Frau von Bernhard (1796–1800), Johan Wenzel Tomaschek (1798), Carl Czerny (c. 1800), Countesses Giulietta and Therese Brunswick (c. 1801), Ignaz von Seyfried (1799–1806), Ferdinand Ries (1801–05), Josef August Röckel (1806), Baron de Trémont — Joseph-Girod de Vienney (1809), Bettina von Arnim and Johann von Wolfgang Goethe (1810–12), Ignaz Moscheles (1810–14), Louis Spohr (1812–

16), Johann Wenzel Tomashek (1814), Cipriani Potter (1818), Anton Schindler (1819), Maurice Schlesinger (1819), Sir John Russell (1821), Gioachino Rossini (1822), Friedrich Johann Rochlitz (1822), Wilhelmine Schröder-Devrient (1822), Louis Schlösser (1822–23), Edward Schulz (1823), Franz Grillparzer (1823), Carl Maria von Weber (1823), Franz Liszt (1823), Anton Schindler (1814–27), Ludwig Rellstab (1825), Sir George Smart (1825), Gerhard von Breuning (1825–27) and Friedrich Wieck (1824–26?).

Oscar George Theodore Sonneck, *Beethoven: Impressions of Contemporaries*, London, Oxford University Press, 1927, republished by Dover Publications, Inc., New York, 1967.

LOUIS SPOHR

In his study of Beethoven's contemporaries, Oscar Sonneck (see above) describes the German composer, conductor and violinist Louis Spohr in the following terms:

> 'Louis Spohr frankly confessed his inability to comprehend Beethoven's music of the last period. He attributed Beethoven's "aesthetic aberrations" to his deafness, but apparently it never occurred to Spohr that his own ears might have been at fault. Considered in his time either the equal of Paganini as a violinist or second only to him, Louis Spohr laid much greater stress on his importance and fame as a composer. As such, his popularity generations ago certainly was not inferior to that of Beethoven.'

Sonneck was doubtless relying, at least in part, on the views that Spohr himself expressed about Beethoven and his music in his *Autobiography* (1865). As remarked by Sonneck, Spohr found Beethoven's later compositions too modern-sounding and attributed their stridency to the composer's hearing misfortune:

> 'But as from this time, owing to his constantly increasing deafness, he could no longer hear any music that, of necessity, must have had a prejudicial influence upon his fancy. His constant endeavour to be original and to open new paths, could no longer, as formerly, be preserved from error by the guidance of the ear. Was it then to be wondered at that his works became more and more eccentric, unconnected, and incomprehensible? It is true there are people who imagine they can understand them, and in their pleasure at that, rank them far above his earlier masterpieces. But I am not of the number, and freely confess that I have never been able to relish the last works of Beethoven. Yes, I must even reckon the much admired *Ninth Symphony* among them, the three first themes of which, in spite of some solitary flashes of genius, are to me worse than all the eight previous Symphonies, the fourth theme of which is in my opinion so monstrous and tasteless, and in its grasp of *Schiller's Ode* so trivial, that I cannot even now understand how a genius like Beethoven could have written it. I find in it another proof of what I already remarked in Vienna, that Beethoven was wanting in aesthetical feeling and in a sense of the beautiful.'

Louis Spohr, *Louis Spohr's Autobiography*, London, Longman, Green, Longman, Roberts, & Green, 1865, pp.

188–9. See also: Henry Pleasants, editor and translator, *The Musical Journeys of Louis Spohr*, Norman, University of Oklahoma Press, 1961.

CHARLES VILLIERS STANFORD

The Irish composer, organist, teacher, and conductor Sir Charles Villiers Stanford is now remembered for his choral works for the church in the Anglican tradition, but he could count amongst his pupils such progressives as Gustav Holst and Ralph Vaughan Williams. Another of his pupils was Margaret Nosek and, according to her account, Stanford was a hard taskmaster:

> 'As a teacher, Stanford was severe and old fashioned in his methods ... Stanford's method of teaching the secrets of Mozart's and Beethoven's Symphonies and their orchestration was to make the pupil initiate himself in them by writing them for orchestra as he thought Mozart and Beethoven would have written them, with only a four-hands piano version of the symphony to guide him. After finishing several pages, the pupil had to take the original full score and copy it above his own version in red ink. This was a most painful and laborious business, yet I doubt if it is possible to gain an intimate knowledge of Mozart and Beethoven by any other means. Having had to do all this for a long time, and having survived, I am very grateful for the lessons I learned from it, although I am just as grateful that I do not have to do it again!'

Paul Rodmell, *Charles Villiers Stanford*, Aldershot, Ashgate, 2002, p. 355.

*

Just before his death, in 1924, Stanford published his reflections on music that include *A Sketch of the Symphony*. At the time of Stanford's writing, Beethoven's symphonies would have been unfamiliar to many audiences. Perhaps with this in mind his observations have something of the propaedeutic about them:

> 'Beethoven was wise and quick to appreciate what his predecessors had done, but he saw far greater possibilities in the symphonic form than they did. His symphonies were nine in number (the "Nine Muses" they have been happily termed), and the very first of them was as advanced and in its way as impressive and new, as those of others who preceded it. Nos. 1 and 2 were mainly Mozartian and Haydnesque in shape and in style (he conformed rather to Haydn than to Mozart), but in No. 3 he became a prophet. The *Eroica* was openly written as a tribute to the genius of Napoleon – a name which he tore off the Title Page when the Frenchman assumed the Imperial purple – and most of it afterwards became rather a memory than a commemoration of a "Great Man". The Symphony is as great as the man it illustrated, and greater than that man's principles. It is difficult not to look upon the slow movement, with its enigmatic title, as other than a lament over fallen greatness in Beethoven's estimation. He was always an ardent Republican. In the finale of this work, he first introduced the variation form into the symphony, which was afterwards used and developed in the Ninth Symphony.
>
> 'The Fourth (called by a great musician

[unnamed] the "Cinderella" of the Symphonies) was delightful in itself but evidently a "réculer pour mieux sauter" ['to put off the inevitable'], and the great C minor, No. 5, squeezed it, a little unfairly, out of the position which by its great inherent value it deserves. In the C minor, No. 5, Beethoven brought rhythm into a powerful position which it had not previously occupied. He also interwove the scherzo and the finale, a tendency to unity which had not previously been tried. He had already practically invented the scherzo (as a development of the minuet and trio, a form which he did not disdain to use in No. 8). In this Symphony he used more instruments, e.g. trombones, a piccolo, and a double bassoon. He had previously added a third horn in No. 3. In No. 6 he betook himself to the countryside, and illustrated it in countless pictorial and humorous ways ... No. 7 was a reversion to the big rhythmical style of No. 5. It was written about the same time as his arrangements of Scotch and Irish melodies for [George] Thomson of Edinburgh. It carries upon the face of it the impression made upon him by Irish music ... The Ninth Symphony, the culminating point of his life-work, was on the largest scale of all (although always on the same lines), and included in the last movement the assistance of the human voice.'

Charles Villiers Stanford, *Interludes: Records and Reflections*, London, John Murray, 1922, pp. 81–85.

PRESTON STEDMAN

The American musicologist and educator Preston Stedman — at the time of writing in his 98th year — published a survey of the symphony that he intended to serve as a research and information guide. Part IV of his survey is titled *The Symphonies of Beethoven*. In this Stedman first adds testimony to the frequently stated view of Beethoven being a 'bridge' between the Classical and Romantic periods and what for him constitutes the essence of Beethoven's music:

> 'Ludwig van Beethoven's position in the history of the symphony is unique. Since his life span [1770—1827] more-or-less bridged the Classical and Romantic periods, we might assume that his musical output was similarly transitional. However, it was much more than this. The conflicting influences of the two periods resulted in what could be considered the perfect symphony, a mark of the composer's character. As he handled musical forms with perfection while at the same time experimenting with these forms. As one of the first romanticists, he infused many of his works with a depth of personal expression that rivals the expressive quality of the music of the nineteenth century. The architectural grandeur of the Third, Fifth, and Ninth Symphonies is equalled only by the expressive impact of each work. On the other hand, a true classical symphonic style can be clearly seen in the movements of the First, Second, Fourth, and Eighth Symphonies.'

Stedman considers Beethoven's expansion of the symphony:

'These is no argument that Beethoven contributed to the growth of the symphony. His expansionist tendencies created larger introductions, development sections, and codas. The coda became in some instances a second development section. He substituted the more easily developed scherzo for the less easily developed minuet. While the frequency of use of variation form did not increase in his symphonies, the scope of the form broadened considerably in some of the symphony movements. Orchestral resources were also expanded with the addition of the trombone, piccolo, contrabassoon, and vocal-choral resources. Most important, however, was the highly articulated sense of formal structure that permeates many of the works. This one feature, more than anything else, points the way for subsequent symphony composers.'

Stedman asks: 'In what ways do the symphonies of Beethoven differ from the classical symphonies of Haydn, and Mozart?' His response:

'From the standpoint of texture, the works have a denser and heavier sound brought about by the increased number of parts and a greater use of wind instruments. There is a compelling logic in the composer's progression of musical thought, created for the most part by the superb articulation of much of the thematic material and by the emphasis on repetition of materials as important breaks in the form. The range of the sound is wider because of the addition of such wind instruments as the piccolo and the contrabassoon and, more importantly, the expanding of the tessituras of the instruments already in use (e.g., lower bass instrument parts and higher soprano instrument parts). The flow of musical materials is often expanded by the composer's use of long and sustained passages where he has dwelt on one idea (either a theme, a chord, or a cadence progression) primarily. Contrapuntal passages are more extended than those by Haydn or Mozart. The handling of dynamics and tempo seems impulsive at times in comparison to that of the classicists.'

Beethoven sketches reveal that he worked on several compositions at the same time, turning from one to another to impart to each work its own individual character. As he was given to say: 'I never repeat myself.' Stedman reflects how this found expression in the odd-numbered symphonies and the even-numbered symphonies — including also the composer's first venture into the symphonic genre:

'In the nine symphonies there is a division of style into two different categories. Symphonies 1, 2, 4, and 8 closely adhere to the style norms of the classical symphony as represented by the mature works of Haydn and Mozart. These works are more concise, of smaller dimensions, and less expansive in the use of developmental principles. Symphonies 3, 5, 7, and 9 are of greater length, expressive import, and developmental complexity. The Sixth Symphony, the composer's sole programme symphony, has the same extended dimensions of the more complex works but in its depiction of mood avoids the developmental and formal intricacies of that group.'

Stedman concludes:

'If one were to isolate the single factor that probably contributed more than any other to the greatness of Beethoven's symphonies, he would have to select the composer's architectural-expressive line. By Beethoven's time, it was no longer enough to construct a work so that it met certain formal expectations; the manner of composition must also unfold continuously, almost imperceptibly, and have an overpowering logic and expressive impact. In the more expansive symphonies Beethoven was able to accomplish this. By so doing he left a challenge to all composers who followed him.'

Preston Stedman, *The Symphony: A Research and Information Guide*, Englewood Cliffs, New Jersey, London, Prentice-Hall, 1979, pp. 62–66.

KARL HEINRICH STOCKHAUSEN

Sometime in the early 1970s, the musicologist Karl Heinrich Wörner interviewed the German composer Karl Heinrich Stockhausen concerning his thoughts on 'the philosophy of music'. Stockhausen — widely acknowledged for his groundbreaking work in the field of recorded and electronic music — recalled how, on 17 December 1970, he was requested to give a lecture to celebrate the bicentenary of Beethoven's birth. Stockhausen's initial response was to offer his audience an evening 'meditating' on Beethoven's music 'in performance' with a quartet of selected musicians — i.e., musicians sympathetic to Stockhausen's contemporary modernist views and personal style of expression. In the event, Stockhausen required his musicians to play recorded fragments of Beethoven's music so as to, in Stockhausen's word's, 'transform *found* music into *new music*' [Stockhausen's italics]. Stockhausen himself selected and recorded the musical extracts. He justified his actions on the grounds that Beethoven himself was a tireless searcher for new forms in the creative process:

> 'It is certainly in keeping with the spirit of Beethoven — that timelessly universal spirit — that we should use the whole of his music (and not merely a "theme" from it) as the material for a *development without mediation*, in which not merely sections, but *even the single notes and sounds are spontaneously "developed" the moment they are heard.*' [Stockhausen's italics]

Stockhausen closes:

> 'For this music [Beethoven's music 'transformed' by the performers] is not fenced off and dead, but is rather a living generative force: an immediate cause and pre-text for the new and unknown.'

Karl Heinrich Wörner, *Stockhausen: Life and Work*, London, Faber, 1973, p. 77. This recollection is also published, with some variation in the translation, in: Michael Kurtz, *Stockhausen: A Biography*, London, Faber and Faber, 1992, p. 176.

We have remarked that Robert Simpson (see above) wanted the listener to hear music with an unprejudiced ear — what he called an 'innocent ear'. Stockhausen expressed similar thoughts. He first suggests how our sense of musical appreciation is formed:

> 'It is no longer primarily music that we hear, but always music associated with the names of composers and the type or genre to which a piece of music belongs. This begins when we learn an instrument; already we are playing under a suggestion. The effect continues throughout our whole life. Every concert advertisement "lures" us by the programmes just as much as by the names of the performers.'

Stockhausen continues:

> 'If a symphony by Beethoven is announced, we always hear it in the concert in a prejudiced way, influenced by the experiences that have already accumulated for us around the name of Beethoven, and aware of the knowledge that everyone associates with this composer in particular.'

Karl Heinrich Wörner, *Stockhausen: Life and Work*, London, Faber, 1973, pp. 173–74.

RICHARD STRAUSS

In 1904 the Austrian pianist, conductor and writer on music August Göllerich published a collection of illustrated musical studies, the first volume of which was titled *Beethoven* (Bard, Marquart & Co.). Richard Strauss was invited to contribute an introduction. His opening remarks provide insights into his views on the nature of art, taken in the widest sense of the meaning:

> 'Art is a product of civilisation. It is not its "calling" to lead a self-sufficient, isolated existence in accordance with "laws" which are first arbitrarily formulated or designed to meet the needs of the moment and then proclaimed to be "eternal": its natural calling is to bear witness to the civilisation of an age and of a people.'

Turning his attention to music, Strauss comments:

> 'We observe in the history of music, as in the development of the other arts, an evolution from the representation of indefinite or general and typical concepts to the expression of an orbit of ideas which become increasingly more definite, individual and intimate.'

In commending Göllerich's study of Beethoven, Strauss expatiates:

> 'A monograph on Beethoven would appear to be best suited to form the first volume of such a collection, because the appreciation of Beethoven's position with regard to our civilisation may well offer today the largest field of agreement between friend and foe. It may be hoped that more-or-less general agreement on this interpretation of Beethoven's life and work will form a sure foundation for agreement on greater and more hotly disputed issues of musical aesthetics.'

Willi Schuh, editor: *Richard Strauss: Recollections and Reflections*, London, New York, Boosey & Hawkes, 1953, pp. 10–11.

Strauss, the conductor, has been described as 'a musical literalist with a tiny beat and an anti-romantic approach'. He once told an orchestra, rehearsing the slow movement of a Beethoven symphony: 'Gentlemen, please, not so much emotion. Beethoven wasn't nearly as emotional as our conductors.' Not surprisingly he advocated a restrained style of conducting:

> 'It is decisive for the technique of conducting that the shorter the movements of the arm, and the more confined to the wrist, then the more precise is the execution. If the arm is allowed to be involved in conducting — which results in a kind of lever-action the effects of which are incalculable — the orchestra is apt to be paralysed and misdirected, unless it is determined from the start (and this is frequently the case with conductors whose downbeat is imprecise) to play according to its own judgement in tacit agreement as it were, without paying too much attention to the antics of the conductor.'

Strauss agreed with Wagner who urged conductors to 'grasp the fundamental tempo correctly'. This, Strauss considered, was 'all-important for the proper performance of a piece of music, especially in slow movements'. Turning to a consideration of performing Beethoven, Strauss remarked:

> 'A conductor who interprets the *adagio* theme of Beethoven's Fourth Symphony will never allow himself to be led by the rhythmical figure accompanying the first bar into chopping this fine melody up into quavers. Always conduct in periods, never scan bars.'

Although Strauss preferred a restrained style of conducting, his recollection of the conducting style of Franz Liszt suggests his gestures were too spare:

> 'At a music festival in the Rhineland eighty years ago, Franz Liszt, when conducting the last movement of Schubert's C major Symphony, adapted his beat to the period, i.e. he only used a down beat once in every four bars. The poor orchestra, unused as it was to the ways of genius, was at a loss how to squeeze in the triplets and concluded that [Liszt] was no conductor.'

Hans von Bülow was both a virtuoso pianist and one of the nineteenth century's most respected orchestral conductors. At the start of his career Strauss was von Bülow's protégé with the Meiningen Orchestra and — despite the challenges he had to confront — he greatly admired his teacher's interpretation of Beethoven. Of the experience he relates:

> 'As a pedagogue he could be relentlessly pedantic and his motto, "Learn to read the score of a Beethoven symphony *accurately* first, and you will have found its interpretation", would be an adornment to the main door of any conservatoire to this day ... The exactitude of his phrasing, his intellectual penetration of the score combined with almost

pedantic observation of the latter, his analysis of the period structure and, above all, his understanding of the psychological content of Beethoven's symphonies, and of Wagner's preludes in particular, have been a shining example to me to this day, although I have myself at times modified his incisive dissection of some movements — e.g. of the first movement of the *Eroica* — I endeavour to achieve a greater uniformity of tempo.'

Willi Schuh, editor, *Richard Strauss: Recollections and Reflections*, London, New York, Boosey & Hawkes, 1953, pp. 44–50, and p. 121.

IGOR STRAVINSKY

As a child Stravinsky showed an aptitude for the piano and by the age of fifteen he had mastered Mendelssohn's Piano Concerto in G minor. In his student days he had lessons in orchestration with Rimsky-Korsakov. He was required to set passages of Beethoven sonatas and Schubert quartets, which the master then criticised and corrected. When in conversation with the American conductor and writer Robert Craft, Stravinsky reflected on Beethoven and summed up his feelings as they then were towards him:

> 'I did not hero-worship Beethoven, nor have I ever done so, and the nature of Beethoven's talent and work are more "human" and more comprehensible to me than are, say the talents and works of more "perfect" composers like Bach and Mozart; I think I know how Beethoven composed. I have little enough Beethoven in me, alas, but some people have found I have some.'

Igor Stravinsky and Robert Craft, *Memories and Commentaries*, London, Faber and Faber, 2002, p. 39.

In his *Autobiography*, Stravinsky recalls how his youthful encounters with Beethoven initially proved too much for him:

> 'In our early youth we were surfeited by his works, his famous *weltschmerz* [world weariness] being forced upon us at the same, together with his "tragedy" and all the commonplace utterances voiced for more than a century about the composer who must be regarded as one of the world's greatest musical geniuses.
>
> 'Like many other musicians, I was disgusted by this intellectual and sentimental attitude, which had little to do with serious musical appreciation. This deplorable pedagogy did not fail in its result. It alienated me from Beethoven for many years.'

Stravinsky admits that he soon gained respect for Beethoven and his music:

> 'Cured and matured by age, I could now approach him objectively so that he wore a different aspect for me ... Just as in his pianistic work, Beethoven lives on in the piano, so, in his symphonies, and chamber music he draws sustenance from his instrumental ensemble. With him the instrumentation is never apparel, and that is why it never strikes one. The profound wisdom with which groups, the carefulness of his instru-

mental writing, and the precision with which he indicates his wishes — all these testify to the fact that we are above all in the presence of a tremendous constructive force.

'I do not think I am mistaken in asserting that it was just his manner of moulding his musical material which logically led to the erection of those monumental structures which are his supreme glory.'

Igor Stravinsky, *An Autobiography*, London, Calder and Boyars, 1975, pp. 115–18.

Some ten years after Robert Craft held his first interview with Stravinsky, he had a further meeting with him and asked the composer to remark on his 'favourite events' in Beethoven's symphonies. Stravinsky responded:

'The Eighth Symphony is a miracle of growth and development and I am therefore reluctant to cite my particular admirations out of context. Nevertheless, the entrance of the trumpets and drums in F major in the last movement, after the F sharp minor episode, is the most wonderful moment ... For me, the Ninth Symphony contains no event of comparable force. But then, for me, nothing in the Ninth is as perennially surprising and delightful as the development section of the last movement of the Fourth Symphony, or the repeated B flat A in the Trio of the Fourth, or the *tutti*, measures 50–54, in the adagio of the Fourth.'

Igor Stravinsky and Robert Craft, *Dialogues and a Diary*, London, Faber and Faber 1968, p. 112.

JOHN WILLIAM NAVIN SULLIVAN

Sullivan was a British born journalist and author whose polymath interests and abilities encompassed a wide range of subjects. These are reflected in his circle of gifted contemporaries who included T. S Eliot, Aldous Huxley, Wyndham Lewis and John Middleton Murray. In addition to being the author of a widely respected study *Beethoven: His Spiritual Development* (1927) Sullivan published some of the earliest accounts of Einstein's Theory of Relativity, studies on the nature of atoms and the universe, and addressed contemporary questions concerning God and religion.

In the Preface to his Beethoven study, Sullivan writes:

> 'I believe that in his greatest music, Beethoven was primarily concerned to express his personal vision of life. This vision was, of course, the product of his character and his experience. Beethoven the man and Beethoven the composer are not two unconnected entities, and the known history of the man may be used to throw light upon the character of his music.'

In his formulation of the Beethoven symphonies, Sullivan states:

> 'The transition from the Fourth to the Fifth Symphony is not the transition from one "mood" to another, both equally valid and representative; it is the transition from one level of experience and realization to another; one might say that the transition is vertical, not horizontal. And the Third and Fifth Symphonies are more important than the Fourth in the history of Beethoven because it was the deepest things in him that

conditioned his development. The greater importance the world has always attributed to the Third, Fifth, Seventh and Ninth Symphonies, compared with the Fourth, Sixth and Eighth, is not because of any purely musical superiority they possess, but because everyone is more-or-less clearly aware that greater issues are involved, that something more important for mankind is being expressed.'

J. W. N. Sullivan, *Beethoven: His Spiritual Development*, 1927, pp. 155—6.

KAROL SZYMANOWSKI

The Polish composer and pianist Karol Szymanowski is regarded as being one of his country's foremost musical personalities of the late nineteenth — early twentieth-century modernist movement. Notwithstanding, his writings reveal a deep respect for the European musical tradition and its inheritance. Of Beethoven, he remarks:

'I believe that Beethoven was the most profoundly eloquent symbol of his time. We know that he was born into the classical tradition, and that this was his starting-point in the quest for a new Ideal. As such he bridged two eras. The colossal burden of historical catastrophes and events of great power and consequence roared like a storm through his consciousness and channelled deep furrows in it. His music became a true likeness reflected on some mystical screen of the immediate historical substance (in the deepest sense of the word) of the fifty years that was his span on earth.'

*

Placing the composer in the context of his time, Szymanowski continues:

> 'Along with his contemporaries he searched for "that new word which would become flesh", and his seemingly abstract art is clearly marked by the traces of his search and discovery of it. In effect his creative drive depended on the conscious breaking-down of the artistic forms inherited from his ancestors. The psychological source of this apparently destructive, yet in reality *constructive*, work was doubtless a sensitive subconscious state that did not confine itself merely to the sphere of aesthetic matters. In their essence these aesthetic ideas were inherited from his great predecessors; we have eloquent testimony to this in all those works of his first period.'

Turning to Beethoven's later achievements, Szymanowski singles out for special mention the *Choral* Symphony:

> 'The choice of text for the finale of the Ninth Symphony was by no means fortuitous, the result perhaps of purely poetic considerations. The decisive factor was undoubtedly the intellectual and ideological content of Schiller's hymn in which the full gravity and substance of the "word" is positively and specifically expressed. In creating his greatest masterpiece, Beethoven was certainly far removed from purely aesthetic concepts. Instead he was at his closest to the very fountainhead of contemporary life, that internally glowing and uncontrollably coursing Life which is, day in,

day out, posing questions of untold importance for those of course who are capable of understanding their full significance. Without doubt, Beethoven was one of those who "understood" and who shouldered part of the ideological burden of his era, and perhaps his true greatness lies in his ethical qualities, rather than in the now slightly faded aesthetic qualities of his music.'

Szymanowski affirms the value of Beethoven to him as a composer:

'What does Beethoven mean to me? Or rather, what did he mean? I need not say anything about his objective greatness. It is only a question of how I, subjectively, perceive his work. He was a profound experience for me in my artistic youth. For the first time in the *Kingdom of Art* I understood how one could be consumed by the flames of one's own fire.'

Alistair Wightman, editor, *Szymanowski on Music: Selected Writings of Karol Szymanowski,* London, Toccata Press, 1999, pp. 166–8.

PETER TCHAIKOVSKY

Tchaikovsky studied piano and composition at the nascent Saint Petersburg Conservatory where he received instruction in the formal Western-oriented musical tradition. Later in life he was befriended by the influential patron of the arts Nadezhda von Meck. She was herself a capable pianist, familiar with the classical repertoire and regarded Tchaikovsky as her ideal composer and philosopher-friend. Their extensive correspondence sheds light on many aspects of Tchaikovsky's views on music. In December 1878, Von Meck wrote to her protégée with her thoughts concerning the programmatic nature she considered evident in certain of Beethoven's piano sonatas — unspecified. Her letter prompted the following responses from Tchaikovsky:

> 'In my opinion, any music is programme music. There's no other kind because, for example, symphonies have a programme, overtures even more so, and operas definitely. I know Beethoven sonatas, one of which represents the movement of a wheel [Tchaikovsky is probably thinking here of the *Les Adieux* Piano Sonata, Op. 81a with its associations of a coach taking leave of Beethoven's patron the Archduke Rudolph.] and another a quarrel between husband and wife [Tchaikovsky is probably thinking here of the Piano Sonata, Op. 90, with its alleged associations between Count Moritz Lichnowsky and Josepha (Johanna) Stummer.] ... Programme music was invented by *Beethoven*, to some extent in the *Eroica* Symphony, but more particularly in the Sixth, the *Pastoral* ... I think Beethoven was wrong not to give a programme for the sonatas you mention. In any case, as I see it, both kinds of music (instrumental and orchestral) have an equal raison d'être, and I don't understand those gentlemen who recognize only one category to the exclusion of the other.'

Tchaikovsky affirmed to his patron he was a champion of 'great artists who will show art new paths' rather than 'pathetic weakness disguised as serious creation' that Tchaikovsky believed 'you get with Germans like Brahms'. 'They're hopelessly insipid'. As for the French, Tchaikovsky acknowledged Berlioz had been 'a strong progressive force' but complained how, ten years after his death, his works were only now being performed. He lamented:

> 'In art, the French are terrible conservatives. They were the last to acknowledge *Beethoven*. Even in the 1840s, they thought him nothing more than an impetuous eccentric. The leading French critic, Fétis, complained that Beethoven had made mistakes in harmony and absolutely had to correct those mistakes twenty-five years later.'

Edward Garden and Nigel Gottrei, editors, '*To My Best Friend*': *Correspondence between Tchaikovsky and Nadezhda von Meck, 1876–1878,* Oxford: Clarendon Press, 1993, pp. 122–3. See also: Jay Leyda and Sergi Bertensson, *The Mussorgsky Reader: A Life of Modeste Petrovich Musorgsky in Letters and Documents*, New York, W.W. Norton, 1947, p. 367.

Writing a long letter to von Meck from Florence on 16–18 February 1878, Tchaikovsky enthused on the delights of Florence telling her that the greatest impression made on him was the Medici Chapel in San Lorenzo. The greatness of Michelangelo prompted Tchaikovsky to find a parallel between him and Beethoven – as others have done:

> 'Here, at last, I've begun to appreciate Michelangelo's immense genius for the first time. I've begun to recognize a vague kinship with Beethoven. There is the same breadth and strength, the same

boldness bordering on uncouthness, and the same sombre mood. Perhaps this idea is not new. Taine perspicaciously compared Raphael with Mozart. Has Michelangelo been compared to Beethoven, I wonder?' [Hippolyte Taine was a French writer and critic.]

The next month Tchaikovsky raised a subject very dear to him: 'I don't just like Mozart – I idolize him. For me, *Don Giovanni* is the best opera ... ever written.'

He adds:

'It is true that Mozart spread himself too thinly and often wrote not from inspiration but from necessity. But, if you read Otto Jahn's beautifully written biography of him, you will see that he could not help it. Anyway, both Beethoven and Bach have plenty of inferior compositions, unworthy to stand alongside their masterpieces. Such was the force of circumstance that they sometimes had to turn their art into a craft.'

An English edition of Jahn's *Biography of Mozart* was published in 1891. The cited quotation is derived from: Edward Garden, and Nigel Gottrei, editors, *'To My Best Friend': Correspondence between Tchaikovsky and Nadezhda von Meck, 1876–1878*, Oxford: Clarendon Press, 1993, p. 182, p. 195, and p. 219.

In a letter to von Meck written in 1888, Tchaikovsky enthused:

'There is no padding in Beethoven. It is astonishing how equal, how significant and forceful

this giant among musicians always remains and
how well he understands the art of curbing this
vast inspiration, never losing sight of balanced,
traditional form.'

Ferruccio Bonavia, *Musicians on Music*, London, Routledge
& Kegan Paul, 1956, p. 262.

One night, in order to rest from the preoccupation with his own
music, Tchaikovsky played through a piano reduction of Bizet's
Carmen from beginning to end. He considered Bizet's Opera
to be a '*chef d'oeuvre*' — a masterpiece. This prompted him to
reflect on past and present-day music, his views on which he
shared with von Meck in a letter of 30 July 1889:

> 'It seems to me that the era we live in differs from
> the preceding in one way; our composers are
> *searching* — and first of all, they *are* searching for
> pretty and piquant effects — a thing which Mozart
> and Beethoven and Schubert and Schumann
> never did.'

Catherine Drinker Bowen, *Beloved Friend: The story of
Tchaikovsky and Nadejda von Meck*, London, Hutchinson
& Co., 1937, p. 411.

In a diary entry for 1886, headed 'My Taste in Music',
Tchaikovsky communed with himself, reflecting that after his
death people would probably be interested to know what were
his musical predilections — especially since he seldom confided these in general conversation. He resolved 'to speak to
the point' and to start with Beethoven, of whom he remarks:

> 'It is usual to praise [Beethoven] unconditionally

and whom it is commanded to worship as though he were a god ... And what is Beethoven to me? ... I bow before the greatness of some of his works — but I do not *love* Beethoven. My attitude toward him reminds me of what I experienced in childhood toward the God Jehovah. I had toward Him (and even now my feelings have not changed) a feeling of wonder, but at the same time also of fear. He created Heaven and earth, He too created me — and still even though I bow before Him, there is no *love*. Christ, on the contrary, inspires truly and exclusively the feeling of *love*. Though He was *God*, He was at the same time man. He suffered like us. We *pity* Him, we love in Him His ideal *human* side. And if Beethoven occupies a place in my heart analogous to the God Jehovah, then Mozart I love as the musical Christ.'

Jacques Barzun, *Pleasures of Music: An Anthology of Writing about Music and Musicians*, London, Cassell, 1977, pp. 266–7.

ALEXANDER WHEELOCK THAYER

Alexander Wheelock Thayer is acknowledged — and much admired — for being Beethoven's first scholarly biographer. In the opinion of the present writer, Thayer's biography of Beethoven stands equally alongside James Boswell's celebrated *Life of Samuel Johnson*. Thayer's study of Beethoven's life and work has been justly described as 'the classic biography of Beethoven' and, notwithstanding its several editorial revisions (see below), Thayer's researches on Beethoven, and his objective manner of writing about him, have set a benchmark that still remains a point of reference for modern-day studies of the composer.

Thayer travelled extensively in Europe to gather materials for his study of the composer. Whenever possible, he met with those who had direct contact with him or had reliable first-hand accounts to relate. Thayer's credo was: 'I fight for no theories and cherish no prejudices; my sole point of view is the truth.' In pursuit of this ideal, he objectively studied the sources available to him, endeavoring 'to clear away the romantic fiction' that was then accumulating about Beethoven.

The first edition of Thayer's biography was published, in German, in three volumes that appeared between 1866 and 1879. These covered Beethoven's life to the year 1816. Thayer did not live to complete his monumental study. His German colleagues Herman Deiters and Hugo Rieman published volume four in 1907 and volume 5 the following year — making use of such of Thayer's original source materials that had survived; regrettably, it is believed some of Thayer's notes were lost. In 1921, the American music critic and musicologist Henry Edward Krehbiel published the first English edition. This was substantially revised and edited by Elliot Forbes (1964 and 1967) to universal acclaim — '[A] model of objective biography one that is amazingly modern and as valuable today as when it was written ... Thayer's *Life* remains the definitive biography'. (Harold C. Schonberg, *New York Times*)

The subsequent studies and reinterpretation of the life and work of Beethoven, by, such authorities as, Maynard Solomon and Barry Cooper, have further enriched and enlarged our understanding of the enigmatic composer in ways that would assuredly have won the approval of Thayer himself.

With regard to Beethoven's symphonies — as, indeed, with his other compositions — Thayer traces their composition origins, publication, first and subsequent performances, critical reception, and a veritable mass of related musicological desiderata.

VIRGIL THOMSON

In his long life, Virgil Thomson divided his gifts between composition, essay writing and music criticism — in the latter role for many years as music critic to the *New York Herald-Tribune*. We consider first the views Thomson expressed about music and musicians in his writings.

From an essay titled *Why Composers Write*, originally published in 1939 as *The State of Music*, Thomson discussed patronage in music. He advanced the proposition that composers, living on subsidies, 'tend to write introspective music of strained harmonic texture and emphatic instrumental style'. He considered such composers 'were not bothered about charm, elegance, sentiment, or comprehensibility'. Rather, he maintained, 'they go for high-flown lyricism and dynamic punch ... they are revolters against convention.' Having set forth his theory, Thomson considered the case of Beethoven, who was himself the beneficiary of patronage who received an annuity from his middle years onwards. With this circumstance in mind, Thomson asserts:

> 'Beethoven is their ideal; and they think of themselves as prophets in a wilderness, as martyrs unappreciated, as persecuted men. Appearing to be persecuted is, of course, their way of earning their living. The minute they lose the air of being brave men downed by circumstances, they cease to get free money. Because people with money to give away don't like giving it to serene or successful characters, no matter how poor the latter may be.'

*

In an essay from 1940, titled *Mozart's Leftism*, Thomson took up the theme of politics in music. He opens with the remarks: 'Persons of humanitarian, libertarian, and politically liberal orientation have for a century used Beethoven as their musical standard-bearer.' Thomson was not, however, personally convinced on the grounds that he maintained (controversially):

> '[It] is hard to find much in Beethoven's life or music — beyond the legend of his having torn up the dedication of his "Heroic" Symphony to Napoleon [Symphony No. 3, the *Eroica*] when the defender of the French Revolution allowed himself to be crowned Emperor — to justify the adoration in which he has always been held by political liberals.'

Later, Thomson reserves further venom for Beethoven:

> 'Mozart was not, like Wagner, a political revolutionary. Nor was he, like Beethoven, an old fraud, who just talked about human rights and dignity but who was really an irascible, intolerant, and scheming careerist, who allowed himself the liberty, when he felt like it, of being unjust toward the poor, lickspittle toward the rich, dishonest in business, unjust and unforgiving toward the members of his own family [!]'

In 1941, Thomson discussed the concept of the masterpiece in music. He first suggested the expression could be taken to mean an artist's 'most accomplished work, the high point of his production'. He adds: 'And certain composers (Beethoven was the first of them) are considered to have worked exclusively in this vein.' Regarding Beethoven's legacy, Thomson continues:

> '[All] the successors of Beethoven who aspired to his authority — Brahms and Bruckner, Wagner and Mahler and Tchaikovsky — quite consciously imbued their music with the "masterpiece" tone.'

Richard Kostelanetz, editor, *Virgil Thomson: A Reader; Selected Writings, 1924–1984*, New York; London: Routledge, 2002, p. 27, pp. 48–9 and p. 101.

Writing to a catholic priest on 26 May 1943, Thomson discussed the nature of broadcast music. In the course of this letter, he is more generous to Beethoven than in his earlier pronouncements:

> 'You are quite right. My radio is not a very good instrument, though there are worse on the market. I still think I am right that the narrow range of dynamics which any microphone will carry makes Beethoven one of the least effective composers for broadcasting purposes. This does not mean that I consider Beethoven's music, even in its distorted radio-sound, to be uninteresting. Quite to the contrary. The way it survives processing is to its eternal glory.'

Tim Page, and Vanessa Weeks, editors: *Selected Letters of Virgil Thomson*, New York, Summit Books, 1988, pp. 186–7.

Many of Thomson's writings for the *New York Herald-Tribune* were collected and published as *The Musical Scene*.

From the 1940s period we have selected the following texts in which he makes reference to Beethoven and his music:

Haydn, Beethoven, and Mozart, 21 December 1941:

> 'Beethoven really was an old bachelor. But he never liked it. All his music is cataclysmic, as if he were constantly trying to break out of his solitude. His first movements state the problem squarely. His slow movements are less interesting because they try, unsuccessfully, to avoid it; they tread water. His minuets and scherzos reopen the problem and announce the hope of a solution. The finales, almost always the finest and certainly the most characteristic movements in Beethoven, are the solution that the whole piece has been working up to. That solution is usually of a religious nature. It represents redemption, the victory of soul over flesh. It varies from calm serenity to active triumph but joy is its thesis.'

In the 2 May 1942 issue of the *New York Herald-Tribune*, Thomson reported on the fifth concert that formed part of a Beethoven festival. At this, Arturo Toscanini conducted the Philharmonic Symphony Orchestra:

> 'A Beethoven cycle is always profoundly satisfactory, no matter who conducts it. A Toscanini concert is always stimulating to an audience, no matter what the programme is. That public enthusiasm about the present series should run high is not surprising. That I am unable to share it wholeheartedly is a matter of sincere regret to me.'

*

Thomson gives the reasons for having such reservations:

> 'The Seventh Symphony was not so much the full Seventh Symphony as a highly dramatized outline or syllabus of the Seventh Symphony. Its main melodic material, its harmonic progress, and especially the dynamic pattern, the chiaroscuro of it, were wholly clear. Unfortunately, many of the rapid string passages were not audible in detail. This skimping of the fast work was probably unavoidable at the given speed, but it is not usually considered the best musical style to play non-theatrical works at a speed at which their detail cannot be executed satisfactorily by the group performing them.'

Beethoven in the Home, May 1943:

In this essay, Thomson considered the limitations of hearing Beethoven's symphonies on the radio. His thoughts were prompted by a concert broadcast from the Carnegie Hall in which Bruno Walter directed the Philharmonic Symphony Orchestra in an all-Beethoven programme that included performances of his Fifth and Eighth Symphonies. Of Walter's interpretation, and choice of music, Thomson mused:

> 'There is nothing banal about Bruno Walter's Beethoven. It is plain, sensible, eloquent, and clear. And the tempos are all reasonable ones. I presume it was as a statement of faith and a proof of orthodoxy that he chose to begin the summer broadcasts with a full programme of this music,

which has been for over a century now the Credo
and Gloria of the symphony-orchestra business.'

In the 1940s orchestral music, broadcast over the radio, was impaired by the limitations of the technology then available. Just one or two microphones were used to capture the sounds of the entire orchestra, disposing Thomson to reiterate:

> 'In spite of Mr. Walter's lucid exposition and the charming way he has of making solo instruments sing, Beethoven, heard over the radio, sounds disjointed and picayune. The limited range that a microphone will carry has something to do with this distortion; and so, I imagine, has the placing of the microphones. Yesterday, for instance, the fortes all lacked background, as if the violins were too close; and so the essential majesty of Beethoven, which comes from his constant contrasts of loud and soft, was reduced both by the radio's inability, at best, to transmit a really loud ensemble of musical sounds ... There was continuity in the rhythmic layout but no real strength in the dynamic pattern or any massiveness in individual chords. The lyrical passages came off prettily, as they always do in broadcast music; but the dramatic eloquence that constitutes such a large part of Beethoven's thought sounded puny.'

THE FRENCH STYLE,
16 JANUARY 1944:

In this text, Thomson considered the French style of musical expression and its emphasis on rhythm. Turning to such considerations in Beethoven's music, he comments: 'It was Beethoven who first among the great masters of music made a serious effort to introduce rhythmic and dynamic exactitude into musical notation.'

TRANSCRIPTIONS,
4 JUNE 1944:

In this essay Thomson considered the legitimacy of transcribing music from one musical medium into another:

> 'Whether the transcribing and arranging of classical pieces, for executional conditions different from those conceived by their authors, is a legitimate practice or not is a question that frequently bothers music-lovers. Persons of refined taste are likely to disapprove it, in principle, but to tolerate it when it is carried out with brilliance or with some authoritative reference to the past.'

Thomson defended transcriptions on the grounds:

> 'All musical execution entails transformation, and it is not necessarily the part of taste to keep this minimal. Knowledge and skill and authority are valuable. But so is a commonsense approach ... It has never accomplished much to have symphony orchestras play Beethoven's string quartets on sixty instruments. But the execution in the home of classical overtures and symphonies transcribed as piano duets, is the very fundamental of our musical culture.'

TEMPOS,
11 JUNE 1944:
Thomson considered pieces of music require to be played at a given speed 'in order to make sense'. In his opinion: '[Speed] itself is not nearly so expressive an element in musical communication as clear phraseology and exact rhythmic articulation are.' He recognised this called for the close study of the composition to be performed and elaborated:

> 'No element of musical execution is more variable from one interpreter to another than tempo. No problem, indeed, is more bothering to any musician, even to the composer, than that of determining the exact metronomic speed at which he wishes or advises that a piece be made to proceed in performance, unless it is that of sticking to his tempo once he has decided on it. Many musical authors, beginning with Beethoven, have indicated in time-units per minute their desire in this matter. And yet interpreters do not hesitate to alter these indications when conviction, based on reasoning or on feeling or on exceptional circumstances, impels them to do so.'

Virgil Thomson, *The Musical Scene*, New York, Greenwood Press, 1968, pp. 54–55, p. 71, pp. 259–60, p. 272, pp. 275–77, and p. 299. See also Toscanini.

MICHAEL TIPPETT

The English composer Sir Michael Tippett studied composition at the Royal College of Music under the guidance of Charles Wood. Tippett relates how Wood used Bach, Mozart and Beethoven as models to inculcate 'a solid understanding of musical forms and syntax'. Beethoven, in particular, became a central influence on Tippett from his earliest years and remained with him until his last as he himself acknowledged:

> 'When I was a student I submitted entirely to the music of Beethoven. I explored his music so exhaustively that for a long time later on I listened to every other music but his. But as a student I was fascinated by his music and his personality, though I had also a very catholic taste, to which little was foreign. I doubt if in adolescence one can be absorbed by Beethoven and have a real understanding of Mozart. In so far as I have acquired that it has come later.'

Michael Tippett, *Moving into Aquarius*, London, Routledge and Kegan Paul, 1959, p. 101.

Writing of his earliest musical experiences, Tippett remarks on the value he derived from the Henry Wood Promenade Concerts: 'Thus began the springtime of my life, as a human being and as a musician.' Of the concerts themselves he remarks:

> 'In those days, Henry Wood did all the conducting, except for the last items in the second half of each concert, which were always instrumental solos, vocal ballads etc. plus a final orchestral item conducted by the leader: and on successive Fridays he presented all the Beethoven symphonies, in order from 1 to 9. These I followed with the scores John had lent me. Their impact was devastating: Beethoven became my musical god and has remained so ever since.'

John, to whom Tippett makes reference, was his first close

friend and the object of his affections. John's proper name was Herbert Sumison.

Wood's allocating Friday night exclusively to the music of Beethoven persisted until well into the 1950s, as the present writer recalls, with much the same enthusiasm as Tippett, but, alas, with *much less* musical insight! Composition was the central focus of Tippett's studies at the Royal College of Music. He discovered that Charles Wood admired Beethoven as much as he did, 'especially the string quartets and piano sonatas'. Tippett though was not a particularly adept student as he admits:

> 'At the examinations I was hopelessly at sea, in reality because I could not hear in my head the notes I was writing "by calculation" on the manuscript paper ... The tradition at the RCM was that one never used a piano for such work. I quickly realised that this was impossible for me. Beethoven may have been deaf, but that didn't mean everyone else had to be.'

Michael Tippett, *Those Twentieth Century Blues: An autobiography*, London, Hutchinson, 1991, p. 13.

Tippet discussed music as an independent art form in the context of change and the emergence of the composer in the, sometimes stereotyped, image of the artist as a lone prophet, misunderstood by an increasingly unreceptive society. In this context, in Arnold Whittall's phrase 'Beethoven stood for an attitude to art'. Tippett writes:

> 'When music as an independent art form flowered at the end of the eighteenth century, the European climate of opinion was already deeply involved in

the swift and shattering process by which value was going over from the world of imagination to the world of technics [see below]. And the artistic consequences of the depreciation of value given to the imaginative world, meant that the effort of imaginative creation began to assume, already in Beethoven's time, that superhuman quality, that desperate struggle to restore spiritual order by increasingly transcendent and extraordinary works of art.'

Originally published in: Michael Tippett, *Moving into Aquarius*, London, Routledge and Kegan Paul, 1959, p. 77 and quoted in: Suzanne Robinson, editor: *Michael Tippett: Music and Literature*, Aldershot, Ashgate, 2002, p. 39. See also: Arnold Whittall, *Exploring Twentieth-Century Music: Tradition and Innovation*, Cambridge, New York, Cambridge University Press, 2003, pp. 118–9.

In her study of Tippett's writing about music, Suzanne Robinson discusses the composer's 'truth-value' concept in the music of Beethoven. By this, as Robinson remarks, Tippett was alluding to

'that quality of music that reflects the problems of society and attempts to reconcile the world of technics [Tippetts's way of referring to the 'real world' — the world as it is] and the world of imagination [the 'ideal world'].

She continues:

'Tippett's deep admiration for Beethoven, for both his music and personality, can be explained in part by the fact that the 'truth-value' of

Beethoven's music ... is still relevant [today].'

In substantiating this proposition, Robinson quotes the following from Tippett's reference to Beethoven's music:

'At least ninety-per-cent of all music lovers of *all ages* need the experience which great works of music in this humanistic tradition provide, just as theatre-lovers need Shakespeare. (In my private jargon, I call this the Shakespeare-Beethoven archetype.)'

In pursuing the notion of 'art mirroring society', Robinson cites the utopian message of hope and brotherhood that Beethoven sought to embody in his setting of Schiller's text *Ode to Joy* in the Ninth Symphony. She contrasts this, as did Tippett himself, with the horrors of Auschwitz as 'the ultimate symbol of our society's utter failure'.

Suzanne Robinson, editor: **Michael Tippett: Music and Literature**, Aldershot, Ashgate, 2002, pp. 50–1.

With the outbreak of war, Tippett's beliefs compelled him to become a Conscientious Objector. Subsequently, for failing to carry out his conditions of exemption he was required to serve a prison sentence in Wormwood Scrubbs, disposing him 'to feel like an outcast'. At the conclusion of hostilities, when the full extent of mankind's suffering became known, Tippett's despair was complete. Later he wrote:

'The climax of my sense of isolation came shortly afterwards when the noble Christian allies decided to put their faith in that masterpiece of technics — the atom bomb. Simultaneously, the concentration camps were opened. I found in these obscenities, as did many others, a most violent and enduring shock of my sense of what humanity might be at all. A denial of any and every affirmation which the poet might make, whether in the name of God or of Mankind.'

Tippett asked the question, 'What price Beethoven now?' Could we any longer, he propositioned, find solace in Beethoven's setting of Schiller's *Ode to Joy*?

Michael Tippett, *Moving into Aquarius*, London, Routledge and Kegan Paul, 1959, p. 153.

In his study of twentieth-century music, the English musicologist Robert Hines devotes a chapter to Michael Tippet. In this he cites Tippett's interpretation of the meaning of 'symphony' in a contemporary sense:

'I feel that much of the confusion that may arise when a contemporary instrumental work is called a "symphony" is due to the fact that we have two differing uses of the word, implying two contrasting conceptions ... The two contrasting conceptions, or ideas of what is meant by a symphony, are: that we imply by the title a *historical archetype* (from which we depart and return), e.g., the middle symphonies of Beethoven; and that we imply a *notional archetype* (permitting endless variations to the end of time), e.g., the Mahler symphonies, as variations of a notional archetype, are as much symphonies as those of Beethoven (irrespective, of course, of pure value judgement).'

Robert Stephan Hines, *The Orchestral Composer's Point of View: Essays on Twentieth-Century Music by those who Wrote It*, Norman, University of Oklahoma Press, 1970, p. 204.

ARTURO TOSCANINI

The Italian conductor Arturo Toscanini inspired and intimidated orchestral players in equal measure. He approached the interpretation of music with intensity bordering on religious fervour. Writing of his realisation of Beethoven, the British composer Spike Hughes states:

> 'Toscanini always gave the impression that he had never heard of Beethoven until the moment he had begun rehearsing for the concert you were listening to. There was a unique quality of wide-eyed innocence, of deliberate refusal to be wise about Beethoven's symphonies after the event — that is, to adopt any musico-historical attitude towards Beethoven by suggesting that there was any such thing as "early" or "middle period" or "late" Beethoven ... Toscanini did not observe any "tradition" in the performance of ... any Beethoven symphony, because he could not ... It was his ability to regard every Beethoven symphony he ever performed as "a brand-new work" which made Toscanini's performances so uniquely illuminating — and with his Beethoven particularly it was, as Constant Lambert [see above] once wrote, "as though Beethoven himself had become endowed with conducting technique".'

Spike Hughes, *The Toscanini Legacy: A Critical Study of Arturo Toscanini's Performances of Beethoven, Verdi, and other Composers*, London, Putnam, 1959, p. 24.

In his survey *The Great Conductors*, the American music critic Harold C. Schonberg writes of what he regarded as

Toscanini's cautious approach to considerations of style and authenticity:

> 'He had read a great deal about stylistic problems, and he had come to the conclusion that there was no conclusion. He said that it was futile to try to achieve an "authentic" style. Instruments had changed, pitch had changed, concepts had changed, and Beethoven would hardly recognize a twentieth-century performance of his music. Thus, the only thing — *the only thing* — a musician has is the notes, and those he must observe as honestly and scrupulously as possible. And not only must he observe the notes, but he must keep a steady rhythmic flow, avoiding the heaving and hauling that characterized the rhythms and tempos that in a previous age had been used in the name of "expression". Conductors like Furtwängler who (according to Toscanini) were constantly over-interpreting in the name of "style" aroused his scorn and derision.'

Harold C. Schonberg *The Toscanini Mystique: The Great Conductors*, Simon & Schuster, 1967, p. 254.

Bernard H. Haggin was an American music critic who wrote reviews for *The Nation* and *The New York Herald Tribune*. He was a staunch admirer of Toscanini and enjoyed a personal friendship with him. The respect he had for Toscanini's conducting is evident in his review of a concert given on 13 June 1942 by the New York Philharmonic Society. The concert in question was one of a series that prompted Haggin to enthuse:

'Though the concerts were interesting, primarily for their presentation of Beethoven's works, they were interesting incidentally for other things. Involved in the presentations was the New York Philharmonic Symphony Orchestra to which, in the ten or more seasons that he had conducted it, Toscanini had given a discipline, a sound, a style as distinctive as those of the Philadelphia Orchestra when conducted by Stokowski, or of the Boston Symphony when conducted by Koussevitzky. This discipline, sound and style had departed from the orchestra when he had departed in 1936; and it was interesting to note their return with him at these Beethoven concerts ... Nothing at the concerts was more breath-taking than what happened at the first moments of the first rehearsal when Toscanini, with no preliminaries, simply began to conduct the orchestra for the first time after six years, and the orchestra began at once to play as though the interval had been only one day — when, that is, he began to convey his wishes through those largely moulding movements of the right arm, those subtly inflecting movements of the left hand, and the orchestra began to produce the razor-edge attacks, the radiant and beautifully shaped sonorities, the sharply contoured phrases, the transparent textures of balanced sounds, that those movements had elicited in April 1936.'

Bernard H. Haggin, *Music Observed*, New York, Oxford University Press, 1964, pp. 35–36. See also: Virgil Thomson.

In 1937 the National Broadcasting Company (NBC) founded *The Symphony of the Air* that performed regular concerts, initially with Toscanini and later with other conductors, notably, Leopold Stokowski. It is from this time that many of Toscanini's 'NBC' gramophone recordings have their origin — Toscanini then being in his seventieth year. In the NBC Orchestra was the distinguished violinist Samuel Antek — himself an assistant conductor with the Chicago Symphony Orchestra. Of Toscanini's demeanour when conducting his relates:

> 'One of Toscanini's most enigmatic qualities was the almost unbelievable combination of saint and demon, poet and peasant, that was such an essential and paradoxical part of his temperament. As he stood on the podium at rehearsal in his severe black alpaca jacket with a thin white piping made by a handkerchief tucked in underneath the high collar, sharply creased striped trousers and finely shaped ankle-high slippers, he looked the personification of a priestly leader or a venerable saint. His face was transfigured with a spiritual light as he worked on a passage of beauty. He seemed lost in the mood.'

George Richard Marek, *Toscanini*, London, Vision, 1976, p. 103.

Following Toscanini's death on 16 January 1957, the BBC invited Arthur Bliss to contribute an obituary notice. We select the following passages:

> 'We in England haven't seen as much of Arturo

Toscanini as we should have wished. He came to London three times in the thirties, and he paid us what was virtually a farewell visit in 1952.

'I shall never forget the first concerts he gave here in the old Queen's Hall: no library of gramophone recordings can ever really conjure up those rehearsals. They had to be seen and lived through. I see today, as vividly as then, the orchestral players on the Queen's Hall platform. In the circle of the auditorium there are groups of prominent musicians, all silent, all waiting for one man, who suddenly, a slight figure, enters, carrying his baton. He quickly mounts the rostrum, flicks his stick against the metal stand, and launches straight into rehearsal. His beat seems big, his baton carves geometrical figures in the air; he uses it like a rapier or stiletto. There is no difference in intensity between rehearsal and concert performance — no relaxation of effort.'

During one of Toscanini's London visits, Bliss became personally acquainted with the celebrated conductor. Much to his surprise — astonishment even — he was asked: 'Tell me, Mr Bliss, do you as an Englishman think that I, an Italian, take the slow movements of Beethoven symphonies too fast?'

Regretfully, Bliss does not reveal what he said in reply and simply recalls: 'The name Toscanini is only another word for single-minded artistic integrity.'

Arthur Bliss, *As I Remember*, London, Thames Publishing, 1989, pp. 243–44. See also: Arthur Bliss. The Queen's Hall, to which Bliss makes reference, was London's principal concert venue until it was destroyed in 1941.

Thereafter, the Royal Albert Hall became the venue for the Promenade Concerts and the Royal Festival Hall for the general concert season.

DONALD FRANCIS TOVEY

The British musicologist, composer, pedagogue and conductor Sir Donald Francis Tovey is best known for his *Essays in Musical Analysis*. They had their origins as programme notes written by him to accompany the concerts given by the Ried Orchestra, Edinburgh — performed largely under Tovey's direction. The *Essays* were published in six volumes with each volume focusing on a particular category of Beethoven's music. Volumes I and II were devoted to the symphonies; Volume III, the concertos; Volume IV, illustrative music, Volume V, vocal music; and Volume VI, supplementary essays. A seventh volume was published posthumously dealing with chamber music. These writings are still respected today for their musicological erudition that Tovey interspersed with passages of wit and mordant humour. His musical analyses seek 'to facilitate the listener's appreciation of [the music's] artistic content and technical merits'. In addition to the *Essays*, Tovey paid tribute to Beethoven and his music in a series of articles that were published in the 1911 edition of the *Encyclopaedia Britannica*. Writing of Beethoven's artistic development, Tovey observes:

> 'The peculiar interest and difficulty in tracing Beethoven's artistic development are that the changes in the materials and range of his art were as great as those in the form, so that he appears in the light of a pioneer, while the art with which he started was nevertheless already a perfectly mature and highly organized thing.'

*

In an essay from 1902, Tovey discussed 'progress and achievement' in music:

> 'What after all is the progress of art? Certainly not the same as the progress of science. In science new theories supersede the old, but a great work of art is never superseded. It stands by its own consistency. The symphonies of Beethoven have not superseded those of Mozart; for what difference can it make to the perfection of a Mozart symphony that Beethoven afterwards produced equally perfect symphonies on a larger scale? The only indisputable fact on art, to which the name of progress can be applied, is that fundamental principle which we deduce from the nature of organic unity, the principle that every perfect work of art must differ in material and treatment in its own identity. And if we apply this principle to some of the great names in musical history, we shall find the results to be very varied indeed.'

In *The Musical Gazette*, July 1902, Tovey makes reference to Beethoven's creative progress:

> 'With Beethoven, progress seems to start out in all directions and all of them lead to truth. The real fact is that in his case the differences between one work and another are evident in outward form, and the range covered by each work increased with enormous rapidity throughout his career. But his early works certainly do not stand

towards the later as exercises to works of art: they are perfect masterpieces of smaller range. What is right for them would be inadequate for later: what is right for the later would be nonsensical in the earlier.'

Writing on 4 March 1920, Tovey considered 'the needs of an orchestra':

'[Nobody] with an appreciation of Beethoven's style could wish to add a note to his scores. But adding notes is a very different matter from getting the right balance of tone in complicated passages, and no one with the smallest pretentions to musical common sense, or to an appreciation of Beethoven's style, will deny the necessity of such work as has been mapped out by Weingartner in his treaties on the conducting of Beethoven's symphonies. In that work he points out, with an accuracy that leaves no room for doubt, that a complete performance of most of Beethoven's orchestral music requires a microscopically careful use of double wind, in order that the many important passages Beethoven gives to the wind instruments, in a position where they cannot penetrate through the other parts, may be reinforced without altering the quality of tone. [Tovey is referring here to: Felix Weingartner, *Ratschläge für Aufführungen der Symphonien Beethovens*, Leipzig, 1906]

'Beethoven's imagination of quality of tone is as vivid as anything in the history of art, nor did his deafness have the smallest adverse effect on it; but his deafness prevented him from detecting and correcting miscalculations of mere balance of tone, and none of his pupils or contemporaries could follow well enough to help him. It is essential to correct a performance of a Beethoven symphony that the woodwind should contain a reserve force which can set the balance right without altering the colour scheme, and which can retire the instant that it is necessary for any wind instrument to have the pure quality of a solo.'

Donald Francis Tovey, *Ludwig van Beethoven*, in: Michael Tilmouth, editor: *Donald Francis Tovey: The Classics of Music: Talks, Essays, and other Writings Previously Uncollected*, Oxford, Oxford University Press, 2001, p. 333, p. 674, p. 677, and pp. 751–52

In 1975, the American critic and musicologist Joseph Kerman wrote an essay to commemorate the hundredth anniversary of Tovey's birth, titled *Tovey's Beethoven*. In this, he makes a measured critique of the British musicologist's contribution to Beethoven musicology:

'To Tovey ... and I think many naïve listeners [i.e. not musically trained] ... Beethoven's music more than any other suggested links with life-experience. Darkness, mystery, fierceness, ghostliness: Beethoven puts words like these into the critic's mouth in a way that Bach and even Haydn and Brahms do not. Beethoven also suggests psychological states of mind.'

In his summing up of Tovey's achievement, Kerman reflects:

> '[In] some sense [Tovey] ... was ... one of the completest musicians who ever lived. Our latest musical dictionary calls him a "musical historian, pianist, composer and conductor".'

Kerman's reference here is to the entry in *Collins Music Encyclopedia*, London and Glasgow, 1959. Kerman adds: '[A] list which is obviously half as long as it should be: [Tovey] was also a legendary teacher, a musical analyst, theorist, music critic, and aesthetician.' We should also add that Tovey was an accomplished contributor to radio broadcasts, illustrating his remarks at the piano. Kerman concludes:

> 'Beethoven ... brought out the best in [Tovey], and for him richness, consistency, and completeness, *Tovey's Beethoven* stands out as the most impressive achievement, perhaps yet produced, by the art of music criticism.'

Joseph Kerman, *Write All These Down: Essays on Music*, Berkeley, California, London, University of California Press, 1994, pp. 155–70.

COSIMA WAGNER

Cosima Wagner was the illegitimate daughter of the Hungarian pianist and composer Franz Liszt and his mistress Marie d'Agoult. Her second marriage, to Richard Wagner, was an act of sustained veneration for the man and his music. Much of this is preserved in the 2,500 pages of her Diary. From Volume I, we have extracted the following remarks in which she recorded her, and Wagner's views concerning Beethoven:

22 JANUARY 1871:

'Richard considers: "Everybody should improvise, every good musician can produce something interesting in his improvisation. But writing it down is quite a different process, then it has to be turned into a sonata, a suite, and so on, and it takes a lot to revitalize a familiar, defined form ... Beethoven was the first to write music which was listened to purely as music, all previous things were designed to enliven social gatherings or to accompany what was going on in the church or on the stage".' pp. 325–6.

15 FEBRUARY 1871:

'I told [Richard] that for me the difference between Beethoven's music and that of the others also seemed to me to lie in the fact that his melodies arise out of the whole tonal fabric, in the way that a flower arises out of the whole plant, whereas other composers think up a theme with more-or-less ease, then append to it their musical work, their fugues, canons, counter-themes, etc. When yesterday we exclaimed, "Ah, that is Beethoven," I asked myself what we meant by that. With other composers, Mendelssohn for example, when we say "That is he," we are defining some routine, an inborn or assumed manner which crops up in unthinking moments; with Beethoven, however, we are recognizing the spirits which he alone can conjure up.' pp. 337–8.

31 MAY 1871:

'At lunch R. sang a theme by Beethoven (the second in the first movement of the F-minor

Sonata [Op. 57]) and says: "No one before him or after him has ever given us anything like that; it is sublimity when it becomes pleasurable; when it has been caught and one floats in it".'

4 NOVEMBER 1872:
[From this entry from Cosima Wagner's Diary, we learn of Wagner's views concerning Beethoven's Hammerklavier Sonata]
'[Richard] tells me he has been going through the first movement of Beethoven's B flat Sonata and was quite overwhelmed by the beauty and tenderness and richness of its detail, which passes by in such a way that nobody notices all that has been put into it ... He talks about orchestrating this sonata, in order to make it more accessible.' At this point Wagner himself remarked: "As it is, only the greatest of virtuosos can play it, but if it were performed as orchestrated by me, a sort of tradition could be established." Cosima concludes: 'We read though the sonata together with incredible delight, its richness of detail is like flowers hidden in a meadow.' p. 551.

30 OCTOBER 1874:
'In the evening R. studies [Beethoven's] *Les Adieux* Sonata with Herr [Josef] Rubenstein. In his [Wagner's] playing the usual fault of making an emotional work of this kind almost unrecognisable through an unfeeling, unaccented rendition can be discerned again.' A later entry of Cosima's suggests Wagner justified his style of interpretation to Rubinstein: 'R. explains to him that the difficulty of interpreting the works of

B.'s middle period lies in the fact that they appear to preserve the old forms, whereas the themes and figurations go far beyond them — they are full of passion and deep emotion.' p. 798.

25 SEPTEMBER 1877:
[From this entry of Cosima Wagner's Diary, we gain an insight into the intellectual nature of her relationship with Wagner and of his estimation of the second movement of Beethoven's C minor Piano Sonata, Op. 111:] 'In the evening ... [Richard] reads me ... Voltaire's article on Aristotle in the *Dictionnaire philosophique*. The boldness of its flights of imagination leads to Beethoven, and R. says that were he to try to visualize Beethoven "in all his starry glory", he would surely think of the second movement of Op. 111 (adagio with variations); he knows nothing more ecstatic, he says, yet at the same time it is never sentimental.' pp. 983–4.

Gregor-Dellin and Dietrich Mack, editors, *Cosima Wagner's Diaries, Vol. 1, 1869–1877,* London, Collins, 1978–80.

RICHARD WAGNER

We learn of Wagner's admiration of Beethoven from his biographer, the composer, teacher and writer on music Ferdinand Praeger. His, *Wagner As I Knew Him* appeared in 1892 — the first-full length biography of the composer to be published in English. It earned the endorsement of the Wagner enthusiast George Bernhard Shaw but was later criticized for Praeger's alleged misrepresentations. If we place our trust in the less controversial aspects of Praeger's account, we derive the following impressions.

Beethoven's youthful influences on Wagner:

> 'Wagner at fifteen was a poet, and the energetic, suggestive music of Beethoven was mentally transformed into living personalities. He has said that he felt as if Beethoven addressed him "personally." Every movement formed itself into a story, glowed with life, and assumed a clear, distinct shape. I do not forget the earlier influence of Weber over him, but then that was more due to emotion than to reason. The novelty of *Der Freischütz*, the freshness of its melodic stream, and the wild imaginative treatment of the romantic story captivated his first affection and enchained it to the last. The whole of his impressions of Beethoven (whom, by the way, Wagner never saw) were embodied by him in a sketch written for a periodical and entitled, *A Pilgrimage to Beethoven*. Although the incidents painted there are not to be taken as having happened to the pilgrim, Wagner, yet the story is clear on one point — the unbounded spell Beethoven exercised over him.'

Wagner's youthful absorption in the music of Beethoven:

> 'Beethoven was his daily study. He was carefully storing all the grand thoughts of the great master, but his fiery enthusiasm had not yet come to that burning-point when it should ignite his own latent powers. His acquaintance

with the scores of Beethoven has never been equalled. It was extraordinary. He had them so much by heart that he could play on the piano, with his own awkward fingering, whole movements.'

Wagner's estimation of the variable standard of orchestral conducting in 1856:

'At Leipzig, the entire music was particularly slovenly played ... And yet the very men who played so reprehensively in the stage orchestra, when performing at the famous Gewandhaus concerts, seemed to be moved by feelings of reverence for their work, unknown to them in the theatre. It would be an interesting investigation to discover why this was. The symphonies of Beethoven, in the concert-room, compelled their whole worship; the symphonies of Haydn, in the theatre, were treated like "dinner" music. Perhaps the explanation is, that the symphonic movements played in the theatre bore no relation to the drama enacted, whereas music played for itself went with a verve and spirit, and attention to its meaning quite unknown to the stop-gap-music scrambling of the theatre.'

Ferdinand Praeger, *Wagner as I knew Him*, London, New York, Longmans, Green, 1892, p. 35, p. 37, and p. 40.

Wagner outlined his own debt to Beethoven in his Autobiography *My Life* from which we cite the following:

'I sketched out a musical composition about this

time [1834], a symphony in E major, whose first movement (3/4 time) I completed as a separate piece. As regards style and design, this work was suggested by Beethoven's Seventh and Eighth Symphonies, and, so far as I can remember, I should have had no need to be ashamed of it, had I been able to complete it, or keep the part I had actually finished. But I had already begun at this time to form the opinion that, to produce anything fresh and truly noteworthy in the realm of symphony, and according to Beethoven's methods, was an impossibility. Whereas opera, to which I felt inwardly drawn, though I had no real example I wished to copy, presented itself to my mind in varied and alluring shapes as a most fascinating form of art.'

Wagner's response to learning of the death of Beethoven:

'Another work also exercised a great fascination over me, namely, the overture to *Fidelio* in E major, the introduction to which affected me deeply. I asked my sisters about Beethoven, and learned that the news of his death had just arrived. Obsessed as I still was by the terrible grief caused by Weber's death, this fresh loss, due to the decease of this great master of melody, who had only just entered my life, filled me with strange anguish, a feeling nearly akin to my childish dread of the ghostly fifths on the violin. It was now Beethoven's music that I longed to know more thoroughly; I came to Leipzig, and found his music to *Egmont* on the piano at my sister Louisa's. After that I tried to get hold of his sonatas. At last, at a concert at the Gewandhaus, I heard one of the master's symphonies for the first time; it was the Symphony in A major. The effect on me was indescribable. To this must be added the impression produced on me by Beethoven's features, which I saw in the lithographs that were circulated everywhere at that time, and by the fact that he was deaf, and lived a quiet secluded life. I soon conceived an image of him in my mind as a sublime and unique supernatural being, with whom none could compare. This image was associated in my brain with that of Shakespeare; in ecstatic dreams I met both of them, saw and spoke to them, and on awakening found myself bathed in tears.'

Richard Wagner, *My Life*, London, Constable and Company Ltd., 1911, pp. 35–6, p. 37, and pp. 111–12.

Wagner's prose works extend to eight substantial volumes, English editions of which appeared in translation over the period 1895–1907 from the hand of William Ashton Ellis. In Volume I, Wagner reveals facets of his respect for Beethoven.

On Beethoven's powers of invention:

'Assuredly there had never been an artist who pondered less upon his art. The brusque impetuosity of his nature shows he felt as an actual personal injury, almost as direct as every other shackle of convention, the ban imposed on his genius by these forms. Yet his rebellion consisted in nothing but the exuberant unfolding of his inner genius, unrestrained by those outward forms themselves. He never did radically alter an existing form of instrumental music; in his last sonatas, quartets, symphonies and so forth, we may demonstrate beyond dispute a structure such as of the first. But compare these works with one another; compare for example the Eighth Symphony in F with the Second in D, and marvel at the wholly new world that fronts us in well-nigh the identical form.'

Wagner compares Beethoven with Columbus:

'Did Columbus teach us to take ship across the ocean, and thus to bind in one each continent of Earth; did his world-historical discovery convert the narrow-seeing national-man into a universal and all-seeing *Man*: so, by the hero who explored the broad and seeming shoreless sea of absolute Music unto its very bounds, are won the new and never dreamt-of coasts which this sea no longer now divorces from the old and primal continent of man, but *binds together* with it for the newborn, happy art-life of the Manhood of the Future. And this hero is none other than — Beethoven.'

On Beethoven's instrumental music:

'It was *Beethoven* who opened up the boundless faculty of Instrumental Music for expressing elemental storm and stress. His power it was, that took the basic essence of the Christian's Harmony, that bottomless sea of unhedged fullness and unceasing motion, and clove in twain the fetters of its freedom. *Harmonic Melody* — for so must we designate this melody divorced from speech, in distinction from the Rhythmic Melody of dance — was capable, though merely borne by instruments, of the most limitless expression together with the most unfettered treatment. In long, connected tracts of sound, as in larger, smaller, or even smallest fragments, it turned beneath the Master's poet hand to vowels, syllables, and words and phrases of a speech in which a message hitherto unheard, and never spoken yet, could promulgate itself. Each letter of this speech was an infinitely soul-full element; and the measure of the joinery of these elements was utmost free commensuration, such as could be exercised by none but a tone-poet who longed for the unmeasured utterance of this unfathomed yearning.'

On the Fifth Symphony:

'What inimitable art did Beethoven employ in his "C-minor Symphony," in order to steer his ship from the ocean of infinite yearning to the haven of fulfilment! He was able to raise the utterance of his music *almost* to a moral resolve, but not to speak aloud that final word; and after every onset of the Will, without a moral handhold, we feel tormented by the equal possibility of falling back again to suffering, as of being led to lasting victory. Nay, this falling-back must almost seem to us more "necessary" than the morally ungrounded triumph, which therefore —

not being a necessary consummation, but a mere arbitrary gift of grace — has not the power to lift us up and yield to us that *ethical* satisfaction which we demand as outcome of the yearning of the heart.'

On the Seventh Symphony:

'This symphony is the *Apotheosis of Dance* herself: it is Dance in her highest aspect, as it were the loftiest Deed of bodily motion incorporated in an ideal mould of tone. Melody and Harmony unite around the sturdy bones of Rhythm to firm and fleshy human shapes, which now with giant limbs' agility, and now with soft, elastic pliance, *almost before our very eyes,* close up the supple, teeming ranks; the while now gently, now with daring, now serious, now wanton, now pensive, and again exulting, the deathless strain sounds forth and forth; until, in the last whirl of delight, a kiss of triumph seals the last embrace.'

On the Ninth Symphony:

'The Last Symphony of Beethoven is the redemption of Music from out her own peculiar element into the realm of *universal Art.* It is the human Evangel of the art of the Future. Beyond it no forward step is possible; for upon it the perfect Art-work of the Future alone can follow, the *universal Drama* to which Beethoven has forged for us the key ... "*Freude!*" *("Rejoice!") ... With this word he cries to men: "Breast to breast, ye mortal millions! This one kiss to all the world!*"

— And *this Word* will be the language of the *Art-work of the Future.*'

William Ashton Ellis, *Richard Wagner's Prose Works: Vol. 1, The Art-Work of the Future*, edited and translated by William Ashton Ellis, London, Kegan Paul, Trench, Trübner, 1895. The quotations cited above are derived from: p. 83, p. 115, p. 121, p. 123, pp. 124–25, and p. 126.

In 1870, Wagner published his study *Beethoven* to correspond with the centenary celebrations then arising in connection with the composer's birth. An English translation appeared in 1893 by Edward Dannreuther. Wagner's stated aim, as he outlined in his *Preface*, was 'to deliver an oration ... in honour of the great musician ... at a greater length than would have been possible had he actually addressed an audience'. We cite the following passages, some of which overlap with the texts from which we have previously quoted.

Beethoven and sonata form:

> 'It may be said that Beethoven was and remained a composer of sonatas, for in far the greater number and the best of his instrumental compositions, the outline of the sonata-form was the veil-like tissue through which he gazed into the veil-like realm of sounds; or, through which, emerging from that realm, he made himself intelligible; whilst other forms, particularly the mixed ones of vocal music, despite the most extraordinary achievements in them, he only touched upon in passing, as if by way of experiment.'

Beethoven's debt to his predecessors:

> 'Beethoven's earlier works are not incorrectly held to have sprung from Haydn's model; and a closer relationship to Haydn than Mozart may be traced even in the later development of his genius ... Beethoven would not recognise Haydn as his teacher, though the latter was generally taken for such, and he even suffered injurious expressions of youthful arrogance to escape him about Haydn. It seems as though he felt himself related to Haydn like one born a man to a childish elder. As regards form he agreed with his teacher, but the unruly demon of his inner music, fettered by that form, impelled him to a disclosure of his power, which, like everything else in the doings of gigantic musicians, could only appear incomprehensibly rough.'

Beethoven's youthful independence of mind:

> 'We see young Beethoven ... facing the world at once with that defiant temperament which, throughout his life, kept him in almost savage independence: his enormous self-confidence, supported by haughtiest courage, at all times prompted him to defend himself from the frivolous demands made upon music by a pleasure-seeking world. He had to guard a treasure of immeasurable richness against the importunities of effeminate taste. He was the soothsayer of the innermost world of tones, and he had to act as such in the very forms in which music was displaying itself as a merely diverting art.'

Beethoven's capacity to enrich traditional musical forms:

> 'He never altered any of the extant forms of instrumental music on principle; the same structure can be traced in his last sonatas, quartets, symphonies, etc., as unmistakably as in his first. But compare these works with one another; place the Eighth Symphony in F major beside the Second in D, and wonder at the entirely new world, almost in precisely the same form!'

Beethoven's powers of invention:

> '[The] feature in Beethoven's musical productions which is so particularly momentous for the history of art is this; that in every technical detail, by means of which for clearness' sake the artist places himself in a conventional relation to the external world, is raised to the highest significance of a spontaneous effusion.'

Beethoven's response to nature:

> 'He cast his glance upon phenomena that answered in wondrous reflex, illuminated by his inner light. The essential nature of things now again speaks to him, and he sees things displayed in the calm light of beauty. Again, he understands the forest, the brook, the meadow, the blue sky, the song of birds, the flight of clouds, the roar of storms, the beatitude of blissfully moving repose. All he perceives and constructs is permeated with that wondrous serenity which

music has gained through him ... Who does not hear the Redeemer's word when listening to the *Pastoral* Symphony?'

On Beethoven's setting of Schiller's *Ode to Joy*:

'It is quite evident that Schiller's words have only been made to fit the main melody as best they could; for that melody is at first fully developed, and emitted by instruments alone, when it inspires us with inexpressible emotions of joy at the "paradise regained". The most consummate art has never produced anything artistically more simple than that melody, the childlike innocence of which, when it is first heard in the most equable whisper of the bass stringed-instruments, in unison, breathes upon us with a saintly breath ... there is nothing like the sweet fervour to which every newly-added voice further animates this prototype of purest innocence, until every embellishment, every glory of elevated feeling, unites in it and around it, like the breathing world round a finally revealed dogma of purest love.'

Wagner compares Beethoven with Shakespeare:

'Shakespeare ... remained wholly incomparable, until German genius produced in *Beethoven* a being that can only be analogically explained by comparison with him.'

Wagner's concluding celebratory tribute to Beethoven:

'[Nothing] can more inspiringly stand beside the triumphs of [the] bravery [of the German people] in this wonderful year of 1870 than the memory of our great *Beethoven*, who just a hundred years ago was born to the German people ... Let us then celebrate the great pathfinder in the wilderness of degenerate paradise! But let us celebrate him worthily — not less worthily than the victories of German bravery: for the world's benefactor takes precedence of the world's conqueror!'

Richard Wagner, *Beethoven: With [a] Supplement from the Philosophical Works of A. Schopenhauer*, translated by E. Dannreuther, London, Reeves, 1893. The quotations cited above are derived from: p. 36, pp. 37–38, p. 39, p. 42, p. 45, pp. 54–55, pp. 70–71, p. 79, and pp. 112–13.

In other of his prose works, Wagner pays further tribute to Beethoven's orchestral writing. He first reiterates his conviction of the significance of the rhythmic impulse of the dance:

> 'The *harmonized dance* is the basis of the richest art-work of the modern *Symphony* ... This artwork, in its highest culmination, is *the symphony of Haydn, of Mozart, and Beethoven.*' [Wagner's italics]

Wagner likens orchestral sound to that of the human voice:

> 'The orchestra indisputably possess a *faculty of speech*, and the creations of modern instrumental music have disclosed it to us. In the Symphonies of Beethoven, we have seen this faculty

develop to a height whence it felt thrust to speak out. That which, by its very nature, it cannot speak out. Now that in the word-verse melody we have brought it that which *it* could not speak out, and have assigned to it, as carrier of this kindred melody, the office in which — completely eased in mind — it is to speak nothing but what its nature fits *it* alone to speak: now we have plenty to denote this speaking-faculty of the orchestra as the faculty of uttering the *unspeakable*.' [Wagner's italics]

Wagner compares Beethoven's orchestral construction with that of Mozart's:

'*Mozart* still commenced his symphonies with an entire melody, which he then, as though in sport, divided contrapuntally into smaller and smaller portions. *Beethoven's* most distinctive creation began with these divided pieces, from which he built before our very eyes an ever loftier and richer edifice.'

Wagner offers a summary of Beethoven's symphonic inheritance and pays tribute to the pioneering achievements of his precursors Haydn and Mozart:

'HAYDN was the genius who first developed this form to a broader compass, and gave it power of deep expression through an exhaustless play of motives, as also of their traditional links and working-out ... It was MOZART who became aware of this charm, and while he brought to Italian Opera the richer *development* of the

German mode of instrumental composition, he imparted in turn to the orchestral melody the full *euphony* of the Italian mode of song.

'This ample heritage and promise of both these masters was taken up by BEETHOVEN: he matured the Symphonic artwork to so engrossing a breadth of form, and filled that form with so manifold and enthralling a melodic content, that we stand today before the Beethovenian Symphony as before the landmark of an entirely new period in the history of universal Art; for through it there came into the world a phenomenon not even remotely approached by anything that art of any age or any people has shown us.' [Wagner's italics and capitalization]

William Ashton Ellis, Richard Wagner's prose works: Vol. 3, *The Theatre*, edited and translated by William Ashton Ellis, London, Kegan Paul, Trench, Trübner, 1907 (*et seq.*), p.120; Vol. 2, *Opera and Drama*, p. 316; Vol. 4, *Art and Politics*, p. 79; and Vol. 5, *Actors and Singers*, pp. 317–18.

ERNEST WALKER

Ernest Walker was an Indian-born English composer, pianist, teacher, and writer on music. He held the post of Director of music at Baliol College, Oxford, contributed articles to *Grove's Dictionary of Music and Musicians* (1902), and wrote the entry ***Beethoven*** in the pioneering *Music of the Masters* series (1905). In his capacity as a pianist, he wrote cadenzas for Beethoven's Third Piano Concerto. Writing in the December 1930 issue of *The Monthly Musical News*, Walker considered 'Some Questions of Tempo' in connection with the metronome:

'Theoretically the metronome ought of course to have solved forever what Mozart judged to be the most difficult of all a performer's problems, the decision of the tempo. But, practically, we all know that it has not; and there must indeed be any number of performers — conductors, ensemble-players, soloists — who never trouble themselves about even more-or-less authoritative metronome marks.

'The rigidity of the metronome we of course discount; the indication, whatever it is, is understood to be both approximate and fluctuating. Except for contrasts of other special effects, no performance worth anything, of any music, remains mathematically level, either in time or tone, for more than a very limited period. This we all take for granted; but the vital questions remain — do the indications really represent the composer's fully considered wishes, and even if they do, is he to be the only judge of tempo? Conductors of unimpeachable classical-mindedness will no doubt know Beethoven's own metronomizations of his symphonies; but very rarely indeed will they feel bound by them.'

Ernest Walker, *Free Thought and the Musician, and other Essays*, London, New York, Oxford University Press, 1946, pp. 134–35.

FELIX WEINGARTNER

The Austrian conductor, composer and pianist Felix Weingartner is today primarily remembered for his interpretations of Beethoven's symphonies — he was the first conductor to make commercial recordings of all nine symphonies. Whilst they are still recognized for being pioneering, many consider his interpretations to be subjective by today's performance-standards on the basis, for example, of tempo fluctuations that are inconsistent with the printed score.

When on holiday as a young boy, Weingartner recalls his first awakening interest in Beethoven that was to set the course of his future destiny as a major interpreter of the composer's works:

> 'While in Baden, I had for the first time heard the name of Beethoven; my grandfather had related that he had once, in his youth, sat at the same table as the master. It happened at an inn and my grandfather, without knowing who the other was, had been struck by his strange appearance, his air of living apart from the world, his loud tones when he spoke, and the large ear-trumpet he held at his ear when anybody addressed him. On inquiry, my grandfather had been told who his fellow guest had been. This tale made such a deep impression on me that I remembered the name of Beethoven and connected it with something vast, like St. Stephen's Tower and the Danube, so that now I readily comprehend why, when my mother — or another member of my family — suddenly said: "Beethoven lived here", I was strangely thrilled.'

Felix Weingartner, *Buffets and Rewards: A Musician's Reminiscences*. London: Hutchinson & Co., 1937, p. 18.

In his memoirs, the Hungarian violinist recalls his impressions of Weingartner:

> '[Arthur] Nikisch's rival in the favour of the Berlin public was Felix Weingartner ... I remember him as an exceptionally handsome man, well-proportioned in his figure and features like a Greek sculpture ... His beat was far more conventional and old-fashioned than Nikisch's. What was remarkable, however, was the difference in quality between his performances. While his interpretations of the first movement of Beethoven's Fifth, in Amsterdam in 1903, was one of the greatest re-creations I have ever heard, his *Eroica*, at Moscow in 1910, seemed like a feeble average performance of a provincial conductor. The effect left by his interpretations depended above all on whether he found it possible to compel the orchestra to surrender entirely to his will. Thus, his art rested primarily on psychic foundations, whereas his pure craftsmanship, both in his baton technique and in rehearsing the orchestra, was on a comparatively primitive level. His state of mind was decisive for the achievement or failure of his intentions, since purely technically he was unable to produce, up to a point, a substitute for any missing inspiration.'

Hans Keller, editor, *The Memoirs of Carl Flesch*, New York, Macmillan, 1958, pp. 150–51.

HUGO WOLF

The Austrian composer Hugo Wolf was regarded as a child prodigy, commencing study of the piano and violin at the age of four. He eventually enrolled at the Vienna Conservatory where, his friend Peter Miller recalls, he applied himself diligently to the study of Beethoven's piano sonatas:

> 'He spent day after day in the big Vienna library, absorbed in music of every kind, chiefly that of Beethoven and of Bach, dissecting it, committing it to memory.'

Years later, Miller called upon Wolf and happened to see in his room a dilapidated copy of Beethoven's sonatas. Turning the leaves over, he noticed many indications on them of careful study, and remarked upon them to Wolf:

> 'Yes', said Wolf, very seriously, 'those were bad days. I lived in a garret, and had no piano; so, I used to take out the sonatas separately, and study them in the Prater.'

Ernest Newman, *Hugo Wolf*, New York, Dover Publications, 1966, p. 14.

As his studies progressed, Wolf was seized with enthusiasm for the classical composers:

> 'His musical interests were no longer confined to operatic pot-pourri: he talked now of Haydn, Mozart, and Beethoven and other composers, but principally with fanatical zeal, of Beethoven, whose symphonies he played in piano arrange-

ments. His colleagues loved to make game of him on account of these Beethoven transports, but when they exasperated him beyond bearing he used to fly at them with raised fists and pummel them into displaying more reverence before his idols.'

Frank Walker, *Hugo Wolf: A Biography*, London, J. M. Dent, 1951, p. 13.

In February 1883, Richard Wagner died — a circumstance that affected Wolf deeply. The following year, *The Vienna Academic Wagner Society* sponsored an anniversary concert — 'In Memory of Richard Wagner'. The celebrated virtuoso pianist Anton Rubinstein was invited to play a selection of Beethoven's piano sonatas. Wolf was in the audience and wrote a review of the recital — in characteristically trenchant terms — that give an insight into Rubinstein's style of performance:

'Rubinstein moves among our ivory crushers like Gulliver among the Lilliputians ... As for Beethoven's sonatas, he must bow to Bülow [Hans von Bülow], who, three years ago, played the last six sonatas for us, and so perfectly as to persuade us immediately that Beethoven should be played in this way and in no other. The dreadfully hurried tempi, the unexampled interpretive liberties, the nonchalance with which Rubinstein treats particularly prominent passages such as the recitative phrase in the first movement of the Sonata in D minor, etc., all these [are] dark blemishes on the luminous glory of his heroic deeds.

> Perhaps it was simply not Anton Rubinstein's night for Beethoven?'

Frank Walker, Hugo *Wolf: A Biography*, London, J. M. Dent, 1951, p. 158.

Wolf earned much of his living as a music critic, notably for the *Vienna Salonblatt*. Ernest Newman, writing of Wolf's acerbic style in *The Times* (1 August 1912) declared: 'His sharp pen ... makes everything live that it describes ... The writing is always fresh, and often witty.' On attending a concert in the 1884 music season — that evidently displeased him — Wolf protested:

> 'If you want symphonies today, as Beethoven wrote them, then turn back our century, waken the master from the dead, but don't set up in his place our epigones, these impotent symphony writers of the present day ... Beethoven as absolute musician, has in the symphony spoken the last word.'

At the period when Wolf was writing his music criticism, the symphonies of Anton Bruckner were being performed after years of neglect. In an article of 28 December 1884, Wolf acknowledged the grandeur of the Austrian composer's music but considered it to be flawed and over-reliant on Beethovenian influences:

> 'It is a certain want of intelligence that makes Bruckner's symphonies, for all their originality, grandeur, power, imagination, and invention so difficult to grasp. There is always and everywhere the will, the colossal strivings — but no satisfaction, no artistic resolution ... Thus, he wavers, rooted

halfway between Beethoven and the new advances of the moderns ... [In] all of Bruckner's symphonies we detect in the grandiose themes and their thoughtful elaboration the language of Beethoven.'

Henry Pleasants editor and translator, *The Music Criticism of Hugo Wolf,* New York, Holmes & Meier Publishers, 1978, p. 99.

In April 1884, Wolf reflected on the music season and gave expression to his views on music. He singled out for praise Schubert's Symphony in B minor that he described as 'a faithful mirror of its creator's artistic individuality'. He lamented, as so many others have, that it is 'but a fragment ... [whose] form resembles the composer's own mortal life, cut off by death in the bloom of life, at the summit of his creative power'. Wolf closed with further remarks about Schubert in the context of Beethoven, the composer whom he so revered. His moving words make a fitting close to our *Anthology*:

'As if by agreement between muses and fates, the fruitful isle of song was Schubert's birthright from the former, to be transformed by the bubbling spring of his melodies, in the short span of his mortal existence, into a fabulous magic garden whose freshness and fragrance will never, never fade. From this enchanted island he now beheld the giant Beethoven crossing the ocean in the storm, defying the elements in his furious passage. Then was the islander's heart seized by a mighty urge. To follow Beethoven in his desolate and dangerous course was now Schubert's only thought. But that was hard, for that Titan loved to sail among rocks, sandbanks, reefs and whirlpools and surf. And if he made for the open sea, he surged ahead on the wings of the storm, calling down thunder and lightning, a god annihilating with a mere glance whomever he encountered.'

Henry Pleasants, editor and translator, *The Music Criticism of Hugo Wolf*, New York, Holmes & Meier Publishers, 1978, pp. 12–13 and pp. 37–38.

BIBLIOGRAPHY

The author has individually consulted all the publications listed in this bibliography and can confirm that each makes reference, in some way or other, to Beethoven and his works. It will be evident from their titles which of these are publications devoted exclusively to the composer. Others that make only passing reference to Beethoven and his compositions, nevertheless unfailingly bear testimony to his genius and humanity. The diversity of the titles listed testifies to the centrality of Beethoven to western culture and beyond; the mere survey of these should be of itself a rewarding experience for a lover of so-called classical music. The entries are confined to book publications, reflecting the scope of the author's researches. The cut-off date for this was 2007; no works after this date are listed, notwithstanding the author is mindful that Beethoven musicology, and related publication, continue to be a major field of endeavour.

Abraham, Gerald. *Beethoven's second-period quartets*. London: Oxford University Press: Humphrey Milford, 1944.

Abraham, Gerald. *Essays on Russian and East European music*. Oxford: Clarendon Press: New York: Oxford University Press, 1985.

Abraham, Gerald, Editor. *The age of Beethoven, 1790-1830*. London: Oxford University Press, 1982.

Abraham, Gerald. *The tradition of Western music*. London: Oxford University Press, 1974.

Abse, Dannie and Joan. *The Music lover's literary companion*. London: Robson Books, 1988.

Adorno, Theodor W., Translator. *Alban Berg: master of the smallest link*. Cambridge: Cambridge University Press, 1991.

Adorno, Theodor W. *Beethoven: the philosophy of music; fragments and texts*. Cambridge: Polity Press, 1998.

Albrecht, Daniel, Editor. *Modernism and music: an anthology of sources*. Chicago; London: University of Chicago Press, 2004.

Albrecht, Theodore, Translator and Editor. *Letters to Beethoven and other correspondence*. Lincoln, New England: University of Nebraska Press, 3 vols., 1996.

Allsobrook, David Ian. *Liszt: my travelling circus life*. London: Macmillan, 1991.

Anderson, Christopher, Editor and Translator. *Selected writings of Max Reger*. New York; London: Routledge, 2006.

Anderson, Emily, Editor and Translator. *The letters of Beethoven*. London: Macmillan, 3 vols.,1961.

Anderson, Martin, Editor. *Klemperer on music: shavings from a musician's workbench*. London: Toccata Press, 1986.

Antheil, George. *Bad boy of music*. London; New York: Hurst & Blackett Ltd., 1945.

Appleby, David P. *Heitor Villa-Lobos: a bio-bibliography*. New York: Greenwood Press, 1988.

Aprahamian, Felix, Editor. *Essays on music: an anthology from The Listener*. London, Cassell, 1967.

Armero, Gonzalo and Jorge de Persia. *Manuel de Falla : his life & works*. London: Omnibus Press, 1999.

Arnold, Ben, Editor. *The Liszt companion*. Westport, Connecticut; London: Greenwood Press, 2002.

Arnold, Denis and Nigel Fortune, Editors. *The Beethoven companion*. London: Faber and Faber, 1973.

Ashbrook, William. *Donizetti*. London: Cassell, 1965.

Auner, Joseph Henry. *A Schoenberg reader: documents of a life*. New Haven Connecticut; London: Yale University Press, 2003.

Avins, Styra, Editor. *Johannes Brahms: life and letters*. Oxford: Oxford University Press, 1997.

Azoury, Pierre H. *Chopin through his contemporaries: friends, lovers, and rivals*. Westport, Connecticut: Greenwood Press, 1999.

Badura-Skoda, Paul. *Carl Czerny: On the Proper Performance of all Beethoven's Works for the Piano*. Universal Edition: A. G. Wien, 1970.

Bailey, Cyril. *Hugh Percy Allen*. London: Oxford University Press, 1948.

Bailey, Kathryn. *The life of Webern.* Cambridge: Cambridge University Press, 1998.

Barenboim, Daniel. *A life in music.* London: Weidenfeld & Nicolson, 1991.

Barlow, Michael. *Whom the gods love: the life and music of George Butterworth.* London: Toccata Press, 1997.

Barrett-Ayres, Reginald. *Joseph Haydn and the string quartet.* New York: Schirmer Books, 1974.

Bartos, Frantisek. *Bedrich Smetana: Letters and reminiscences.* Prague: Artia, 1953.

Barzun, Jacques. *Pleasures of music: an anthology of writing about music and musicians.* London: Cassell, 1977.

Bauer-Lechner, Natalie. *Recollections of Gustav Mahler.* London: Faber Music, 1980.

Bazhanov, N. Nikolai. *Rakhmaninov.* Moscow: Raduga, 1983.

Beaumont, Antony, Editor. *Ferruccio Busoni: Selected letters.* London: Faber and Faber, 1987.

Beaumont, Antony, Editor. *Gustav Mahler, letters to his wife.* London: Faber and Faber, 2004.

Beecham, Thomas. *A mingled chime: an autobiography.* New York: Da Capo Press, 1976.

Bekker, Paul. *Beethoven.* London: J. M. Dent & Sons, 1925.

Bellasis, Edward. *Cherubini: memorials illustrative of his life.* London: Burns and Oates, 1874.

Bennett, James R. Sterndale. *The life of William Sterndale Bennett.* Cambridge: University Press, 1907.

Benser, Caroline Cepin. *Egon Wellesz (1885–1974): chronicle of twentieth-century musician.* New York: P. Lang, 1985.

Berlioz, Hector. *Evenings in the orchestra.* Harmondsworth: Penguin Books, 1963.

Berlioz, Hector. *The musical madhouse (Les grotesques de la musique).* Rochester, New York: University of Rochester Press, 2003.

Bernard, Jonathan W., Editor. *Elliott Carter: collected essays and lectures, 1937-1995.* Rochester, New York; Woodbridge: University of Rochester Press, 1998.

Bernstein, Leonard. *The joy of music.* New York: Simon and Schuster, 1959.

Bertensson, Sergei. *Sergei Rachmaninoff: a lifetime in music.* London: G. Allen & Unwin, 1965.

Biancolli, Louis. *The Flagstad manuscript.* New York: Putnam, 1952.

Bickley, Nora, Editor. *Letters from and to Joseph Joachim.* London: Macmillan, 1914.

Bie, Oskar. *A history of the pianoforte and pianoforte players.* New York: Da Capo Press, 1966.

Blaukopf, Herta. *Mahler's unknown letters.* London: Gollancz, 1986.

Blaukopf, Kurt and Herta. *Mahler: his life, work and world.* London: Thames and Hudson, 1991.

Bliss, Arthur. *As I remember.* London: Thames Publishing, 1989.

Block, Adrienne Fried. *Amy Beach, passionate Victorian: the life and work of an American composer, 1867–1944.* New York: Oxford University Press, 1998.

Bloch, Ernst. *Essays on the philoso-*

phy of music. Cambridge: Cambridge University Press, 1985.
Blocker, Robert. *The Robert Shaw reader*. New Haven; London: Yale University Press, 2004.
Blom, Eric. *A musical postbag*. London: J. M. Dent, 1945.
Blom, Eric. *Beethoven's pianoforte sonatas discussed*. London: J. M. Dent, 1938.
Blom, Eric. *Classics major and minor: with some other musical ruminations*. London: J. M. Dent, 1958.
Blum, David. *The art of quartet playing: the Guarneri Quartet in conversation with David Blum*. London: Gollancz, 1986.
Blume, Friedrich. *Classic and Romantic music: a comprehensive survey*. London: Faber and Faber, 1972.
Boden, Anthony. *The Parrys of the Golden Vale: background to genius*. London: Thames Publishing, 1998.
Bonavia, Ferruccio. *Musicians on music*. London: Routledge & Kegan Paul, 1956.
Bonds, Mark Evan *After Beethoven: imperatives of originality in the symphony*. Cambridge, Massachusetts; London: Harvard University Press, 1996.
Bonis, Ferenc, Editor. *The selected writings of Zoltán Kodály*. London; New York: Boosey & Hawkes, 1974.
Bookspan, Martin. *André Previn: a biography*. London: Hamilton, 1981.
Boros, James and Richard Toop, Editors. *Brian Ferneyhough: Collected writings*. Amsterdam: Harwood Academic, 1995.
Boulez, Pierre. *Stocktakings from an apprenticeship*. Oxford: Clarendon Press, 1991.
Boult, Adrian. *Boult on music: words from a lifetime's communication*. London: Toccata Press, 1983.
Boult, Adrian. *My own trumpet*. London, Hamish Hamilton, 1973.
Boult, Adrian with Jerrold Northrop Moore. *Music and friends: seven decades of letters to Adrian Boult from Elgar, Vaughan Williams, Holst, Bruno Walter, Yehudi Menuhin and other friends*. London: Hamish Hamilton, 1979.
Bovet, Marie Anne de. *Charles Gounod: his life and his works*. London: S. Low, Marston, Searle & Rivington, Ltd., 1891.
Bowen, Catherine Drinker. *Beloved friend: the story of Tchaikowsky and Nadejda von Meck*. London: Hutchinson & Co., 1937.
Bowen, Meiron, Editor. *Gerhard on music: selected writings*. Brookfield, Vermont: Ashgate, 2000.
Bowen, Meirion. *Michael Tippett*. London: Robson Books, 1982.
Bowen, Meiron, Editor. *Music of the angels: essays and sketchbooks of Michael Tippett*. London: Eulenburg, 1980.
Bowen, Meiron, Editor. *Tippett on music*. Oxford: Clarendon Press, 1995.
Bowers, Faubion. *Scriabin: a biography*. Mineola: Dover; London: Constable, 1996.
Boyden, Matthew. *Richard Strauss*. London: Weidenfeld & Nicolson, 1999.
Bozarth, George S., Editor. *Brahms*

studies: *analytical and historical perspectives; papers delivered at the International Brahms Conference, Washington, DC, 5-8 May 1983*. Oxford: Clarendon Press, 1990.

Brand, Juliane, Christopher Hailey and Donald Harris, Editors. *The Berg-Schoenberg correspondence: selected letters*. Basingstoke: Macmillan, 1987.

Brandenbugh, Sieghard, Editor. *Haydn, Mozart, & Beethoven: studies in the music of the classical period: essays in honor of Alan Tyson*. Oxford: Clarendon Press, 1998.

Braunstein, Joseph. *Musica Æterna, program notes for 1961–1971*. New York: Musica Æterna, 1972.

Braunstein, Joseph. *Musica Æterna, program notes for 1971–1976*. New York: Musica Æterna, 1978.

Brendel, Alfred. *Alfred Brendel on music: collected essays*. Chicago, Illinois: A Cappella Books, 2001.

Brendel, Alfred. *The veil of order: Alfred Brendel in conversation with Martin Meyer*. London: Faber and Faber, 2002.

Breuning, Gerhard von. *Memories of Beethoven: from the house of the black-robed Spaniards*. Cambridge: Cambridge University Press, 1992.

Briscoe, James R., Editor. (Brief Description): *Debussy in performance*. New Haven: Yale University Press, 1999.

Brott, Alexander Betty Nygaard King. *Alexander Brott: my lives in music*. Oakville, Ontario; Niagara Falls, New York: Mosaic Press, 2005.

Brown, Alfred Peter. *The symphonic repertoire. Vol. 2, The first golden age of the Viennese symphony: Haydn, Mozart, Beethoven, and Schubert*. Bloomington, Indiana: Indiana University Press, 2002.

Brown, Maurice John Edwin. *Schubert: a critical biography*. London: Macmillan; New York: St. Martin's Press, 1958.

Broyles, Michael. *Beethoven: the emergence and evolution of Beethoven's heroic style*. New York: Excelsior Music Publishing Co., 1987.

Brubaker, Bruce and Jane Gottlieb, Editors. *Pianist, scholar, connoisseur: essays in honor of Jacob Lateiner*. Stuyvesant, N.Y., Pendragon Press, 2000.

Buch, Esteban. *Beethoven's Ninth: a political history*. Chicago; London: University of Chicago Press, 2003.

Burk, John N., Editor. *Letters of Richard Wagner: the Burrell collection*. London: Gollancz, 1951.

Burnham, Scott G. *Beethoven hero*. Princeton, New Jersey: Princeton University Press, 1995.

Burnham, Scott G and Michael P. Steinberg, Editors. *Beethoven and his world*. Princeton, New Jersey; Oxford: Princeton University Press, 2000.

Burton, William Westbrook, Editor. *Conversations about Bernstein*. New York; Oxford: Oxford University Press, 1995.

Busch, Fritz. *Pages from a musician's life*. London: Hogarth Press, 1953.

Busch, Hans, Editor. *Verdi's Aida: the history of an opera in letters and documents*. Minneapolis: University of Minnesota Press, 1978.

Busch, Hans, Editor. *Verdi's Falstaff in letters and contemporary reviews*. Bloomington: Indiana University Press, 1997.

Busch, Marie, Translator. *Memoirs of Eugenie Schumann*. London: W. Heinemann, 1927.

Bush, Alan Dudley. *In my eighth decade and other essays*. London: Kahn & Averill, 1980.

Busoni, Ferruccio. *Letters to his wife*. Translated by Rosamond Ley. New York: Da Capo Press, 1975.

Byron, Reginald. *Music, culture, & experience: selected papers of John Blacking*. Chicago: University of Chicago Press, 1995.

Cairns, David. *Responses: musical essays and reviews*. New York: Da Capo Press, 1980.

Cardus, Neville. *Talking of music*. London: Collins, 1957.

Carley, Lionel. *Delius: a life in letters*. London: Scolar Press in association with the Delius Trust, 1988.

Carley, Lionel. *Grieg and Delius: a chronicle of their friendship in letters*. London: Marion Boyars, 1993.

Carner, Mosco. *Major and minor*. London: Duckworth, 1980

Carner, Mosco. *Puccini: a critical biography*. London: Duckworth, 1958.

Carroll, Brendan G. *The last prodigy: a biography of Erich Wolfgang Korngold*. Portland, Oregon: Amadeus Press, 1997.

Carse, Adam von Ahn. *The life of Jullien: adventurer, showman-conductor and establisher of the Promenade Concerts in England, together with a history of those concerts up to 1895*. Cambridge England: Heffer, 1951.

Carse, Adam von Ahn. *The orchestra from Beethoven to Berlioz: a history of the orchestra in the first half of the 19th century, and of the development of orchestral baton-conducting*. Cambridge: W. Heffer, 1948.

Casals, Pablo. *Joys and sorrows: reflections by Pablo Casals as told to Albert E. Kahn*. London: Macdonald, 1970.

Casals, Pablo. *The memoirs of Pablo Casals as told to Thomas Dozier*. London: Life en Español, 1959.

Chappell, Paul. *Dr. S. S. Wesley, 1810–1876: portrait of a Victorian musician*. Great Wakering: Mayhew-McCrimmon, 1977.

Chasins, Abram. *Leopold Stokowski, a profile*. New York: Hawthorn Books, 1979.

Charlton, Davi, Editor and Martyn Clarke Translator. *E.T.A. Hoffmann's musical writings: Kreisleriana, The Poet and the Composer*. Cambridge: Cambridge University Press, 1989.

Chávez, Carlos. *Musical thought*. Cambridge: Harvard University Press, 1961.

Chesterman, Robert, Editor. *Conversations with conductors: Bruno Walter, Sir Adrian Boult, Leonard Bernstein, Ernest Ansermet, Otto Klemperer, Leopold Stokowski*. Totowa, New Jersey: Rowman and Littlefield, 1976.

Chissell, Joan. *Clara Schumann: a dedicated spirit; a study of her life and work*. London: Hamilton, 1983.

Chua, Daniel K. L. *The "Galitzin" quartets of Beethoven: Opp.127, 132, 130.* Princeton: Princeton University Press, 1995.

Citron, Marcia, Editor. *The letters of Fanny Hensel to Felix Mendelssohn.* Stuyvesant, New York: Pendragon Press, 1987.

Clark, Walter Aaron. *Enrique Granados: poet of the piano.* Oxford, England; New York, N.Y.: Oxford University Press, 2006.

Clark, Walter Aaron. *Isaac Albéniz: portrait of a romantic.* Oxford; New York: Oxford University Press, 1999.

Clive, Peter. *Beethoven and his world.* Oxford University Press, 2001.

Closson, Ernest. *History of the piano.* Translated by Delano Ames and edited by Robin Golding. London: Paul Elek, 1947.

Cockshoot, John V. *The fugue in Beethoven's piano music.* London: Routledge & Kegan Paul, 1959.

Coe, Richard N, Translator. *Life of Rossini by Stendhal.* London: Calder & Boyars, 1970.

Coleman, Alexander, Editor. *Diversions & animadversions: essays from The new criterion.* New Brunswick, New Jersey; London: Transaction Publishers, 2005.

Colerick, George. *From the Italian girl to Cabaret: musical humour, parody and burlesque.* London: Juventus, 1998.

Coleridge, A. D. *Life of Moscheles, with selections from his diaries and correspondence by his wife.* London: Hurst & Blackett, 1873.

Colles, Henry Cope. *Essays and lectures.* London: Humphrey Milford, Oxford University Press, 1945.

Cone, Edward T., Editor. *Roger Sessions on music: collected essays.* Princeton, New Jersey: Princeton University Press, 1979.

Cone, Edward T. *The composer's voice.* Berkeley; London: University of California Press, 1974.

Cook, Susan and Judy S. Tsou, Editors. *Cecilia reclaimed: feminist perspectives on gender and music.* Urbana: University of Illinois Press, 1994.

Cooper, Barry. *Beethoven: The master musicians series.* Oxford: Oxford University Press, 2000.

Cooper, Barry. *Beethoven and the creative process.* Oxford: Clarendon Press, 1990.

Cooper, Barry. *Beethoven's folksong settings: chronology, sources, style.* Cambridge: Cambridge University Press, 1991.

Cooper, Barry. *The Beethoven compendium: a guide to Beethoven's life and music.* London: Thames and Hudson, 1991.

Cooper, Martin. *Beethoven: the last decade, 1817–1827.* London: Oxford University Press, 1970.

Cooper, Martin. *Judgements of value: selected writings on music.* Oxford; New York: Oxford University Press, 1988.

Cooper, Martin. *Ideas and music.* London: Barrie and Rockliff, 1965.

Cooper, Victoria L. *The house of Novello: the practice and policy of a Victorian music publisher, 1829–1866.* Aldershot, Hants: Ashgate, 2003.

Coover, James. *Music at auction: Puttick and Simpson (of London), 1794–1971: being an annotated, chronological list of sales of musical materials*. Warren, Michigan: Harmonie Park Press, 1988.

Copland, Aaron. *Copland on music*. London: Deutsch, 1961.

Corredor, J. Ma. *Conversations with Casals*. London: Hutchinson, 1956.

Cott, Jonathan. *Stockhausen: conversations with the composer*. London: Picador, 1974.

Cottrell, Stephen. *Professional music making in London: ethnography and experience*. Aldershot: Ashgate, 2004.

Cowell, Henry. *Charles Ives and his music*. New York: Oxford University Press, 1955.

Cowling, Elizabeth. *The cello*. London: Batsford, 1983.

Crabbe, John. *Beethoven's empire of the mind*. Newbury: Lovell Baines, 1982.

Craft, Robert. *An improbable life: memoirs*. Nashville: Vanderbilt University Press, 2002.

Craft, Robert, Editor. *Stravinsky: selected correspondence*. London: Faber and Faber, 3 Vols. 1982–1985.

Craw, Howard Allen. *A biography and thematic catalog of the works of J. L. Dussek: 1760–1812*. Ann Arbor: Michigan, 1965.

Crawford, Richard, R. Allen Lott and Carol J. Oja, Editors. *A Celebration of American music: words and music in honor of H. Wiley Hitchcock*. Ann Arbor: University of Michigan Press, 1990.

Craxton, Harold and Tovey, Donald Francis. *Beethoven: Sonatas for Pianoforte*. London: The Associated Board, [1931].

Crichton, Ronald: Editor. *The memoirs of Ethel Smyth*. New York: Viking, 1987.

Crist, Stephen A. and Roberta M. Marvin, Editors. *Historical musicology: sources, methods, interpretations*. Rochester, New York: University of Rochester Press, 2004.

Crofton, Ian and Donald Fraser, Editors. *A dictionary of musical quotations*. London: Croom Helm, 1985.

Crompton, Louis, Editor. *Shaw, Bernard: The great composers: reviews and bombardments*. Berkeley; London: University of California Press, 1978.

Csicserry-Ronay, Elizabeth, Translator and Editor. *Hector Berlioz: The art of music and other essays: (A travers chants)*. Bloomington: Indiana University Press, 1994.

Curtiss, Mina Kirstein. *Bizet and his world*. London: Secker & Warburg, 1959.

Cuyler, Louise Elvira. *The symphony*. New York: Harcourt Brace Jovanovich, 1973.

Dahlhaus, Carl. *Ludwig van Beethoven: approaches to his music*. Oxford: Clarendon Press, 1991.

Dahlhaus, Carl. *Nineteenth-century music*. Translated by J. Bradford Robinson. Berkeley; London: University of California Press, 1989.

Daniels, Robin. *Conversations with Cardus*. London: Gollancz, 1976.

Daniels, Robin. Conversations with Menuhin. London: Macdonald General Books, 1979.

Day, James. *Vaughan Williams*. London: Dent, 1961.

Davies, Peter Maxwell. *Studies from two decades*. Selected and introduced by Stephen Pruslin. London: Boosey & Hawkes, 1979.

Dean, Winton. *Georges Bizet: his life and work*. London: J.M. Dent, 1965.

Deas, Stewart. *In defence of Hanslick*. London: Williams and Norgate, 1940.

Debussy, Claude. *Debussy on music*. London: Secker & Warburg, 1977.

Delbanco, Nicholas. *The Beaux Arts Trio*. London: Gollancz, 1985.

Demény, Janos, Editor. *Béla Bartók: letters*. London: Faber and Faber, 1971.

Dent, Edward Joseph. *Selected essays*. Edited by Hugh Taylor. Cambridge; New York: Cambridge University Press, 1979.

Deutsch, Otto Erich. *Mozart: a documentary biography*. London: Adam & Charles Black, 1965.

Deutsch, Otto Erich. *Schubert: a documentary biography*. London: J.M. Dent, 1946

Deutsch, Otto Erich. *Schubert: memoirs by his friends*. London: Adam & Charles Black, 1958.

Dibble, Jeremy. *C. Hubert H. Parry: his life and music*. Oxford: Clarendon Press, 1992.

Dibble, Jeremy. *Charles Villiers Stanford: man and musician*. Oxford: Oxford University Press, 2002.

Donakowski, Conrad L. *A muse for the masses: ritual and music in an age of democratic revolution, 1770–1870*. Chicago: University of Chicago Press, 1977.

Dower, Catherine. *Alfred Einstein on music: selected music criticisms*. New York: Greenwood Press, 1991.

Downs, Philip G. *Classical music: the era of Haydn, Mozart, and Beethoven*. New York: W.W. Norton, 1992.

Drabkin, William. *Beethoven: Missa Solemnis*. Cambridge: Cambridge University Press, 1991.

Dreyfus, Kay. *The farthest north of humanness: letters of Percy Grainger, 1901–1914*. South Melbourne; Basingstoke: Macmillan, 1985.

Dubal, David, Editor. *Remembering Horowitz: 125 pianists recall a legend*. New York: Schirmer Books, 1993.

Dubal, David. *The world of the concert pianist*. London: Victor Gollancz, 1985.

Dvorák, Otakar. *Antonín Dvorák, my father*. Spillville, Iowa: Czech Historical Research Center, 1993.

Dyson, George. *The progress of music*. London: Oxford University Press, Humphrey Milford, 1932.

Eastaugh, Kenneth. *Havergal Brian: the making of a composer*. London: Harrap, 1976.

Edwards, Allen. *Flawed words and stubborn sounds: a conversation with Elliott Carter*. New York: Norton & Company, 1971.

Edwards, Frederick George. *Musical haunts in London*. London: J. Curwen & Sons, 1895.

Ehrlich, Cyril. *First philharmonic: a history of the Royal Philharmonic Society*. Oxford: Clarendon Press, 1995.

Einstein, Alfred. *A short history of music*. London: Cassell and Company Ltd., 1948.

Einstein, Alfred. *Essays on music*. London: Faber and Faber, 1958.

Einstein, Alfred. *Mozart: his character, his work.* London: Cassell and Company Ltd., 1946.

Einstein, Alfred. *Music in the Romantic era.* London: J.M. Dent Ltd., 1947.

Ekman, Karl. *Jean Sibelius, his life and personality.* New York: Tudor Publishing. Co., 1945.

Elgar, Edward. *A future for English music: and other lectures*, Edited by Percy M. Young. London: Dobson, 1968.

Elkin, Robert. *Queen's Hall, 1893–1941.* London: Rider, 1944.

Ella, John. *Musical sketches, abroad and at home: with original music by Mozart, Czerny, Graun, etc., vocal cadenzas and other musical illustrations.* London: Ridgway, Vol. 1., 1869.

Ellis, William Ashton. *The family letters of Richard Wagner.* Edited and translated by William Ashton Ellis and enlarged with introduction and notes by John Deathridge. Basingstoke: Macmillan, 1991.

Ellis, William Ashton. *Richard Wagner's prose works: Vol. 1, The art-work of the future.* Edited and translated by William Ashton Ellis. London: Kegan Paul, Trench, Trübner, 1895.

Ellis, William Ashton. *Richard Wagner's prose works: Vol. 2, Opera and drama.* Edited and translated by William Ashton Ellis. London: Kegan Paul, Trench, Trübner, 1900.

Ellis, William Ashton. *Richard Wagner's prose works: Vol. 3, The theatre.* Edited and translated by William Ashton Ellis. London: Kegan Paul, Trench, Trübner, 1907.

Ellis, William Ashton. *Richard Wagner's prose works: Vol. 4, Art and politics.* Edited and translated by William Ashton Ellis. London: Kegan Paul, Trench, Trübner, 1895.

Ellis, William Ashton. *Richard Wagner's prose works: Vol. 5, Actors and singers.* Edited and translated by William Ashton Ellis. London: Kegan Paul, Trench, Trübner, 1896.

Ellis, William Ashton. *Richard Wagner's prose works: Vol. 6, Religion and art.* Edited and translated by William Ashton Ellis. London: Kegan Paul, Trench, Trübner, 1897.

Ellis, William Ashton. *Richard Wagner's prose works: Vol. 7, In Paris and Dresden.* Edited and translated by William Ashton Ellis. London: Kegan Paul, Trench, Trübner, 1898.

Ellis, William Ashton. *Richard Wagner's prose works: Vol. 8, Posthumous.* Edited and translated by William Ashton Ellis. London: Kegan Paul, Trench, Trübner, 1899.

Elterlein, Ernst von. *Beethoven's pianoforte sonatas: explained for the lovers of the musical art.* London: W. Reeves, 1898.

Engel, Carl. *Musical myths and facts.* London: Novello, Ewer & Co.; New York: J.L. Peters, 1876.

Eosze, László. *Zoltán Kodály: his life and work.* London: Collet's, 1962.

Etter, Brian K. *From classicism to modernism: Western musical culture and the metaphysics of order.* Aldershot: Ashgate, 2001.

Ewen, David. *From Bach to Stravinsky: the history of music by its *foremost critics.* New York, Greenwood Press, 1968.

Ewen, David. *Romain Rolland's Essays on music.* New York: Dover Publications, 1959.

Fay, Amy. *Music-study in Germany: from the home correspondence of Amy Fay.* New York: Dover Publications, 1965.

Fenby, Eric. *Delius as I knew him.* London: Quality Press, 1936.

Ferguson, Donald Nivison. *Masterworks of the orchestral repertoire: a guide for listeners.* Minneapolis: University of Minnesota Press, 1954.

Fétis, François-Joseph. *Curiosités historiques de la musique: complément nécessaire de la Musique mise à la portée de tout le monde.* Paris: Janet et Cotelle, 1830.

Fifield, Christopher. *Max Bruch: his life and works.* London: Gollancz, 1988.

Fifield, Christopher. *True artist and true friend: a biography of Hans Richter.* Oxford: Clarendon Press, 1993.

Finson, Jon and R. Larry Todd, Editors. *Mendelssohn and Schumann: essays on their music and its context.* Durham, N.C.: Duke University Press, 1984.

Fischer, Edwin. *Beethoven's pianoforte sonatas: a guide for students & amateurs.* London: Faber and Faber, 1959.

Fischer, Edwin. *Reflections on music.* London: Williams and Norgate, 1951.

Fischer, Hans Conrad and Erich Kock. *Ludwig van Beethoven: a study in text and pictures.* London: Macmillan; New York, St. Martin's Press, 1972.

Fischmann, Zdenka E. Janác̆ek-*Newmarch correspondence. 1st limited and numbered edition.* Rockville, MD: Kabel Publishers, 1986.

Fitzlyon, April. *Maria Malibran: diva of the romantic age.* London: Souvenir Press, 1987.

FitzLyon, April. *The price of genius: a life of Pauline Viardot.* London: John Calder, 1964.

Forbes, Elliot, Editor. *Thayer's life of Beethoven.* Princeton, New Jersey: Princeton University Press, 1967.

Foreman, Lewis. *Bax: a composer and his times.* London: Scolar Press, 1983.

Foreman, Lewis, Editor. *Farewell, my youth, and other writings by Arnold Bax.* Aldershot: Scolar Press, 1992.

Foster, Myles Birket. *History of the Philharmonic Society of London, 1813–1912: a record of a hundred years' work in the cause of music.* London: Bodley Head, 1912.

Foulds, John. *Music today: its heritage from the past, and legacy to the future.* London: I. Nicholson and Watson, limited, 1934.

Frank, Mortimer H. *Arturo Toscanini: the NBC years.* Portland, Oregon: Amadeus Press, 2002.

Fraser, Andrew Alastair. *Essays on music.* London: Oxford University Press, H. Milford, 1930.

Frohlich, Martha. *Beethoven's Appassionata' sonata.* Oxford: Clarendon Press, 1991.

Gal, Hans. *The golden age of Vienna.* London: Max Parrish & Co. Limited, 1948.

Gal, Hans. *The musician's world:*

great composers in their letters. London: Thames and Hudson, 1965.

Galatopoulos, Stelios. *Bellini: life, times, music*. London: Sanctuary, 2002.

Garden, Edward and Nigel Gottrei, Editors. *'To my best friend': correspondence between Tchaikovsky and Nadezhda von Meck, 1876–1878*. Oxford: Clarendon Press, 1993.

Geck, Martin. Beethoven. London: Haus, 2003.

Gerig, Reginald. *Famous pianists & their technique*. Washington: R. B. Luce, 1974.

Gilliam, Bryan. *The life of Richard Strauss*. Cambridge: Cambridge University Press, 1999.

Gilliam, Bryan, Editor. *Richard Strauss and his world*. Princeton, New Jersey: Princeton University Press, 1992.

Gillies, Malcolm and Bruce Clunies Ross, Editors. *Grainger on music*. Oxford; New York: Oxford University Press, 1999.

Gillies, Malcolm and David Pear, Editors. *The all-round man: selected letters of Percy Grainger, 1914–1961*. Oxford: Clarendon Press, 1994.

Gillies, Malcolm, Editor. *The Bartók companion*. London: Faber and Faber, 1993.

Gillmor, Alan M. *Erik Satie*. Basingstoke: Macmillan Press, 1988.

Glehn, M. E. *Goethe and Mendelssohn : (1821–1831)*. London: Macmillan, 1874.

Glowacki, John, Editor. *Paul A. Pisk: Essays in his honor*. Austin, Texas: University of Texas, 1966

Gollancz, Victor. *Journey towards music: a memoir*. London: Victor Gollancz Ltd., 1964.

Good, Edwin Marshall. *Giraffes, black dragons, and other pianos: a technological history from Cristofori to the modern concert grand*. Stanford, California: Stanford University Press, 1982.

Gordon, David. *Musical visitors to Britain*. London: Routledge, 2005.

Gordon, Stewart. *A history of keyboard literature: music for the piano and its forerunners*. Schirmer Books: New York: London : Prentice Hall International, 1996.

Gorrell, Lorraine. *The nineteenth-century German lied*. Portland, Oregon: Amadeus Press, 1993.

Goss, Glenda D. *Jean Sibelius: the Hämeenlinna letters: scenes from a musical life, 1875–1895*. Esbo, Finland: Schildts, 1997.

Goss, Madeleine. *Bolero: the life of Maurice Ravel*. New York: Tudor, 1945.

Gotch, Rosamund Brunel, Editor. *Mendelssohn and his friends in Kensington: letters from Fanny and Sophy Horsley, written 1833–36*. London: Oxford University Press, 1938.

Gounod, Charles. *Charles Gounod; autobiographical reminiscences: with family letters and notes on music; from the French*. London: William Heinemann, 1896.

Grabs, Manfred, Editor. *Hanns Eisler: a rebel in music; selected writings*. Berlin: Seven Seas Publishers, 1978.

Grace, Harvey. *A musician at large*. London: Oxford University Press, H. Milford, 1928.

(La) Grange, Henry-Louis de. *Gustav Mahler*. Oxford: Oxford University Press, 1995.

Graves, Charles L. *Hubert Parry: his life and works*. London: Macmillan, 1926.

Graves, Charles L. *Post-Victorian music: with other studies and sketches*. London: Macmillan and Co., limited, 1911.

Graves, Charles L. *The life & letters of Sir George Grove, Hon. D.C.L. (Durham), Hon. LL.D. (Glasgow), formerly director of the Royal college of music*. London: Macmillan and Co., Ltd.; New York: The Macmillan Co., 1903.

Gray, Cecil. *Musical chairs, or, between two stools: being the life and memoirs of Cecil Gray*. London: Home & Van Thal, 1948.

Gregor-Dellin and Dietrich Mack, Editors. *Cosima Wagner's diaries.: Vol. 1, 1869 - 1877*. London: Collins, 1978-1980.

Griffiths, Paul. *Modern music: the avant-garde since 1945*. London: J. M. Dent & Sons Ltd., 1981.

Griffiths, Paul. *Olivier Messiaen and the music of time*. London: Faber and Faber, 1985.

Griffiths, Paul. *Peter Maxwell Davies*. London: Robson Books, 1988.

Griffiths, Paul. *The sea on fire: Jean Barraqué*. Rochester, New York: Woodbridge: University of Rochester Press, 2003.

Griffiths, Paul. *The string quartet*. London: Thames and Hudson, 1983.

Grout, Donald Jay and Claude V. Palisca, Editors. *A history of Western music*. London: J. M. Dent, 1988.

Grove, George. *Beethoven and his nine symphonies*. London: Novello, Ewer, 1896.

Grover, Ralph Scott. *Ernest Chausson: the man and his music*. London: The Athlone Press, 1980.

Grover, Ralph Scott. *The music of Edmund Rubbra*. Aldershot: Scolar Press, 1993.

Grun, Bernard. *Alban Berg: letters to his wife*. Edited and translated by Bernard Grun. London: Faber and Faber, 1971.

Gutman, David. *Prokofiev*. London: Omnibus Press, 1990.

Hadow, William Henry. *Collected essays*. London: H. Milford at the Oxford University Press, 1928.

Hadow, William Henry. *Beethoven's Op. 18 Quartets*. London: H. Milford at the Oxford University Press, 1926.

Haggin, Bernard H. *Music observed*. New York: Oxford University Press, 1964.

Hailey, Christopher. *Franz Schreker, 1878–1934: a cultural biography*. Cambridge: Cambridge University Press, 1993.

Hall, Michael. *Leaving home: a conducted tour of twentieth-century music with Simon Rattle*. London: Faber and Faber, 1996.

Hall, Patricia and Friedemann Sallis, Editors. (Brief Description): *A handbook to twentieth-century musical sketches*. Cambridge: Cambridge University Press, 2004.

Hallé, C. E. *Life and letters of Sir Charles Hallé: being an autobiography (1819–1860) with correspondence and diaries*. London: Smith, Elder & Co., 1896.

Halstead, Jill. *The woman composer: creativity and the gendered politics of musical composition.* Aldershot: Ashgate, 1997.

Hamburger, Michael, Editor and Translator. *Beethoven letters, journals, and conversations.* New York: Thames and Hudson, 1951.

Hammelmann, Hanns A. and Ewald Osers. *The correspondence between Richard Strauss and Hugo von Hofmannsthal.* London: Collins, 1961.

Hanson, Lawrence and Elisabeth Hanson. *Tchaikovsky: the man behind the music.* New York: Dodd, Mead & Co, 1967.

Harding, James. *Massenet.* London: J. M. Dent & Sons Ltd., 1970.

Harding, James. *Saint-Saëns and his circle.* London: Chapman & Hall, 1965.

Harding, Rosamond E. M. *Origins of musical time and expression.* London: Oxford University Press, 1938.

Harman, Alec with Anthony Milner and Wilfrid Mellers. *Man and his music: the story of musical experience in the West.* London: Barrie & Jenkins, 1988.

Harper, Nancy Lee. *Manuel de Falla: his life and music.* Lanham, Maryland; London: The Scarecrow Press, 2005.

Hartmann, Arthur. *'Claude Debussy as I knew him' and other writings of Arthur Hartmann.* Edited by Samuel Hsu, Sidney Grolnic, and Mark Peters. Rochester, New York; Woodbridge: University of Rochester Press, 2003.

Haugen, Einar and Camilla Cai. *Ole Bull: Norway's romantic musician and cosmopolitan patriot.* Madison: The University of Wisconsin Press, 1993.

Headington, Christopher. *The Bodley Head history of Western music.* London: The Bodley Head, 1974.

Heartz, Daniel. *Music in European capitals: the galant style, 1720–1780.* New York; London: W. W. Norton, 2003.

Hedley, Arthur, Editor. *Selected correspondence of Fryderyk Chopin: abridged from Fryderyk Chopin's correspondence.* London: Heinemann, 1962.

Heiles, Anne Mischakoff. *Mischa Mischakoff: journeys of a concertmaster.* Sterling Heights, Michigan: Harmonie Park Press, 2006.

Henderson, Sanya Shoilevska. *Alex North, film composer: a biography, with musical analyses of a Streetcar named desire, Spartacus, The misfits, Under the volcano, and Prizzi's honor.* Jefferson, N.C.; London: McFarland, 2003.

Henschel, George. *Personal recollections of Johannes Brahms: some of his letters to and pages from a journal kept by George Henschel.* Boston: R G. Badger, 1907.

Henze, Hans Werner. *Bohemian fifths: an autobiography.* London: Faber and Faber, 1998.

Henze, Hans Werner. *Music and politics: collected writings 1953–81.* London: Faber and Faber, 1982.

Herbert, May, Translator. *Early letters of Robert Schumann.* London: George Bell and Sons, 1888.

Heyman, Barbara B. *Samuel Barber:*

the composer and his music. New York: Oxford University Press, 1992.

Heyworth, Peter. *Otto Klemperer, his life and times.* Cambridge: Cambridge University Press, 2 Vols. 1983–1996.

Hildebrandt, Dieter. *Pianoforte: a social history of the piano.* London: Hutchinson, 1988.

Hill, Peter. *The Messiaen companion.* London: Faber and Faber, 1995.

Hill, Peter and Nigel Simeone. *Messiaen.* New Haven Connecticut; London: Yale University Press, 2005.

Hiller, Ferdinand. *Mendelssohn: Letters and recollections.* New York: Vienna House, 1972.

Hines, Robert Stephan. *The orchestral composer's point of view: essays on twentieth-century music by those who wrote it.* Norman: University of Oklahoma Press, 1970.

Ho, Allan B. *Shostakovich reconsidered.* London: Toccata Press, 1998.

Hodeir, André. *Since Debussy: a view of contemporary music.* New York: Da Capo Press, 1975.

Holmes, Edward. *The life of Mozart: including his correspondence.* London: Chapman and Hall, 1845.

Holmes, John L. *Composers on composers.* New York: Greenwood Press, 1990.

Hopkins, Anthony. *The concertgoer's companion.* London: J.M. Dent & Sons Ltd., 1984.

Hopkins, Anthony. *The seven concertos of Beethoven.* Aldershot: Scolar Press, 1996.

Holt, Richard. *Nicolas Medtner (1879–1951): a tribute to his art and personality.* London: D. Dobson, 1955.

Honegger, Arthur. *I am a composer.* London: Faber and Faber, 1966.

Hoover, Kathleen and John Cage. *Virgil Thomson: his life and music.* New York; London: T. Yoseloff, 1959.

Horgan, Paul. *Encounters with Stravinsky: a personal record.* London: The Bodley Head, 1972.

Horowitz, Joseph. *Conversations with Arrau.* London: Collins, 1982.

Horowitz, Joseph. Understanding Toscanini. London: Faber and Faber, 1987.

Horwood, Wally. *Adolphe Sax, 1814–1894: his life and legacy.* Bramley: Bramley Books, 1980.

Howie, Crawford. *Anton Bruckner: a documentary biography.* Lewiston, N.Y.; Lampeter: Edwin Mellen Press, 2002.

Hueffer, Francis. *Correspondence of Wagner and Liszt.* New York: Greenwood Press, 2 Vols.1969.

Hughes, Spike. *The Toscanini legacy: a critical study of Arturo Toscanini's performances of Beethoven, Verdi, and other composers.* London: Putnam, 1959.

Hullah, Annette. *Theodor Leschetizky.* London and New York: J. Land & Co., 1906.

Le Huray, Peter and James Day, Editors. *Music and aesthetics in the eighteenth and early-nineteenth centuries.* Cambridge: Cambridge University Press, 1988.

D' Indy, Vincent. *César Franck.* New York: Dover Publications, 1965.

Jacobs, Arthur. *Arthur Sullivan: A*

Victorian musician. Aldershot: Scolar Press, 1992.

Jahn, Otto. *Life of Mozart.* London: Novello, Ewer & Co., 1882.

Jefferson, Alan. *Sir Thomas Beecham: a centenary tribute.* London: World Records Ltd., 1979.

Jezic, Diane. *The musical migration and Ernst Toch.* Ames: Iowa State University Press, 1989.

Johnson, Douglas Porter, Editor. *The Beethoven sketchbooks: history, reconstruction, inventory.*

Oxford: Clarendon, 1985.

Johnson, Stephen. *Bruckner remembered.* London: Faber and Faber, 1998.

Jones, David, Wyn. *Beethoven: Pastoral symphony.* Cambridge: Cambridge University Press, 1995.

Jones, David Wyn. *The life of Beethoven.* Cambridge: Cambridge University Press, 1998.

Jones, David Wyn. *The symphony in Beethoven's Vienna.* Cambridge: Cambridge University Press, 2006.

Jones, J. Barrie, Editor. *Gabriel Fauré: a life in letters.* London: Batsford, 1989.

Jones, Peter Ward, Editor and Translator. *The Mendelssohns on honeymoon: the 1837 diary of Felix and Cécile Mendelssohn Bartholdy, together with letters to their families.* Oxford: Clarendon Press, 1997.

Jones, Timothy. *Beethoven, the Moonlight and other sonatas, Op. 27 and Op. 31.* Cambridge; New York, N.Y.: Cambridge University Press, 1999.

Kalischer, A. C., Editor. *Beethoven's letters: a critical edition.* London: J. M. Dent, 1909.

Kárpáti, János. *Bartók's chamber music.* Stuyvesant, New York: Pendragon Press, 1994.

Keefe, Simon P. *The Cambridge companion to the concerto.* Cambridge, New York, N.Y.: Cambridge University Press, 2005.

Keller, Hans. *The great Haydn quartets: their interpretation.* London: J. M. Dent, 1986.

Keller, Hans, Editor. *The memoirs of Carl Flesch.* New York: Macmillan, 1958.

Keller, Hans, and Christopher Wintle. *Beethoven's string quartets in F minor, Op. 95 and C minor, Op. 131: two studies.* Nottingham: Department of Music, University of Nottingham, 1995.

Kelly, Thomas Forrest. *First nights at the opera: five musical premiers.* New Haven: Yale University Press, 2004.

Kennedy, Michael. *Adrian Boult.* London: Hamish Hamilton, 1987.

Kennedy, Michael. *Barbirolli, conductor laureate: the authorised biography.* London: Hart-Davis, MacGibbon, 1973.

Kennedy, Michael, Editor. *The autobiography of Charles Hallé; with correspondence and diaries.*

London: Paul Elek, 1972.

Kennedy, Michael. *Hallé tradition: a century of music.* Manchester: Manchester University Press, 1960.

Kennedy, Michael. *The works of Ralph Vaughan Williams.* London: Oxford University Press, 1964.

Kemp, Ian. *Tippett: the composer and his music.* London; New York: Eulenburg Books, 1984.

Kerman, Joseph. *The Beethoven quartets.* London: Oxford University Press, 1967, c1966.

Kerman, Joseph. *Write all these down: essays on music.* Berkeley, California; London: University of California Press, 1994.

Kildea, Paul, Editor. *Britten on music.* Oxford: Oxford University Press, 2003.

Kinderman, William. *Beethoven.* Oxford: Oxford University Press, 1997.

Kinderman, William. *Beethoven's Diabelli variations.* Oxford: Clarendon Press; New York: Oxford University Press, 1987.

Kinderman, William, Editor. *The string quartets of Beethoven.* Urbana, Ilinois: University of Illinois Press, 2005.

King, Alec Hyatt. *Musical pursuits: selected essays.* London: British Library, 1987.

Kirby, F. E. *Music for piano: a short history.* Amadeus Press: Portland, 1995.

Kirkpatrick, John, Editor. *Charles E. Ives: Memos.* New York: W.W. Norton, 1972.

Knapp, Raymond. *Brahms and the challenge of the symphony.* Stuyvesant, N.Y.: Pendragon Press, c.1997.

Knight, Frida. *Cambridge music: from the Middle Ages to modern times.* Cambridge, England.: New York: Oleander Press, 1980.

Knight, Max, Translator. *A confidential matter: the letters of Richard Strauss and Stefan Zweig, 1931–1935.* Berkeley; London: University of California Press, 1977.

Kok, Alexander. *A voice in the dark: the philharmonia years.* Ampleforth: Emerson Edition, 2002.

Kopelson, Kevin. *Beethoven's kiss: pianism, perversion, and the mastery of desire.* Stanford, California: Stanford University Press, 1996.

Kostelanetz, Richard, Editor. *Aaron Copland: a reader; selected writings 1923–1972.* New York; London: Routledge, 2003.

Kostelanetz, Richard. *Conversing with Cage.* New York; London: Routledge, 2003.

Kostelanetz, Richard. *On innovative musicians.* New York: Limelight Editions, 1989.

Kostelanetz, Richard, Editor. *Virgil Thomson: a reader ; selected writings, 1924–1984.* New York; London: Routledge, 2002.

Kowalke, Kim H. *Kurt Weill in Europe.* Ann Arbor, Michigan: UMI Research Press, 1979.

Krehbiel, Henry Edward. *The pianoforte and its music.* New York: Cooper Square Publishers, 1971.

Kruseman, Philip, Editor. *Beethoven's own words.* London: Hinrichsen Edition, 1948.

Kurtz, Michael. *Stockhausen: a biography.* London: Faber and Faber, 1992.

Lam, Basil. *Beethoven string quartets.* Seattle: University of Washington Press, 1975.

Lambert, Constant. *Music ho!: a study of music in decline.* London: Faber and Faber, Ltd. 1934.

Landon, H. C. Robbins. *Beethoven: a documentary study.* London: Thames and Hudson, 1970.

Landon, H. C. Robbins. *Beethoven: his life, work and world.*

Landon, H. C. Robbins. *Essays on the Viennese classical style: Gluck, Haydn, Mozart, Beethoven.* London: Barrie & Rockliff The Cresset Press, 1970.

Landon, H. C. Robbins. *Haydn: chronicle and works/Haydn, the late years, 1801–1809.* Bloomington: Indiana University Press, 1977.

Landon, H. C. Robbins. *Haydn: his life and music.* London: Thames and Hudson, 1988.

Landon, H. C. Robbins. *Haydn in England, 1791–1795.* London: Thames and Hudson, 1976.

Landon, H. C. Robbins. *Haydn: the years of 'The creation', 1796–800.* London: Thames and Hudson, 1977.

Landon, H. C. Robbins. *Mozart: the golden years, 1781–1791.* New York: Schirmer Books, 1989.

Landon, H. C. Robbins. *1791, Mozart's last year.* London: Thames and Hudson, 1988.

Landon, H. C. Robbins *The collected correspondence and London notebooks of Joseph Haydn.* London: Barrie and Rockliff, 1959.

Landon, H. C. Robbins: Editor. *The Mozart companion.* London: Faber, 1956.

Landowska, Wanda. *Music of the past.* London: Geoffrey Bles, 1926.

Lang, Paul Henry. *Musicology and performance.* New Haven: Yale University Press, 1997.

Lang, Paul Henry. *The creative world of Beethoven.* New York: W. W. Norton 1971.

Laurence, Dan H., Editor. *Shaw's music: the complete musical criticism in three volumes.* London: Max Reinhardt, the Bodley Head, 1981.

Lawford-Hinrichsen, Irene. *Music publishing and patronage: C. F. Peters, 1800 to the Holocaust.* Kenton: Edition Press, 2000.

Layton, Robert, Editor. *A guide to the concerto.* Oxford: Oxford University Press, 1996.

Layton, Robert, Editor. *A guide to the symphony.* Oxford: Oxford University Press, 1995.

Lebrecht, Norman. *The maestro myth: great conductors in pursuit of power.* London: Simon & Schuster, 1991.

Lee, Ernest Markham. *The story of the symphony.* London: Scott Publishing Co., 1916.

Leibowitz, Herbert A., Editor. *Musical impressions: selections from Paul Rosenfeld's criticism.* London: G. Allen & Unwin, 1970.

Lenrow, Elbert, Editor and Translator. *The letters of Richard Wagner to Anton Pusinelli.* New York: Vienna House, 1972.

Leonard, Maurice. *Kathleen: the life of Kathleen Ferrier: 1912–1953.* London: Hutchinson, 1988.

Lesure, François and Roger Nichols, Editors. *Debussy, letters.* London: Faber and Faber, 1987.

Letellier, Robert Ignatius, Editor and Translator. *The diaries of Giacomo Meyerbeer.* Madison: Fairleigh Dickinson University Press; London: Associated University Presses, 4 Vols., 1999–2004.

Levas, Santeri. *Sibelius: a personal portrait.* London: J. M. Dent, 1972.

Levy, Alan Howard. *Edward MacDowell, an American master.* Lanham, Md. & London: Scarecrow Press, 1998.

Levy, David Benjamin. *Beethoven: the Ninth Symphony.* New Haven, Connecticut; London: Yale University Press, 2003.

Leyda, Jay and Sergi Bertensson. *The Musorgsky reader: a life of Modeste Petrovich Musorgsky in letters and documents.* New York: W.W. Norton, 1947.

Lewis, Thomas P., Editor. *Raymond Leppard on music: an anthology of critical and personal writings.* White Plains, N.Y.: Pro/Am Music Resources, 1993.

Liébert, Georges. *Nietzsche and music.* Chicago: University of Chicago Press, 2004.

Liszt, Franz. *An artist's journey: lettres d'un bachelier ès musique, 1835–1841.* Chicago: University of Chicago Press, 1989.

Litzmann, Berthold, Editor. *Clara Schumann: an artist's life, based on material found in diaries and letters.* London: Macmillan; Leipzig: Breitkopf & Härtel, 2 Vols. 1913.

Litzmann, Berthold, Editor. *Letters of Clara Schumann and Johannes Brahms, 1853–1896.* New York, Vienna House. 2 Vols. 1971.

Lloyd, Stephen. *William Walton: muse of fire.* Woodbridge, Suffolk: The Boydell Press, 2001.

Locke, Ralph P. and Cyrilla Barr, Editors. *Cultivating music in America: women patrons and activists since 1860.* Berkeley: University of California Press, 1997.

Lockspeiser, Edward. *Debussy: his life and mind.* London: Cassell. 2 Vols. 1962–1965.

Lockspeiser, Edward. *The literary clef: an anthology of letters and writings by French composers.* London: J. Calder. 1958.

Lockwood, Lewis, Editor. *Beethoven essays: studies in honor of Elliot Forbes.* Cambridge, Massachusetts: Harvard University Department of Music: Distributed by Harvard University Press, 1984.

Lockwood, Lewis and Mark Kroll, Editors. *The Beethoven violin sonatas: history, criticism, performance.* Urbana: University of Illinois Press, 2004.

Loft, Abram. *Violin and keyboard: the duo repertoire.* New York: Grossman Publishers. 2 Vols. 1973.

Longyear, Rey Morgan. *Nineteenth-century romanticism in music.* Englewood Cliffs: Prentice-Hall, 1969.

Lowe, C. Egerton. *Beethoven's pianoforte sonatas: hints on their rendering, form, etc., with appendices on definition of sonata, music forms, ornaments, pianoforte pedals, and how to discover keys.* London: Novello, 1929.

Macdonald, Hugh, Editor. *Berlioz: Selected letters.* London: Faber and Faber, 1995.

Macdonald, Malcolm, Editor. *Havergal Brian on music: selections from his journalism: Volume One, British music.* London: Toccata Press, 1986.

MacDonald, Malcolm. *Varèse: astronomer in sound.* London: Kahn & Averill, 2003.

MacDowell, Edward. *Critical and historical essays: lectures delivered at Columbia University*. Edited by W. J. Baltzell. London: Elkin; Boston: A.P. Schmidt, 1912.

MacFarren, Walter. Memories: an autobiography. London: Walter Scott Publishing Co.,1905.

Mackenzie, Alexander Campbell. *A musician's narrative*. London: Cassell and company, Ltd, 1927.

McCarthy, Margaret William, Editor. *More letters of Amy Fay: the American years, 1879–1916*. Detroit: Information Coordinators, 1986.

McClary, Susan. *Feminine endings: music, gender, and sexuality*. Minneapolis: University of Minnesota Press, 1991.

McClatchie, Stephen, Editor and Translator. *The Mahler family letters*. Oxford: Oxford University Press, 2006.

McVeigh, Simon. *Concert life in London from Mozart to Haydn*. Cambridge: Cambridge University Press, 1993.

Mahler, Alma. *Gustav Mahler: memories and letters*. Enlarged edition revised and edited and with and introduction by Donald Mitchell. London: John Murray, 1968.

Mai, François Martin. *Diagnosing genius: the life and death of Beethoven*. Montreal; London: McGill-Queen's University Press, 2007.

Del Mar, Norman. *Orchestral variations: confusion and error in the orchestral repertoire*. London: Eulenburg, 1981.

Del Mar, Norman. *Richard Strauss: a critical commentary on his life and works*. London: Barrie & Jenkins. 3 Vols. 1978.

(La) Mara [pseudonym]. *Letters of Franz Liszt*. London: H. Grevel & Co., 2 Vols. 1894.

Marek, George Richard. *Puccini*. London: Cassell & Co., 1952.

Marek, George Richard. *Toscanini*. London: Vision, 1976.

(De) Marliave, Joseph. *Beethoven's quartets*. New York: Dover Publications (reprint), 1961.

Martin, George Whitney. *Verdi: his music, life and times*. London: Macmillan, 1965.

Martner, Knud, Editor. *Selected letters of Gustav Mahler*. London; Boston: Faber and Faber, 1979.

Martyn, Barrie. *Nicolas Medtner: his life and music*. Aldershot: Scolar Press, 1995.

Martyn, Barrie. *Rachmaninoff: composer, pianist, conductor*. Aldershot: Scolar, 1990.

Massenet, Jules. *My recollections*. Westport, Connecticut: Greenwood Press.1970.

Matheopoulos, Helena. *Maestro: encounters with conductors of today*. London: Hutchinson, 1982.

Matthews, Denis. *Beethoven*. London: J. M. Dent, 1985.

Matthews, Denis. *Beethoven piano sonatas*. London: British Broadcasting Corporation, 1967.

Matthews, Denis. *In pursuit of music*. London: Victor Gollancz Ltd., 1968.

Matthews, Denis. *Keyboard music*. Newton Abbot: London David & Charles, 1972.

Mellers, Wilfrid Howard. *Caliban reborn: renewal in twentieth-century music*. London: Victor Gollancz, 1967.

Mellers, Wilfrid Howard. *The sonata principle (from c. 1750)*. London: Rockliff, 1957.

Mendelssohn Bartholdy. *Letters from Italy and Switzerland.* London: Longman, Green, Longman, and Roberts, 1862.

Mendelssohn Bartholdy, Paul. *Letters of Felix Mendelssohn Bartholdy, from 1833 to 1847.* London: Longman, Green, Longman, Roberts, & Green, 1864.

Menuhin, Yehudi and Curtis W. Davis. *The music of man.* London: Macdonald and Jane's, 1979.

Menuhin, Yehudi. *Theme and variations.* London: Heinemann Educational Books Ltd., 1972.

Menuhin, Yehudi. *Unfinished journey.* London: Macdonald and Jane's, 1977.

Messian, Olivier. *Music and color: conversations with Claude Samuel.* Portland, Oregon: Amadeus, 1994.

Miall, Anthony. *Musical bumps.* London: J.M. Dent & Sons Ltd, 1981.

Michotte, Edmond. *Richard Wagner's visit to Rossini (Paris 1860): and, An evening at Rossini's in Beau-Sejour (Passy), 1858.* Chicago; London: University of Chicago Press, 1982.

Mies, Paul. *Beethoven's sketches: an analysis of his style based on a study of his sketchbooks.*
New York: Johnson Reprint, 1969.

Milhaud, Darius. *My happy life.* London: Boyars, 1995.

Miller, Mina. *The Nielsen companion.* London: Faber and Faber, 1994.

Milsom, David. *Theory and practice in late nineteenth-century violin performance: an examination of style in performance, 1850–1900.* Aldershot: Ashgate, 2003.

Mitchell, Donald, Editor. *Letters from a life: the selected letters and diaries of Benjamin Britten 1913–1976.* London: Faber and Faber. 3 Vols., 1991.

Mitchell, Donald and Hans Keller, Editors. *Music survey: new series 1949–1952.* London: Faber Music in association with Faber & Faber, 1981.

Mitchell, Jon C. *A comprehensive biography of composer Gustav Holst, with correspondence and diary excerpts: including his American years.* Lewiston, New York: Edwin Mellen Press, 2001.

Moldenhauer, Hans. *Anton von Webern: a chronicle of his life and work.* London: Victor Gollancz, 1978.

Monrad-Johansen. Edvard Grieg. New York: Tudor Publishing Co., 1945.

Moore, Gerald. *Am I too loud?: memoirs of an accompanist.* London: Hamish Hamilton, 1962.

Moore, Gerald. *Farewell recital: further memoirs.* Harmondsworth: Penguin Books, 1979.

Moore, Gerald. *Furthermoore: interludes in an accompanist's life.* London: Hamish Hamilton, 1983.

Moore, Jerrold Northrop. *Edward Elgar: a creative life.* Oxford: Oxford University Press, 1984.

Moore, Jerrold Northrop. *Elgar, Edward. The windflower letters: correspondence with Alice Caroline Stuart Wortley and her family.* Oxford: Clarendon

Press; New York: Oxford University Press, 1989.

Moore, Jerrold Northrop. *Elgar, Edward. Edward Elgar: letters of a lifetime.* Oxford: Clarendon Press; New York: Oxford University Press, 1990.

Moore, Jerrold Northrop. *Elgar, Edward. Elgar and his publishers: letters of a creative life.* Oxford: Clarendon, 1987.

Moreux, Serge. *Béla Bartók.* London: Harvill Press, 1953.

Morgan, Kenneth. *Fritz Reiner, maestro and martinet.* Urbana: University of Illinois Press, 2005.

Cone, Edward T., Editor. *Music, a view from Delft: selected essays.* Chicago: University of Chicago Press, 1989.

Morgan, Robert P. *Twentieth-century music: a history of musical style in modern Europe and America.* New York: Norton, 1991.

Morgenstern, Sam., Editor. *Composers on music: an anthology of composers' writings.* London: Faber & Faber, 1956.

Morrow, Mary Sue. *Concert life in Haydn's Vienna: aspects of a developing musical and social institution.* Stuyvesant, New York: Pendragon Press, 1989.

Moscheles, Felix, Editor and Translator. *Letters from Felix Mendelssohn-Bartholdy to Ignaz and Charlotte Moscheles.* London: Trübner and Co., 1888.

Mudge, Richard B., Translator. *Glinka, Mikhail Ivanovich: Memoirs.* Norman: University of Oklahoma Press, 1963.

Munch, Charles. *I am a conductor.* New York: Oxford University Press, 1955.

Mundy, Simon. *Bernard Haitink: a working life.* London: Robson Books, 1987.

Musgrave, Michael. *The musical life of the Crystal Palace.* Cambridge: Cambridge University Press, 1995.

Music & Letters. *Beethoven: special number.* London: Music & Letters, 1927.

Musical Times. *Special Issue.* John A. Fuller-Maitland London: Vol. VIII, No. 2, 1927.

Myers, Rollo H., Editor. *Twentieth-century music.* London: Calder and Boyars, 1960.

National Gallery (Great Britain). *Music performed at the National Gallery concerts, 10th October 1939 to 10th April 1946.* London: Privately printed, 1948.

Nattiez, Jean-Jacques, Editor. *Orientations: collected writings — Pierre Boulez.* London: Faber and Faber, 1986.

Nauhaus, Gerd, Editor. *The marriage diaries of Robert & Clara Schumann.* London: Robson Books, 1994.

Nectoux, Jean Michel. *Gabriel Fauré: a musical life.* Translated by Roger Nichols. Cambridge: Cambridge University Press, 1991.

Nettl, Paul. *Beethoven handbook.* Westport, Connecticut: Greenwood Press, 1975.

Neumayr, Anton. *Music and medicine.* Bloomington, Illinois: Medi-Ed Press, 1994–1997

Newbould, Brian. *Schubert and the symphony: a new perspective.* Surbiton: Toccata Press, 1992.

Newlin, Dika. *Schoenberg remembered: diaries and recollections (1938–76).* New York: Pendragon Press, 1980.

Newman, Ernest. *From the world of music: essays from 'The Sunday Times'*. London: J. Calder, 1956.

Newman, Ernest. Hugo Wolf. New York: Dover Publications, 1966.

Newman, Ernest, Annotated and Translated. *Memoirs of Hector Berlioz from 1803 to 1865, comprising his travels in Germany, Italy, Russia, and England*. New York: Knopf, 1932.

Newman, Ernest. *More essays from the world of music: essays from the 'Sunday Times'*. London: John Calder, 1958.

Newman, Ernest. *Musical studies*. London; New York: John Lane, 1910.

Newman, Ernest. *Testament of music: essays and papers*. London: Putnam, 1962.

Newman, Richard. *Alma Rosé: Vienna to Auschwitz*. Portland, Oregon: Amadeus Press, 2000.

Newman, William S. *The sonata in the classic era*. Chapel Hill: University of North Carolina Press 1963.

Newman, William S. *The sonata in the Classic era*. New York; London: W.W. Norton, 1983.

Newmarch, Rosa Harriet. *Henry J. Wood*. London & New York: John Lane, 1904.

Nicholas, Jeremy. *Godowsky: the pianists' pianist; a biography of Leopold Godowsky*. Hexham: Appian Publications & Recordings, 1989.

Nichols, Roger. *Debussy remembered*. London: Faber and Faber, 1992.

Nichols, Roger. *Mendelssohn remembered*. London: Faber and Faber, 1997.

Nichols, Roger. *Ravel remembered*. London: Faber and Faber, 1987.

Niecks, Frederick. *Robert Schumann*. London: J. M. Dent, 1925.

Nielsen, Carl. *Living music*. Copenhagen, Wilhelm Hansen, 1968.

Nielsen, Carl. *My childhood*. Copenhagen, Wilhelm Hansen, 1972.

Nikolska, Irina. *Conversations with Witold Lutoslawski, (1987–92)*. Stockholm: Melos, 1994.

Nohl, Ludwig. *Beethoven depicted by his contemporaries*. London: Reeves, 1880.

De Nora, Tia. *Beethoven and the construction of genius: musical politics in Vienna, 1792–1803*. Berkeley: University of California Press, 1997.

Norton, Spencer, Editor and Translator. *Music in my time: the memoirs of Alfredo Casella*. Norman: University of Oklahoma Press, 1955.

Nottebohm, Gustav. *Two Beethoven sketchbooks: a description with musical extracts*. London: Gollancz, 1979.

Oakeley, Edward Murray. *The life of Sir Herbert Stanley Oakeley*. London: George Allen, 1904.

Lucas, Brenda and Michael Kerr. *Virtuoso: the story of John Ogdon*. London: H. Hamilton, 1981.

Oliver, Michael, Editor. *Settling the score: a journey through the music of the twentieth century*. London: Faber and Faber, 1999.

Olleson, Philip. *Samuel Wesley: the man and his music*. Woodbridge: Boydell Press, 2003.

Olleson, Philip, Editor. *The letters of Samuel Wesley: professional and social correspondence, 1797–1837*. Oxford; New York: Oxford University Press, 2001.

Olmstead, Andrea. *Conversations with Roger Sessions*. Boston: Northeastern University Press, 1987.

Orenstein, Arbie, Editor. *A Ravel reader: correspondence, articles, interviews*. New York: Columbia University Press, 1990.

Orenstein, Arbie. *Ravel: man and musician*. New York: Columbia University Press, 1975.

Orledge, Robert. *Charles Koechlin (1867–1950): his life and works*. New York: Harwood Academic Publishers, 1989.

Orledge, Robert. *Gabriel Fauré*. London: Eulenburg Books, 1979.

Orledge, Robert. *Satie remembered*. London: Faber and Faber, 1995.

Orledge, Robert. *Satie the composer*. Cambridge: Cambridge University Press, 1990.

Orlova, Alexandra. *Glinka's life in music: a chronicle*. Ann Arbor: UMI Research Press, 1988.

Orlova, Alexandra. *Musorgsky's days and works: a biography in documents*. Ann Arbor: UMI Research Press, 1983.

Orlova, Alexandra. *Tchaikovsky: a self-portrait*. Oxford: Oxford University Press, 1990.

Osborne, Charles, Editor and Translator. *Letters of Giuseppe Verdi*. London: Victor Gollancz, 1971.

Osmond-Smith David, Editor and Translator. *Luciano Berio: Two interviews with Rossana Dalmonte and Bálint András Varga*. New York; London: Boyars, 1985.

Ouellette, Fernand. *Edgard Varèse*. London: Calder & Boyars, 1973.

Paderewski, Ignacy Jan and Mary Lawton. *The Paderewski memoirs*. London: Collins, 1939.

Page, Tim: Editor. *The Glenn Gould reader*. London: Faber and Faber, 1987.

Page, Tim. *Music from the road: views and reviews, 1978–1992*. New York; Oxford: Oxford University Press, 1992.

Page, Tim and Vanessa Weeks, Editors. *Selected letters of Virgil Thomson*. New York: Summit Books, 1988.

Page, Tim. *Tim Page on music: views and reviews*. Portland, Oregon: Amadeus Press, 2002.

Palmer, Christopher. *Herbert Howells, (1892–1983): a celebration*. London: Thames, 1996.

Palmer, Christopher, Editor. *Sergei Prokofiev: Soviet diary 1927 and other writings*. London: Faber and Faber, 1991.

Palmer, Fiona M. *Domenico Dragonetti in England (1794–1846): the career of a double bass virtuoso*. Oxford: Clarendon, 1997.

Palmieri, Robert, Editor. *Encyclopedia of the piano*. New York: Garland, 1996.

Panufnik, Andrzej. *Composing myself.* London: Methuen, 1987.

Parsons, James, Editor. *The Cambridge companion to the Lied*. Cambridge: Cambridge University Press, 2004.

Paynter, John, Editor. *Between old worlds and new: occasional writings on music by Wilfrid Mellers*. London: Cygnus Arts, 1997.

Pestelli, Giorgio. *The age of Mozart and Beethoven*. Cambridge:

Cambridge University Press, 1984.

Peyser, Joan. *Bernstein: a biography: revised & updated.* New York: Billboard Books, 1998.

Phillips-Matz, Mary Jane. *Verdi: a biography.* Oxford: Oxford University Press, 1993.

Piggott, Patrick. *The life and music of John Field, 1782–1837: creator of the nocturne.* London: Faber and Faber, 1973.

Plantinga, Leon. *Beethoven's concertos: history, style, performance.* New York: Norton, 1999.

Plantinga, Leon. *Clementi: his life and music.* London: Oxford University Press, 1977.

Plantinga, Leon. *Romantic music: a history of musical style in nineteenth-century Europe.* New York; London: Norton, 1984.

Plaskin, Glenn. *Horowitz: a biography of Vladimir Horowitz.* London: Macdonald, 1983.

Pleasants, Henry, Editor and Translator. *Hanslick, Eduard: Music criticisms, 1846–99.* Baltimore: Penguin Books, 1963.

Pleasants, Henry, Editor and Translator. *Hanslick's music criticisms.* New York: Dover Publications, 1988.

Pleasants, Henry, Editor and Translator. *The music criticism of Hugo Wolf.* New York: Holmes & Meier Publishers, 1978.

Pleasants, Henry, Editor and Translator. *The musical journeys of Louis Spohr.* Norman: University of Oklahoma Press, 1961.

Pollack, Howard. *Aaron Copland: the life and work of an uncommon man.* New York: Henry Holt, 1999.

Poulenc, Francis. *My friends and myself.* London: Dennis Dobson, 1978.

Powell, Richard, Mrs. *Edward Elgar: memories of a variation.* Aldershot, Hants, England: Scolar Press; Brookfield, Vermont, USA: Ashgate Publishing. Co., 1994.

Poznansky, Alexander, Editor. *Tchaikovsky through others' eyes.* Bloomington: Indiana University Press, 1999.

Praeger, Ferdinand. *Wagner as I knew him.* London; New York: Longmans, Green, 1892.

Previn, Andre. *Anthony Hopkins. Music face to face.* London, Hamish Hamilton, 1971.

Prieberg, Fred K. *Trial of strength: Wilhelm Furtwängler and the Third Reich.* London: Quartet, 1991.

Procter-Gregg, Humphrey. *Beecham remembered.* London: Duckworth, 1976.

Prokofiev, Sergey. *Prokofiev by Prokofiev: a composer's memoir.* London: Macdonald and Jane's, 1979.

Rachmaninoff, Sergei. *Rachmaninoff's recollections told to Oskar von Riesemann.* London: George Allen & Unwin, 1934.

Radcliffe, Philip. *Beethoven's string quartets.* Cambridge: Cambridge University Press, 1978.

Radcliffe, Philip. *Piano Music in: The Age of Beethoven, The New Oxford History of Music, Vol. VIII.* Gerald Abraham, (Editor), 1988, p. 340.

Ratner, Leonard G. *Romantic music: sound and syntax.* New York: Schirmer Books, 1992.

Raynor, Henry. *A social history of music: from the middle ages to*

Beethoven. London: Barrie & Jenkins, 1972.

Rees, Brian. *Camille Saint-Saëns: a life.* London: Chatto & Windus, 1999.

Reich, Willi, Editor. *Anton Webern: The path to the new music.* London; Bryn Mawr: Theodore Presser in association with Universal Edition, 1963.

Reid, Charles. *John Barbirolli: a biography.* London, Hamish Hamilton, 1971.

Reid, Charles. *Malcolm Sargent: a biography.* London: Hamilton, 1968.

Rennert, Jonathan. *William Crotch (1775–1847): composer, artist, teacher.* Lavenham: Terence Dalton, 1975.

Rice, John A. *Antonio Salieri and Viennese Opera.* Chicago, Illinois: University of Chicago Press, 1998.

Rice, John A. *Empress Marie Therese and music at the Viennese court, 1792–1807.* Cambridge: Cambridge University Press, 2003.

Richards, Fiona. *The Music of John Ireland.* Aldershot: Ashgate, 2000.

Rigby, Charles. *Sir Charles Hallé: a portrait for today.* Manchester: Dolphin Press, 1952.

Ringer, Alexander, Editor. *The early Romantic era: between Revolutions; 1789 and 1848.* Basingstoke: Macmillan, 1990.

Roberts, John P.L. and Ghyslaine Guertin, Editors. *Glenn Gould: Selected letters.* Toronto; Oxford: Oxford University Press, 1992.

Robertson, Alec. *More than music.* London: Collins, 1961.

Robinson, Harlow, Editor and Translator. *Selected letters of Sergei Prokofiev.* Boston: Northeastern University Press, 1998.

Robinson, Harlow. *Sergei Prokofiev: a biography.* London: Hale, 1987.

Robinson, Paul A. *Ludwig van Beethoven, Fidelio.* Cambridge: Cambridge University Press, 1996.

Robinson, Suzanne, Editor. *Michael Tippett: music and literature.* Aldershot: Ashgate, 2002.

Rochberg, George. *The aesthetics of survival: a composer's view of twentieth-century music.* Ann Arbor, Michigan: University of Michigan Press, 2004.

Rodmell, Paul. *Charles Villiers Stanford.* Aldershot: Ashgate, 2002.

Roeder, Michael Thomas. *A history of the concerto.* Portland, Oregon: Amadeus Press, 1994.

Rohr, Deborah Adams. *The careers of British musicians, 1750–1850: a profession of artisans.* Cambridge: Cambridge University Press, 2001.

Rolland, Romain. *Goethe and Beethoven.* New York; London: Blom, 1968.

Rolland, Romain. *Beethoven and Handel.* London: Waverley Book Co., 1917.

Rolland, Romain. *Beethoven the creator.* Garden City, New York: Garden City Pub., 1937.

Roscow, Gregory, Editor. *Bliss on music: selected writings of Arthur Bliss, 1920–1975.* Oxford: Oxford University Press, 1991.

Rosen, Charles. *Beethoven's piano sonatas: a short companion.* New Haven, Connecticut:

London: Yale University Press, 2002.

Rosen, Charles. *Critical entertainments: music old and new.* Cambridge, Massachusetts; London: Harvard University Press, 2000.

Rosen, Charles. *The classical style: Haydn, Mozart, Beethoven.* London: Faber and Faber, 1976.

Rosen, Charles. *The romantic generation.* Cambridge, Massachusetts: Harvard University Press, 1995.

Rosenthal, Albi. *Obiter scripta: essays, lectures, articles, interviews and reviews on music, and other subjects.* Oxford: Offox Press; Lanham: Scarecrow Press, 2000.

Rostal, Max. *Beethoven: the sonatas for piano and violin; thoughts on their interpretation.* London: Toccata Press, 1985.

Rostropovich, Mstislav and Galina Vishnevskaya. *Russia, music, and liberty.* Portland, Oregan: Amadeus Press, 1995.

Rubinstein, Arthur. *My many years.* London: Jonathan Cape, 1980.

Rubinstein, Arthur. *My young years.* London: Jonathan Cape, 1973.

Rumph, Stephen C. *Beethoven after Napoleon: political romanticism in the late works.* Berkeley; London: University of California Press, 2004.

Rye, Matthew Rye. *Notes to the BBC Radio Three Beethoven Experience, Friday 10 June 2005,* www.bbc.co.uk/radio3/Beethoven.

Sachs, Harvey. *Toscanini.* London: Weidenfeld and Nicholson, 1978.

Sachs, Joel. *Kapellmeister Hummel in England and France.* Detroit: Information Coordinators, 1977.

Saffle, Michael, Editor. *Liszt and his world: proceedings of the International Liszt Conference held at Virginia Polytechnic Institute and State University, 20–23 May 1993.* Stuyvesant, New York: Pendragon Press, 1998.

Safránek, Milos. *Bohuslav Martinu, his life and works.* London: Allan Wingate, 1962.

Saint-Saëns, Camille. *Outspoken essays on music.* Westport, Connecticut: Greenwood Press, 1970.

Saussine, Renée de. *Paganini.* Westport, Connecticut: Greenwood Press, 1976.

Sayers, W. C. Berwick. *Samuel Coleridge-Taylor, musician: his life and letters.* London; New York: Cassell and Co., 1915.

Schaarwächter, Jürgen. *HB: aspects of Havergal Brian.* Aldershot: Ashgate, 1997.

Schafer, R. Murray. *E.T.A. Hoffmann and music.* Toronto: University of Toronto Press, 1975.

Schafer, R. Murray, Editor. *Ezra Pound and music: the complete criticism.* London: Faber and Faber, 1978.

Schat, Peter. *The tone clock.* Chur, Switzerland; Langhorne, Pa.: Harwood Academic Publishers, 1993.

Schenk, Erich. *Mozart and his times.* Edited and Translated by Richard and Clara Winstin. London: Secker & Warburg, 1960.

Schindler, Anton Felix. *Beethoven as I knew him.* Edited by Donald W. MacArdle and Translated by Constance S. Jolly from the

German edition of 1860 London: Faber and Faber, 1966.

Schlosser, Johann. *Beethoven: the first biography, 1827.* Edited by Barry Cooper. Portland, Oregon: Amadeus Press, 1996.

Schnabel, Artur. *My life and music.* London: Longmans, 1961.

Schnittke, Alfred. *A Schnittke reader.* Bloomington: Indiana University Press, 2002.

Scholes, Percy Alfred. *Crotchets: a few short musical notes.* London: John Lane, 1924.

Schonberg, Harold C. *The great pianists.* London: Victor Gollancz, 1964.

Schrade, Leo. *Beethoven in France: the growth of an idea.* New Haven; London: Yale University Press, H. Milford, Oxford University Press, 1942.

Schrade, Leo. *Tragedy in the art of music.* Cambridge, Massachusetts: Harvard University Press, 1964.

Schuh, Willi. *Richard Strauss: a chronicle of the early years 1864–1898.* Cambridge: Cambridge University Press, 1982.

Schuh, Willi, Editor. *Richard Strauss: Recollections and reflections.* London; New York: Boosey & Hawkes, 1953.

Schuller, Gunther. *Musings: the musical worlds of Gunther Schuller.* New York: Oxford University Press, 1986.

Schumann, Robert. *Music and musicians: essays and criticisms.* London: William Reeves, 1877.

Schuttenhelm, Editor. *Selected letters of Michael Tippett.* London: Faber and Faber, 2005.

Schwartz, Elliott. *Music since 1945: issues, materials, and literature.* New York: Schirmer Books, 1993.

Scott, Marion M. *Beethoven: (The master musicians).* London: Dent, 1940.

Scott-Sutherland, Colin. *Arnold Bax.* London: J. M. Dent, 1973.

Searle, Muriel V. *John Ireland: the man and his music.* Tunbridge Wells: Midas Books, 1979.

Secrest, Meryle. *Leonard Bernstein: a life.* London: Bloomsbury, 1995.

Seeger, Charles. *Studies in musicology II, 1929–1979.* Edited by Anne M. Pescatello. Berkeley; London: University of California Press, 1994.

Selden-Goth, Gisela, Editor. *Felix Mendelssohn: letters.* London: Paul Elek Publishers Ltd, 1946.

Senner, Wayne M., Robin Wallace and William Meredith, Editors. *The critical reception of Beethoven's compositions by his German contemporaries.* Lincoln: University of Nebraska Press, in association with the American Beethoven Society and the Ira F. Brilliant Center for Beethoven Studies, San José State University, 1999.

Seroff, Victor I. *Rachmaninoff.* London: Cassell & Company, 1951.

Sessions, Roger. *Questions about music.* Cambridge, Massachusetts: Harvard University Press, 1970.

Sessions, Roger. *The musical experience of composer, performer, listener.* New York: Atheneum, 1966, 1950.

Seyfried, Ignaz von. *Louis van Beethoven's Studies in thoroughbass, counterpoint and the art of scientific composition*. Leipzig; New-York: Schuberth and Company, 1853.

Sharma, Bhesham R. *Music and culture in the age of mechanical reproduction*. New York: Peter Lang, 2000.

Shaw, Bernard. *How to become a musical critic*. London: R. Hart Davis, 1960.

Shaw, Bernard. *London music in 1888–89 as heard by Corno di Bassetto (later known as Bernard Shaw): with some further autobiographical particulars*. London: Constable and Company, 1937.

Shaw, Bernard. *Music in London, 1890–1894*. London: Constable and Company Limited, 3 Vols., 1932.

Shedlock, John South. *Beethoven's pianoforte sonatas: the origin and respective values of various readings*. London: Augener Ltd., 1918.

Shedlock, John South. *The pianoforte sonata: its origin and development*. London: Methuen, 1895.

Shepherd, Arthur. *The string quartets of Ludwig van Beethoven*. Cleveland: H. Carr, The Printing Press, 1935.

Sheppard, Leslie and Herbert R. Axelrod. *Paganini: containing a portfolio of drawings by Vido Polikarpus*. Neptune City, New Jersey: Paganiniana Publications, 1979.

Short, Michael. *Gustav Holst: the man and his music*. Oxford: Oxford University Press, 1990.

Shostakovich, Dmitry. *Dmitry Shostakovich: about himself and his times*. Moscow: Progress Publishers, 1981.

Simpson, John Palgrave. *Carl Maria von Weber: the life of an artist, from the German of his son Baron, Max Maria von Weber*. London: Chapman and Hall, 1865.

Simpson, Robert. *Beethoven symphonies*. London: British Broadcasting Corporation, 1970.

Sipe, Thomas. *Beethoven: Eroica symphony*. Cambridge: Cambridge University Press, 1998.

Sitwell, Sacheverell. *Mozart*. Edinburgh: Peter Davies Limited, 1932.

Skelton, Geoffrey. *Paul Hindemith: the man behind the music; a biography*. London: Victor Gollancz, 1975.

Smallman, Basil. *The piano trio: its history, technique, and repertoire*. Oxford: Clarendon Press; Oxford; New York: Oxford University Press, 1990.

Smidak, Emil. *Isaak-Ignaz Moscheles: the life of the composer and his encounters with Beethoven, Liszt, Chopin, and Mendelssohn*. Aldershot, Hampshire, England: Scolar Press; Brookfield, Vermont, USA: Gower Publishing Co., 1989.

Smith, Barry. *Peter Warlock: the life of Philip Heseltine*. Oxford: Oxford University Press, 1994.

Smith, Joan Allen. *Schoenberg and his circle: a Viennese portrait*. New York: Schirmer Books, London: Collier Macmillan, 1986.

Smith, Richard Langham, Editor. *Debussy on music: the critical writings of the great French composer Claude Debussy*. London: Secker & Warburg, 1977.

Smith, Ronald. *Alkan*. London: Kahn and Averill, 1976.

Snowman, Daniel. *The Amadeus Quartet: the men and the music*. London: Robson Books, 1981.

Solomon, Maynard. *Beethoven*. New York: Schirmer, 1977.

Solomon, Maynard. *Beethoven essays*. Cambridge, Massachusetts; London: Harvard University Press, 1988.

Solomon, Maynard. *Late Beethoven: music, thought, imagination*. Berkeley; London: University of California Press, 2003.

Solomon, Maynard. *Mozart: a life*. London: Hutchinson, 1995.

Sonneck, Oscar George Theodore. *Beethoven: impressions of contemporaries*. London: Oxford University Press, 1927.

Spalding, Albert. *Rise to follow: an autobiography*. London: Frederick Muller Ltd., 1946.

Spohr, Louis. *Louis Spohr's autobiography*. London: Longman, Green, Longman, Roberts, & Green, 1865.

Stafford, William. *Mozart myths: a critical reassessment*. Stanford, California: Stanford University Press, 1991.

Stanford, Charles Villiers. *Interludes: records and reflections*. London: John Murray, 1922.

Stanley, Glen, Editor. *The Cambridge companion to Beethoven*. Cambridge; New York: Cambridge University Press, 2000

Stedman, Preston. *The symphony*. Englewood Cliffs, New Jersey; London: Prentice-Hall, 1979.

Stedron, Bohumír, Editor and Translator. *Leos Janácek: letters and reminiscences*. Prague: Artia, 1955.

Stein, Erwin, Editor. *Arnold Schoenberg: letters*. London: Faber and Faber, 1964.

Stein, Erwin. *Orpheus in new guises*. London: Rockliff, 1953.

Stein, Jack Madison. *Poem and music in the German lied from Gluck to Hugo Wolf*. Cambridge, Massachusetts: Harvard University Press, 1971.

Stein, Leonard, Editor. *Style and idea: selected writings of Arnold Schoenberg*. London: Faber and Faber, 1975.

Steinberg, Michael P. *Listening to reason: culture, subjectivity, and nineteenth-century music*. Princeton, New Jersey: Princeton University Press, 2004.

Steinberg, Michael. *The concerto: a listener's guide*. New York: Oxford University Press, 1998.

Steinberg, Michael. *The symphony: a listener's guide*. Oxford; New York: Oxford University Press, 1995.

Sternfeld, Frederick William. *Goethe and music: a list of parodies and Goethe's relationship to music; a list of references*. New York: Da Capo Press, 1979.

Stivender, David. *Mascagni: an autobiography compiled, edited and translated from original sources*. New York: Pro/Am Music Resources; London: Kahn & Averill, 1988.

Stone, Else and Kurt Stone, Editors. *The writings of Elliott Carter: an American composer looks at modern music*. Bloomington: Indiana University Press, 1977.

Stowell, Robin. *Beethoven: violin concerto*. Cambridge: Cambridge University Press, 1998.

Stowell, Robin: Editor. *The Cambridge companion to the cello*.

Cambridge: Cambridge University Press, 1999.

Stowell, Robin: Editor. *The Cambridge companion to the string quartet.* Cambridge: Cambridge University Press, 2003.

Stratton, Stephen Samuel. *Mendelssohn.* London: J.M. Dent & Co.; New York: E.P. Dutton & Co., 1901.

Straus, Joseph N. *Remaking the past: musical modernism and the influence of the tonal tradition.* Cambridge, Massachusetts: Harvard University Press, 1990.

Stravinsky, Igor. *An autobiography.* London: Calder and Boyars, 1975.

Stravinsky, Igor. *Themes and conclusions.* London: Faber and Faber, 1972.

Stravinsky, Igor and Robert Craft. *Conversations with Igor Stravinsky.* London: Faber and Faber, 1959.

Stravinsky, Igor and Robert Craft. *Dialogues and a diary.* London: Faber and Faber 1968.

Stravinsky, Igor and Robert Craft. *Memories and commentaries.* London: Faber and Faber, 2002.

Strunk, Oliver. *Source readings in music history, 4: The Classic era.* London: Faber and Faber 1981.

Sullivan, Blair, Editor. *The echo of music: essays in honor of Marie Louise Göllner.* Warren, Michigan: Harmonie Park Press, 2004.

Sullivan, Jack, Editor. *Words on music: from Addison to Barzun.* Athens: Ohio University Press, 1990.

Symonette, Lys and Kim H. Kowalke, Editors and Translators. *Speak low (when you speak love): the letters of Kurt Weill and Lotte Lenya.* London: Hamish Hamilton, 1996.

Swalin, Benjamin F. *The violin concerto: a study in German romanticism.* New York, Da Capo Press, 1973.

Szigeti, Joseph. *With strings attached: reminiscences and reflections.* London: Cassell & Co. Ltd, 1949.

Tanner, Michael, Editor. *Notebooks, 1924–1954: Wilhelm Furtwängler.* London: Quartet Books, 1989.

Taylor, Robert, Editor. *Furtwängler on music: essays and addresses.* Aldershot: Scolar, 1991.

Taylor, Ronald. *Kurt Weill: composer in a divided world.* London: Simon & Schuster, 1991.

Tchaikovsky, Peter Ilich. *Letters to his family: an autobiography.* Translated by Galina von Meck. London: Dennis Dobson, 1981.

Tertis, Lionel. *My viola and I: a complete autobiography; with, 'Beauty of tone in string playing', and other essays.* London: Paul Elek, 1974.

Thayer, Alexander Wheelock. *Salieri: rival of Mozart.* Edited by Theodore Albrecht. Kansas City, Missouri: Philharmonia of Greater Kansas City, 1989.

Thomas, Michael Tilson. *Viva voce: conversations with Edward Seckerson.* London: Faber and Faber 1994.

Thomson, Andrew. *Vincent d'Indy and his world.* Oxford: Clarendon Press, 1996.

Thomson, Virgil. *The musical scene.* New York: Greenwood Press, 1968.

Thomson, Virgil. Virgil Thomson.

London: Weidenfeld & Nicolson, 1967.

Tillard, Françoise. *Fanny Mendelssohn*. Amadeus Press: Portland, 1996.

Tilmouth, Michael, Editor. *Donald Francis Tovey: The classics of music: talks, essays, and other writings previously uncollected.* Oxford: Oxford University Press, 2001

Tippett, Michael. *Moving into Aquarius.* London: Routledge and Kegan Paul, 1959.

Tippett, Michael. *Those twentieth century blues: an autobiography.* London: Hutchinson, 1991.

Todd, R. Larry, Editor. *Nineteenth-century piano music.* New York; London: Routledge, 2004.

Todd, R. Larry, Editor. *Schumann and his world.* Princeton: Princeton University Press, 1994.

Tommasini, Anthony. *Virgil Thomson: composer on the aisle.* New York: W.W. Norton, 1997.

Tortelier, Paul. *A self-portrait: in conversation with David Blum.* London: Heinemann, 1984.

Tovey, Donald Francis. *A Companion to Beethoven's Pianoforte Sonatas.* Revised by Barry Cooper. London: The Associated Board, [1931], 1998.

Tovey, Donald Francis. *Beethoven.* London: Oxford University Press, 1944.

Tovey, Donald Francis. *Essays and lectures on music.* London: Oxford University Press, 1949.

Tovey, Donald Francis. *Essays in musical analysis.* London: Oxford University Press, H. Milford, 7 Vols., 1935–41.

Tovey, Donald Francis. *The forms of music: musical articles from The Encyclopaedia Britannica.* London: Oxford University Press, 1944.

Toye, Francis. *Giuseppe Verdi: his life and works.* London: William Heinemann Ltd., 1931.

Truscott, Harold. *Beethoven's late string quartets.* London: Dobson, 1968.

Tyler, William R. *The letters of Franz Liszt to Olga von Meyendorff, 1871–1886, in the Mildred Bliss Collection at Dumbarton Oaks.* Translated by William R. Tyler. Washington: Dumbarton Oaks, Trustees for Harvard University; Cambridge, Massachusetts: distributed by Harvard University Press, 1979.

Tyrrell, John. *Janácek: years of a life. Vol. 1, (1854–1914) The lonely blackbird.* London: Faber and Faber, 2006.

Tyrrell, John, Editor and Translator. *My life with Janácek: the memoirs of Zdenka Janácková.* London: Faber and Faber, 1998.

Tyson, Alan, Editor. *Beethoven studies 2.* Cambridge: Cambridge University Press, 1977.

Tyson, Alan, Editor. *Beethoven studies 3.* Cambridge: Cambridge University Press, 1982.

Tyson, Alan. *Mozart: studies of the autograph scores.* Cambridge, Massachusetts; London: Harvard University Press, 1987.

Tyson, Alan. *The authentic English editions of Beethoven.* London: Faber and Faber, 1963.

Underwood, J. A., Editor. *Gabriel Fauré: his life through his letters.* London: Marion Boyars, 1984.

Vechten, Carl van, Editor. *Nikolay, Rimsky-Korsakov: My musical life.* London: Martin Secker & Warburg Ltd., 1942.

Vinton, John. *Essays after a dictionary: music and culture at the close of Western civilization.* Lewisburg: Bucknell University Press, 1977.

Volkov, Solomon, Editor. *Testimony: the memoirs of Dmitri Shostakovich.* London: Faber and Faber, 1981.

Volta, Ornella, Editor. *A mammal's notebook: collected writings of Erik Satie.* London: Atlas Press, 1996.

Wagner, Richard. Beethoven: *With [a] supplement from the philosophical works of A. Schopenhauer.* Translated by E. Dannreuther. London: Reeves, 1893.

Wagner, Richard. *My life.* London: Constable and Company Ltd., 1911.

Walden, Valerie. *One hundred years of violoncello: a history of technique and performance practice, 1740–1840.* Cambridge: Cambridge University Press, 1998.

Walker, Alan. *Franz Liszt. Volume 1, The virtuoso years: 1811–1847.* New York: Alfred A. Knopf, 1983.

Walker, Alan. *Franz Liszt. Volume 2, The Weimar years: 1848–1861.* London: Faber and Faber, 1989.

Walker, Alan. *Franz Liszt. Volume 3, The final years, 1861–1886.* London: Faber and Faber, 1997.

Walker, Bettina. *My musical experiences.* London: Richard Bentley and Son, 1890.

Walker, Ernest. *Free thought and the musician, and other essays.* London; New York: Oxford University Press, 1946.

Walker, Frank. *Hugo Wolf: a biography.* London: J. M. Dent, 1951.

Walker, Frank. *The man Verdi.* London: Dent, 1962.

Wallace, Grace, *[Lady Wallace]. Beethoven's letters (1790–1826): from the collection of Dr. Ludwig Nohl. Also his letters to the Archduke Rudolph, Cardinal-Archbishop of Olmutz, K.W., from the collection of Dr. Ludwig Ritter Von Köchel.* London: Longmans, Green, 2 Vols., 1866.

Wallace, Robin. *Beethoven's critics: aesthetic dilemmas and resolutions during the composer's lifetime.* Cambridge; New York: Cambridge University Press, 1986.

Walter, Bruno. *Theme and variations: an autobiography.* London: H. Hamilton, 1948.

Warrack, John Hamilton. *Writings on music.* Cambridge: Cambridge University Press, 1981.

Wasielewski, Wilhelm Joseph von. *Life of Robert Schumann: with letters, 1833–1852.* London: William Reeves, 1878.

Watkins, Glenn. *Proof through the night: music and the Great War.* Berkeley: University of California Press, 2003.

Watkins, Glenn. *Pyramids at the Louvre: music, culture, and collage from Stravinsky to the postmodernists.* Cambridge, Massachusetts; London: Belknap Press of Harvard University Press, 1994.

Watkins, Glenn. *Soundings: music in the twentieth century.* New York: Schirmer Books London: Collier Macmillan, 1988.

Watson, Derek. *Liszt.* London: J. M. Dent, 1989.

Weaver, William, Editor. *The Verdi-Boito correspondence.* Chicago; London: University of Chicago Press, 1994.

Wegeler, Franz. *Remembering Beethoven: the biographical notes of Franz Wegeler and Ferdinand Ries.* London: Andre Deutsch, 1988.

Weingartner, Felix. *Buffets and rewards: a musician's reminiscences.* London: Hutchinson & Co., 1937.

Weinstock, Herbert. *Rossini: a biography.* New York: Limelight, 1987.

Weiss, Piero and Richard Taruskin. *Music in the Western World: a history in documents.* New York: Schirmer; London: Collier Macmillan, 1984.

Weissweiler, Eva *The complete correspondence of Clara and Robert Schumann.* New York: Peter Lang, 2 Vols., 1994.

Whittaker, William Gillies. *Collected essays.* London: Oxford University Press, 1940.

Whittall, Arnold. *Exploring twentieth-century music: tradition and innovation.* Cambridge; New York: Cambridge University Press, 2003.

Whittall, Arnold. *Music since the First World War.* London: J. M. Dent, 1977.

Whitton, Kenneth S. *Lieder: an introduction to German song.* London: Julia MacRae, 1984.

Wightman, Alistair, Editor. *Szymanowski on music: selected writings of Karol Szymanowski.* London: Toccata Press, 1999.

Wilhelm, Kurt. *Richard Strauss: an intimate portrait.* London: Thames and Hudson, 1999.

Will, Richard James. *The characteristic symphony in the age of Haydn and Beethoven.* Cambridge: Cambridge University Press, 2002.

Willetts, Pamela J. *Beethoven and England: an account of sources in the British Museum.* London: British Museum, 1970.

Williams, Adrian, Editor and Translator. *Liszt, Franz: Selected letters.* Oxford: Clarendon Press, 1998.

Williams, Adrian. *Portrait of Liszt: by himself and his contemporaries.* Oxford: Clarendon Press, 1990.

Williams, Ralph Vaughan. *Heirs and rebels: letters written to each other and occasional writings on music.* London; New York: Oxford University Press, 1959.

Williams, Ralph Vaughan. *Some thoughts on Beethoven's Choral symphony: with writings on other musical subjects.* London; Oxford University Press, 1953.

Williams, Ralph Vaughan. *The making of music.* Ithaca, New York: Cornell University Press, 1955.

Williams, Ursula Vaughan. *R.V.W.: a biography of Ralph Vaughan Williams.* London: Oxford University Press, 1964.

Wilson, Conrad. *Notes on Beethoven: 20 crucial works.* Edinburgh: Saint Andrew Press, 2003.

Wilson, Elizabeth. *Shostakovich: a life remembered.* Princeton, New Jersey: Princeton University Press, 1994.

Winter, Robert, Editor. *Beethoven, performers, and critics: the International Beethoven Congress, Detroit, 1977.* Detroit: Wayne State University Press, 1980.

Winter, Robert. *Compositional origins of Beethoven's opus 131.* Ann Arbor, Michigan: UMI Research Press, 1982.

Winter, Robert and Robert Martin, Editors. *The Beethoven quartet companion.* Berkeley: University of California Press, 1994.

Wolf, Eugene K. and Edward H. Roesner, Editors. *Studies in musical sources and style: essays in honor of Jan LaRue.* Madison, Wisconsin: A-R Editions, 1990.

Wolff, Christoph and Robert Riggs. *The string quartets of Haydn, Mozart and Beethoven: studies of the autograph manuscripts: a conference at Isham Memorial Library, March 15–17, 1979.* Cambridge, Massachusetts: Department of Music, Harvard University, 1980.

Wolff, Konrad. *Masters of the keyboard: individual style elements in the piano music of Bach, Haydn, Mozart, Beethoven, Schubert, Chopin, and Brahms.* Bloomington: Indiana University Press, 1990.

Wörner, Karl Heinrich. *Stockhausen: life and work.* London: Faber, 1973.

Wright, Donald, Editor. *Cardus on music: a centenary collection.* London: Hamish Hamilton, 1988.

Wyndham, Henry Saxe. *August Manns and the Saturday concerts: a memoir and a retrospect.* London and Felling-on-Tyne, New York, The Walter Scott Publishing Co., Ltd., 1909.

Yastrebtsev, V.V. Edited and Translated by Florence Jonas. *Reminiscences of Rimsky-Korsakov.* New York: Columbia University Press, 1985.

Yates, Peter. *Twentieth century music: its evolution from the end of the harmonic era into the present era of sound.* London: Allen & Unwin Ltd., 1968.

Young, Percy M. *Beethoven: a Victorian tribute based on the papers of Sir George Smart.* London: D. Dobson, 1976.

Young, Percy M. *George Grove, 1820–1900: a biography.* London: Macmillan, 1980.

Young, Percy M. *Letters of Edward Elgar and other writings.* London: Geoffrey Bles, 1956.

Young, Percy M., Editor. *Letters to Nimrod: Edward Elgar to August Jaeger, 1897–1908.* London: Dennis Dobson, 1965.

Young, Percy M. *The concert tradition: from the middle ages to the twentieth century.* London: Routledge and Kegan Paul, 1965.

Young, Rob, Editor. *(Brief Description): Undercurrents: the hidden wiring of modern music.* London; New York, N.Y.: Continuum, 2002.

Yourke, Electra Slonimsky, Editor. *Nicolas Slonimsky: writings on music.* New York, N.Y.; London: Routledge, 4 Vols. 2003-2005.

Slonimsky, Nicolas. *The great composers and their works.* Edited by Electra Slonimsky Yourke. New York: Schirmer Books, 2 Vols. 2000.

Ysaÿe, Antoine. *Ysaÿe: his life, work and influence.* London: W. Heinemann, 1947.

Zamoyski, Adam. *Paderewski.* London: Collins, 1982.

Zegers, Mirjam, Editor. *Louis Andriessen: The art of stealing time.* Todmorden: Arc Music, 2002.

Zemanova, Mirka, Editor. *Janácek's uncollected essays on music.* London: Marion Boyars, 1989.

INDEX

Gerald Abraham X, 1-3, 207-208
Theodor W. Adorno 3-5, 35, 105, 245
Allgemeine Musikalische Zeitung (Amz) 5-11
Boito Arrigo 11-12,
Vladimir Ashkenazy 12-14

Daniel Barenboim 14-16
Philip Barford 16-18
Béla Bartók 19, 164, 258
Arnold Bax 12-20, 164
Paul Bekker 20-22, 43
Luciano Berio 23
Hector Berlioz 23-29, 37-39, 41, 53, 88, 129, 150, 257, 271, 302
Leonard Bernstein 28, 30-32
Arthur Bliss 32-34, 323-324
Ernst Bloch 3, 34-37, 70, 105-106
Eric Blom 37-40
Mark Evan Bonds 40-42, 43

Leon Botstein 42-45
Pierre Boulez 45-46
Johannes Brahms 41, 46-47, 58, 97-98, 108-140, 145, 147, 158, 160-163, 170, 207, 229, 271, 302, 309, 328
Alfred Brendel 47-48, 238
Gerhard Von Breuning 49-51, 125, 159, 280
Alfred Peter Brown 52-54
Clive Brown 54-55
Michael Broyles 56-58
Anton Bruckner 40, 58-60, 88, 112-113, 207, 214, 270-271, 309, 352, 353

Neville Cardus 60-64, 236
Elliott Carter 64-66
Pablo Casals 67-68
Alfredo Casella 68-69
Carlos Chávez 69-70, 215

Edward T. Cone 70-71
Barry Cooper 72-74, 187, 249-250, 253, 306
Martin Cooper 74-77
Aaron Copland 77-79
John Crabbe 79-81
William Crotch 82
Louise Elvira Cuyler 83-84
Carl Czerny I, 84-86, 171, 173, 270, 279

Carl Dahlhaus 86-89
Peter Maxwell Davies 89-90
Collin Davis 90-92
Basil Deane 92-93
Claude Debussy 41, 93-96, 162, 164, 258
Frederick Delius 97-98
David B. Dennis 98-106
Domenico Dragonetti 106-107
Antonín Dvorák 41, 108, 163, 214

Alfred Einstein 108-109, 297

Frederick Freedman 109-111
Wilhelm Furtwängler 48, 111-117

Hans Gal 118-121, 194, 197
Charles Gounod 121-122
Percy Grainger 122-123
Franz Grillparzer VIII, 51, 101, 124-125, 280
George Grove 37, 125-128, 221, 265

François-Antione Habeneck 129-130, 196-197
William Henry Hadow 130-133
Charles Hallé 133-136,
Christopher Headington 141
E. T. A. Hoffman 100, 142-144
Gustav Holst 144-145, 221, 282
Arthur Honegger 145-147
Anthony Hopkins II, 147-148
Peter Le Huray And James Day 148-149, 153-154

Vincent D'indy 149-151

David Wyn Jones 151-153

Karl August Kahlert 153-154
William Kinderman 154-155
Otto Klemperer 48, 155-157
Raymond Knapp 158, 160
Nikolai Rimsky-Korsakov 159-160, 240, 294
Siegfried Kross 160-162, 269, 320

Constant Lambert 162-165
Paul Henry Lang 165-168
Ernest Markham Lee 168-169
Raymond Leppard 169-171
Franz Liszt 40, 85, 88, 133, 171-174

Edward Macdowell 174-176
Charles Mackerras 176-177
John B. Mcewan 177-179
William Mcnaught 179-180
Gustav Mahler 41-42, 48, 66, 147, 155, 157, 180, 186
Denis Matthews II, 187, 189-191
Wilfrid Mellers 189-191
Felix Mendelssohn 11, 37, 39-42, 88, 96-98, 135, 155, 160 170 191-197, 227, 257, 294, 330
Yehudi Menuhin 197-204
Olivier Messiaen 204-206
Paul Mies 206-208
Darius Milhaud 208-209
Ignaz Moscheles 209-211, 225, 279
Charles Münch 211-212,
Modeste Musorgsky (Mussorgsky, Musorsky) 213-215

Brian Newbould 213
Ernest Newman 24, 29, 215-216

Richard Osborne 219-220

Hubert Parry 221-222

The Philharmonic Society XVII, 107, 209-210, 222-227, 239, 321

Sergei Rachmaninoff 227-228
Simon Rattle 48, 228-229
Maurice Ravel 78, 230-232, 236, 258, 306
Johann Friedrich Reichardt 232-235, 254
Hans Richter 140, 236-237
Ferdinand Ries XVI, 222, 224, 237-240, 279
Nikolay Rimsky-Korsakov 158-160, 240, 294
Romain Rolland 102, 240-243
Stephen Rumph 243-245

Camille Saint-Saëns 94, 211, 231, 245-247
Malcolm Sargent 247-248, 270
Anton Felix Schindler 129, 248-249, 278-280
Johann Aloys Schlosser 250-253, 280
Percy Alfred Scholes 253-254
Harold C. Schonberg 130, 164, 185-186, 254-255, 306, 320-321
Robert Schumann 11, 42, 53, 96, 98, 147, 160, 186, 232, 255-257, 271, 304
Roger Sessions 258-261
Ignaz Von Seyfried 254-255, 261-263, 279
George Bernard Shaw 127-128, 263-267, 332
Jean Sibelius 114, 164-165, 258, 267-269, 289

Robert Simpson VI, 248, 269-272
Nicolas Slonimsky 272-273
Alexander Brent Smith 274-275
Maynard Solomon 18, 49, 51, 91, 245, 275-278, 306
Oscar George Sonneck 125, 278-280
Louis Spohr 165, 255, 279, 280-281
Charles Villiers Stanford 282-284
Preston Stedman 284-288
Karl Heinrich Stockhausen 272, 288-290
Richard Strauss 230, 258, 290-294
Igor Stravinsky 74, 164, 206, 241, 258, 294-296
John William Navin Sullivan 12-13, 226, 297-298
Karol Szymanowsky 298-300
Peter Tchaikovsky 78-79, 98, 141, 163, 300-305, 309
Alexander Wheelock Thayer 106-107, 124, 278, 305-307
Virgil Thomson 307-314, 322
Michael Tippett 314-319
Arturo Toscanini 34, 310, 314, 320-325
Donald Francis Tovey V, 34, 277, 325-329
Cosima Wagner 329-332
Richard Wagner 11, 40, 58-59, 68, 69, 94-95, 111-115, 122, 129, 139-140, 157, 176-177, 185, 208-209, 226, 230, 232, 236, 248, 253, 264, 271, 292-293, 308-309 329-346, 351
Ernest Walker 346-347
Felix Weingartner 139, 248, 327, 347-349
Hugo Wolf 350-354

ABOUT THE AUTHOR

Terence M. Russell graduated with first class honours in architecture and was a nominee for the coveted Silver Medal of the Royal Institute of British Architects. He is a Fellow of the Royal Incorporation of Architects in Scotland (retired), was formerly Reader in the School of Arts, Culture and Environment at the University of Edinburgh, a Fellow of the British Higher Education Academy, and Senior Assessor to the Scottish Higher Education Funding Council. Alongside his professional work in the field of architecture – embracing practice, teaching and research – he has maintained a lifetime's interest in the music and musicology of Beethoven. He has an equal admiration for the work of Franz Schubert and was for many years an active member of the Schubert Institute, UK. His book writings in the field of architecture include the following:

The Built Environment: A Subject Index, Gregg Publishing (1989):
- Vol. 1: Town planning and urbanism, architecture, gardens and landscape design
- Vol. 2: Environmental technology, constructional engineering, building and materials
- Vol. 3: Decorative art and industrial design, international exhibitions and collections, recreational and performing arts
- Vol. 4: Public health, municipal services, community welfare

Architecture in the Encyclopédie of Diderot and D'Alemebert: The Letterpress Articles and Selected Engravings, Scolar Press (1993)

The Encyclopaedic Dictionary in the Eighteenth Century: Architecture, Arts and Crafts, Scolar Press (1997):
- Vol. 1: John Harris, Lexicon Technicum
- Vol. 2: Ephraim Chambers, Cyclopaedia
- Vol. 3: The Builder's Dictionary
- Vol. 4: Samuel Johnson, A Dictionary of the English Language
- Vol. 5: A Society of Gentlemen, Encyclopaedia Britannica

Gardens and Landscapes in the Encyclopédie of Diderot and D'Alemebert: The Letterpress Articles and Selected Engravings, 2 Vols., Ashgate (1999)

The Napoleonic Survey of Egypt: The Monuments and Customs of Egypt, 2 Vols., Ashgate (2001)

The Discovery of Egypt: Vivant Denon's Travels with Napoleon's Army, History Press (2005)